DRAFTING AND ANALYZING CONTRACTS

A Guide to the Practical Application of the Principles of Contract Law

Third Edition

TEACHER'S MANUAL

Scott J. Burnham
Professor of Law
The University of Montana Schoool of Law

LexisNexis™

ISBN#: 0-8205-5789-7

Editorial Offices
744 Broad Street, Newark, NJ 07102 (973) 820-2000
201 Mission St., San Francisco, CA 94105-1831 (415) 908-3200
701 East Water Street, Charlottesville, VA 22902-7587 (804) 972-7600
www.lexis.com

(Pub.3037)

READ THIS FIRST!

While I incorporate drafting exercises throughout the Contracts class, <u>I never review a student's individual draft</u>. I apply the same techniques we all use with case analysis. You expect your students to come prepared, having read and briefed the cases, but you don't collect and read their briefs. Through class discussion, you explore their analyses of the case and expect them to revise their briefs based on the additional learning in class.

Similarly, when I assign a drafting exercise, students bring their drafts to class. I display the original, either by placing a transparency on an overhead projector or by projecting a computer image through a panel placed on the overhead projector. We then start making revisions, which I indicate either with a marker on the transparency or by entering the change on the computer. In a small class, I have found it works well to project the image directly onto the blackboard. Class discussion can get very lively. The students can then self-evaluate how they have done and make appropriate revisions.

Feel free to make material in the book and in the Teacher's Manual into transparencies. You can do this in a number of ways:

1. Put a sheet of transparency film in a photocopier and make a copy (make sure you have the correct sheet for your machine).

2. Put the enclosed disk in a word processor. Put the transparency film in a laser printer and print the document directly onto the sheet.

The advantage of the second method is that you can change fonts to produce a larger image. The instructor working with a draft may wish to save revisions as successive pages. These pages can then be projected from the computer or printed on transparency film to demonstrate the revision process in the classroom.

A number of additional exercises of this sort may be found in F. REED DICKERSON, MATERIALS ON LEGAL DRAFTING (West 1981) and DAVID MELLINKOFF, LEGAL WRITING: SENSE & NONSENSE (West 1982). The use of transparencies is thoroughly developed in Dickerson's Teacher's Manual.

Table of Contents

Introduction

A. Goals of the Book.

As the years have gone by, and I have reflected more and more upon the nature of the judicial process, I have become reconciled to the uncertainty, because I have grown to see it as inevitable. I have grown to see that the process in its highest reaches is not discovery, but creation; and that the doubts and misgivings, the hopes and fears, are part of the travail of mine, the pangs of death and the pangs of birth, in which principles that have served their day expire, and new principles are born.

Cardozo, *The Nature of the Judicial Process* 166 (1921).

The drafting process is similar to the judicial process as described by Cardozo. This is what makes it such a wonderful medium in which to demonstrate the skills of "thinking like a lawyer." There are some right ways to draft and some wrong ways, but mostly there are better ways. Just as the outcome of a case is a function of the facts and the law, so is the language suitable to a particular agreement. There are ways that are better under the particular circumstances and under the applicable substantive rules.

1. To exemplify the principles of contract law.

Educators theorize that there are two kinds of students: formal or abstract learners and concrete or hands-on learners. See, for example, PIAGET, THE PSYCHOLOGY OF INTELLIGENCE (1950). Most teachers consciously or unconsciously put this finding into practice. They know that many students will best grasp a concept when they see examples of its application or when they see it illustrated graphically. The process of drafting suitable language creates for students the immediacy of problem-solving in realistic circumstances. This makes the learning process active rather than passive.

The immediate application also reinforces the learning process, for students appreciate the connection between acquiring substantive knowledge and developing professional skills. This process reinforces the learning of the substantive course, for the concepts learned are seen as resources to draw on. These materials should be particularly rewarding for the concrete learners who are slower to respond to abstract instruction.

2. To illustrate the principles of contract law in a planning context.

Many excellent writings on planning espouse the importance of understanding the client's goals prior to drafting (see the Bibliography). These works often assume that the traditional law school courses have prepared the planner. Ideally, after working through the case method, we should take a step back and ask what the parties might have done to prevent the problem from arising.

This book makes explicit the implicit message of the case method that if the transaction had been planned with greater foresight, the case would not have ended up in court. Through its application to drafting, Contracts becomes more of a planning course, students are made more aware of dispute resolution outside the courtroom, and more skills are integrated into the curriculum.

3. To develop the skills of a lawyer.

Many faculty members wish to incorporate lawyer competencies into their courses. The importance of writing skills is emphasized by the ABA Section of Legal Education and Admissions to the Bar, LAWYER COMPETENCY: THE ROLE OF THE LAW SCHOOL [the Crampton Report] Recommendation 3, which states:

> Law schools should provide instruction in those fundamental skills critical to lawyer competence. In addition to being able to analyze legal problems and do legal research, a competent lawyer must be able effectively to write, communicate orally, gather facts, interview, counsel, and negotiate. Certain more specialized skills are also important for many law graduates.

> Law school should provide every student at least one rigorous legal writing experience in each year of law study. They should provide all students instruction in such fundamental skills as: oral communication, interviewing, counseling and negotiation. Law schools should also offer instruction in litigation skills to all students desiring it.

More recently, drafting skills have been emphasized in the REPORT OF THE ABA TASK FORCE ON LAW SCHOOLS AND THE PROFESSION: NARROWING THE GAP [The MacCrate Report]. With respect to the skill of Factual Investigation, the Report provides:

> 4.3. (b) Document analysis. In order to work with documents effectively, a lawyer should be familiar with the skills and processes required for:

> (iii) Analyzing the documents, including:

> > (A)   Identifying significant passages or portions of the documents and assessing the implications of the facts contained in these passages or portions for the present factual and legal theories;

(B)   Identifying significant omissions (by, for example, analyzing what information logically should be recorded but is not), and assessing the implications of these omissions for the present factual and legal theories;

(C)   Developing a system or process for reviewing the documents at later points in time to identify:

     (I)   Information which does not presently. appear significant but whose significance may become apparent in light of subsequently learned information;

     (II)   Information which is not presently significant because of the current legal or factual theories but which may turn out to be significant in light of later revisions of legal or factual theories;

With respect to the skill of Factual Investigation, the MacCrate Report provides:

5.2 Using Effective Methods of Communication: To communicate effectively, a lawyer should be familiar with:

(a)   The general prerequisites for effective written or oral communication, including:

     (i)   Presenting one's ideas or views in an effective way, which includes:

          (A)   Organizing the presentation effectively;

          (B)   Expressing ideas or views with precision, clarity, logic, and economy;

          (C)   Choosing appropriate terms, phrases, and images;

          (D)   Applying the mechanics of language (grammar, syntax, punctuation) in an effective manner;

          (E)   Attending to detail (for example, using defined terms consistently; proofreading written communications);

     (ii)   Accurately perceiving and interpreting the communications of others (whether these be written, oral, or nonverbal communications); reading, listening and observing receptively; and responding appropriately;

> (iii)   Attending to emotional or interpersonal factors that may be affecting the communications;

(b) Specialized requirements for effective communications in the legal context, such as:

> (iii)   Substantive. and technical requirements for specialized kinds of legal writing, including those applying to:
>
> > (A)   Drafting of executory documents (for example, contracts, wills, trust instruments, covenants, consent decrees, separation agreements, and corporate charters);

At the same time, overburdened faculty members are reluctant to change the existing curriculum. This book teaches lawyer competence not by replacing the analytical model of the case method but by utilizing that learning. If they actively engage in drafting, students may well develop these skills along with other analytical skills. This book is largely self-instructional, with the process of building a contract providing frequent reinforcement. On the interrelationship of various lawyering skills, see Rutter, *A Jurisprudence of Lawyer's Operations*, 13 J. Legal Educ. 301 (1961).

B. Organization of the Book.

I again hasten to add what the book is not: it is not a treatise, nor a formbook, nor a book on drafting style. It is a resource for thinking about substance and applying that substance to a particular skill. It can be debated whether this skill can or should be taught in law school. Needless to say, I believe it can and should.

In teaching drafting, we perform an important service in practicing preventive law. The drafter who is familiar with substance and who considers the personality of the parties has a much better chance of drafting an instrument that, in the words of Kurt Panzer, speaks with a sanction: "It should generate a force of its own, compelling its performance or observance, which derives from its order, English, visual appeal, and its factual, legal and equitable `rightness.'" I found this intriguing quote in the materials for a Work-Shop Institute on Legal Draftsmanship, Southern Methodist University School of Law, April 16 & 17, 1951.

C. How to Use the Book.

1. Contracts. The principal use for the book is to supplement the first-year course in Contracts. The approach is unlike that of any Contracts casebook, but it is designed to complement all of them. The book can be assigned as each topic is studied to illustrate application of the principles. Alternatively, the substantive material can be completed prior to

the end of the semester, leaving time to study the book. It can then pull together the principles, illustrating relationships and reviewing the course. Even if it is not used as assigned reading, as supplementary reading students will find the book interesting and appealing for its practical content. It could also be used as a text, in conjunction with cases chosen by the teacher.

I have found that this approach enables me to write realistic examinations. Instead of inventing imaginative hypothetical fact situations, I present the students with an executed contract. I then ask how certain fact patterns would affect the outcome. One benefit of this approach is that students concentrate more on accounting for the facts, for the provisions of the contract are facts that must be considered in working out a solution. I also ask more sophisticated questions about how the student might redraft a provision to attain a different result.

I have tried to avoid asking questions that inspire thought but are left to the teacher to answer. This Teacher's Manual contains suggestions for answering the questions and completing the Exercises. You may wish to distribute the analysis of a problem to students or place it on reserve. The Manual also provides additional sources, examples, and exercises. Sources for additional materials are cited at the end of this Manual.

2. Legal Writing. Many law schools require legal writing, but are unable to commit substantial resources to the course. Using the book, students could be assigned to draft a document without substantial supervision or instruction. Because the book habituates students to think about the drafting problems raised by substantive law, it prepares them for exercises in legal writing. Because it teaches the process of drafting rather than the substance of particular types of documents, it can be used from year to year in connection with different substantive assignments.

3. Legal Drafting. Most drafting courses emphasize either drafting with clarity or the drafting of documents in a particular substantive area. This book is different in emphasizing the thinking that lies behind drafting. The book's Exercises make useful class activities and when supplemented with a book on style, the book can be used to generate a variety of instruments. This course is generally offered to upper-class students who have completed the course in Contracts, so the application of contract principles to drafting provides a useful review and extension.

4. Office Practice. Students about to leave law school or beginning practitioners can benefit from reading the book before drafting documents. Many drafting books emphasize style rather than substantive law. It is certainly important to know how to say something, but as a first step you have to know why you want to say it.

The main change in drafting in recent years is the increasing use of computers. There are suggestions for using the book in conjunction with such computer-assisted functions as word processing, grammar checking, comparison of drafts, document assembly, and expert systems. As computers increasingly take over the drafting process, it becomes increasingly important that the attorney understand the process so that the attorney remains in control.

D. Planning the Class Hour.

I will assume at this point that you are persuaded that integrating drafting skills with the study of Contracts is a good thing. You want to do it, but you ask two questions: "How can I fit it in and still cover the material?" And perhaps more importantly, "How can I do it and still have time for the rest of my life?"

1. "How can I fit it in and still cover the material?"

Time in the classroom is simply a function of what is important. I recall Bill Whitford saying at an AALS Contracts conference that on top of the rules, policies, and doctrinal analysis, we all can make room for one "extra."

This is my extra. If you believe that this is important, you will make time for it. You may have to cut down on the number of cases discussed. While there are many good reasons for using the case method, conveying information is not one of them. If a case is used merely to state a rule of law, you can take out that case and substitute a *Restatement* section that states that rule. You can then spend time on application of the rule rather than its derivation.

You may also find that your colleagues are doing a terrific job at emphasizing case analysis and synthesis. Instead of duplicating their efforts, you can emphasize other skills such as planning and application. If you are organizing the course around lawyering skills, you might emphasize those aspects of contract law that are seen more often by lawyers. That may involve less time on the formation of contracts and more on their performance. Or if you make room at the end of the course for review, review through drafting applications.

Another approach might involve teaching a unit exclusively through drafting. Assignment and Delegation, for example, is a unit that lends itself well to understanding through drafting (and is often skipped, in spite of its importance, because of its unfortunate location at the end of the casebook). Promise and Condition and Interpretation can also profitably be taught through drafting.

2. "How can I do it and still have time for the rest of my life?"

It has been said that the case method was as much an administrative breakthrough as a pedagogical breakthrough, for it allowed mass production of lawyers. If you are going to teach a skill, you must develop ways to structure the exercises for use in a large class.

Unfortunately, it is not hard to find examples of poor drafting. Most legal drafting is *redrafting*. I often use examples from a formbook. After we have totally rewritten a provision, I tell the students, "that provision came from WEST'S LEGAL FORMS (or the files of a distinguished law firm, etc.). You have used your analytical skills to improve upon it. You can do better than they did." They appreciate that reward. It also teaches them something important about forms. I was never told about forms, and when I discovered them after law school, I thought they were sacred texts that I was unworthy to alter. My students see them merely as first drafts to be altered and improved.

Exercises illustrate the concepts by having students work with contractual language. For example, to illustrate the concept of Indefiniteness, you might present them with an executed Buy-Sell agreement and ask them to detect those provisions that may be too indefinite to be enforceable. They can then evaluate the language in light of the principles of contract law and make suggestions for revision.

3. Pedagogical advantages

Integrating theory and practice may result in more learning by more students. Learning theory tells us that many students are not abstract learners but concrete learners, who do not fully grasp a concept unless they see what it looks like in an example.

The integrated approach also provides the students with rewards. It is possible to go through law school with no one ever saying, "you did a good job." I don't think I could put up with that for three years. I think we alienate a lot of students because they never receive rewards. As Barbara Child points out, you don't teach drafting by biting off whole documents. You break it down into little pieces. With simple drafting exercises, students can successfully solve the problems and feel that they have accomplished something.

As with any skills training, there is a carry-over to other areas of knowledge. I coordinate my class with the teacher of Business Organizations, for example, so that he can employ the students' drafting skills in drafting various corporate documents. Such skills exercises make the students active rather than passive learners. They are not just reading about what someone else has done, but are doing it themselves.

I have many students who get jobs with practitioners during the summer after their first year. They often tell me, "My first assignment was to prepare a contract. I could do it with confidence. I knew what I was doing."

Finally, because drafting is often redrafting, it is fun. As H.G. Wells pointed out:

> No passion in the world, no love or hate, is equal to the passion to alter someone else's draft.

E. Assessment.

It is important that an examination test what has been taught in class. Usually in a case analysis class, the exam represents the first time students actually do what is tested on the exam. On the exam, I ask questions about actual contracts that test the concepts taught in class.

In testing application of knowledge through drafting, I have discovered a number of gaps in the students' knowledge. In the area of consideration, for example, consider this situation. A contract provides:

1. A shall deliver 100 widgets to B on June 1.
2. B shall pay A $1000 on delivery.
3. B shall pay A an additional $10,000 on A's birthday.

When asked to identify problems with this contract, many students will say there is no consideration for B's promise in ¶ 3. Or in a separation agreement in which the parties agree to dissolve their marriage but there is no division of property and no maintenance, students are concerned that there is no consideration.

Once these errors in application become apparent, I can adjust my teaching of substance to remedy them. Thus I frequently obtain feedback that I might not otherwise receive.

F. Additional Works.

I have written a treatise for practitioners, THE CONTRACT DRAFTING GUIDEBOOK (Michie 1992), that examines additional issues as well as the same issues in greater depth. BARBARA CHILD, DRAFTING LEGAL DOCUMENTS (West 2d ed. 1992) and REED DICKERSON, LEGAL DRAFTING (West 1981) both have thorough Teacher's Guides that contain additional suggestions and sources. Dickerson's Teacher's Guide is especially helpful on the use of the overhead projector in class. THOMAS R. HAGGARD, CONTRACT LAW FROM A DRAFTING PERSPECTIVE (West 2003) has a number of exercises that are discussed in the Teacher's Manual. For advanced drafting, I highly recommend Charles M. Fox, WORKING WITH CONTRACTS: WHAT LAW SCHOOL DOESN'T TEACH YOU (PLI 2002).

PART I

How the Principles of Contract Law Are Exemplified in Drafting

Chapter 1
Offer and Acceptance

§ 1.1. Introduction.

1. Most of this book examines drafting problems that arise in negotiated contracts. This chapter is an exception, for where both parties have executed the same agreement, there is rarely a need to demonstrate the occurrence of offer and acceptance. One authority notes that "[i]n defense of traditional analysis, it can still be said that the party who signs first is the offeror." FARNSWORTH, CONTRACTS § 3.5 at 111.

2. MELLINKOFF, LEGAL WRITING: SENSE AND NONSENSE 97 provides this example of a letter agreement:

> Mr. John Doak
> Los Angeles, Calif.
>
> Dear Mr. Doak:
>
> You and I agree:
>
> > 1. . . .
> > 2. . . .
> > 3. . . .
>
> Very truly yours,
>
> Bill Jones
>
> Agreed:
>
> John Doak

3. A negotiated agreement may contain sleeping dogs that will later be roused. The drafter should ask these questions:

- Does it contain the entire understanding of the parties? See Chapter 6, *Parol Evidence*.

- Is it an accurate reflection of the parties' understanding or was there an error in transcription? See Chapter 8, *Mistake*.

- Is it complete enough to constitute an enforceable agreement? Were some of the terms left vague or indefinite or were they to be negotiated later? See Chapter 3, *Indefiniteness*.

4. Unilateral contracts and "reverse unilateral contracts" may require careful drafting to attain the desired results, but are so infrequently encountered that they are not included in this work.

5. For comic relief, it might be fun to show your class the scene from The Marx Brothers' *A Night at the Opera* (1933) in which Groucho and Chico negotiate a contract for the services of an opera singer. Is offer and acceptance found in this negotiation? The negotiations end with this classic exchange:

Groucho: We've got a contract. No matter how small it is.

Chico: Hey, wait. Wait. What does this say here? This thing here?

Groucho: Oh, that. That's the usual clause. That's in every contract. That just says, "If any of the parties participating in this contract are shown not to be in their right mind, the entire agreement is automatically nullified."

Chico: Well, I don't know.

Groucho: It's all right. That's in every contract. That's what they call a sanity clause.

Chico: Ha ha! You can't fool me -- there ain't no sanity clause!

§ 1.2. Firm offers. The language of Example 1 is adapted from *E.A. Coronis Associates v. M. Gordon Construction Co.*, 90 N.J. Super. 69, 216 A.2d 246 (1966).

§ 1.3. Did negotiating parties intend an agreement?

1. Letter of intent. A good example of a letter of intent is found in Canady, *Indemnity, Letters of Intent, and Public Announcements in the Sale of a Business*, 10 ALI-ABA Course Materials J., No.3, 57, 70-72 (1985):

Seller Corporation
San Francisco, California

Dear Sirs:

This letter sets forth our mutual intention that Seller Corporation ("Seller") will be acquired by the undersigned ("Purchaser") on the following terms:

1. The acquisition will be accomplished through the merger of a wholly-owned subsidiary of Purchaser into Seller in a transaction intended to be a reorganization under section 368 of the Internal Revenue Code, as amended. Upon the occurrence of the merger, all of the then-outstanding shares of capital stock of Seller will be converted into 350,000 shares of common stock of Purchaser.

2. The shares of common stock of Purchaser issued to the stockholders of Seller upon the merger becoming effective will not be registered under the Securities Act of 1933 and will constitute "restricted securities" with the limitations on transferability that we have discussed with you. The shares, when issued, will be listed on the New York Stock Exchange.

3. At the closing, X, Y, and Z will execute three-year employment contracts and covenants not-to-compete.

4. Among the conditions to the closing of the contemplated transaction will be the following:

    a. The execution of a definitive agreement containing appropriate representations and warranties by Seller and its principal stockholders, including representations and warranties as to the absence of undisclosed liabilities, as to the Seller's financial statements, and as to the absence of any adverse changes in Seller's business or financial condition since the date of those financial statements;

    b. The approval of the definitive agreement by the Board of Directors and shareholders of Seller and by the Board of Directors of Purchaser;

    c. The satisfactory verification by Purchaser of the financial statements of Seller;

    d. The obtaining by Purchaser of an opinion from Big Eight Accounting Co. to the effect that the transaction contemplated by this Letter of Intent will be given "pooling-of-interests" accounting treatment;

    e. The obtaining by Seller of a ruling from the Internal Revenue Service to the effect that the proposed transaction will constitute a reorganization under Section 368 of the Internal Revenue Code; and

    f. Compliance with any applicable regulatory requirements.

5. Pending execution of the definitive agreement and in any event until _____, _____, Seller has agreed that it will not directly or indirectly enter into an agreement or negotiate with any other party with respect to the sale of its business or any of its subsidiaries and will not engage in any transaction during that period not in the ordinary course of business that might adversely affect the value of the business or assets to be acquired by Purchaser.

6. Neither party will make any public disclosure or publicity release pertaining to the existence of this letter of intent or the subject matter contained herein without the consent of the other signatory hereto; provided, however, that each party shall be permitted to make such disclosures to the public or to governmental agencies as its counsel shall deem necessary to comply with any applicable laws.

7. Other than for the provisions of Paragraph 5 and 6 it is understood that this letter of intent does not bind either of us and that it creates no rights or obligations.

If the foregoing is in accordance with your understanding, please so indicate the attached copy of the letter in the place indicated for your signature and return the same to the undersigned.

Very truly yours,

Acquisition Corporation

By: _____

Seller Corporation

By: _____

Many recent cases indicate the dangers of the parties' neglect to adequately express their intent to enter a contract. See Farnsworth, *Precontractual Liability and Preliminary Agreements: Fair Dealing and Failed Negotiations*, 87 Colum. L. Rev. 217 (1987). Even when parties do draft a "letter of intent," they often draft it carelessly or after an oral commitment has been made. This problem frequently arises in the sale of a business, when the buyer and seller agree on the purchase only to have negotiations break down over the details. See, e.g., *Martin Appalachian Gas Co. v. Haugen, Enochs & Associates, Inc.*, 1987 WL 6207 (E.D. La. 1987); *Rand-Whitney Packaging Corp. v. Robertson Group, Inc.*, 651 F. Supp. 520 (D. Mass. 1986); *California Natural, Inc. v. Nestle Holdings, Inc.*, 631 F. Supp. 465 (D.N.J. 1986). In *California Natural*, the Letter of Intent stated in part:

this letter constitutes only a Letter of Intent and a statement of our present intentions regarding the transactions set forth above, and neither constitutes nor should be construed as evidence of any form of offer or binding contract.

The suggested language is adapted from *Simplicio v. National Scientific Personnel Bureau, Inc.*, 180 A.2d 500 (D.C. 1962). See also Knapp, *Enforcing the Contract to Bargain*, 44 N.Y.U. L. Rev. 637 (1969).

In *Smissaert v. Chiodo*, 163 Cal. App. 2d 827, 330 P.2d 98 (1958), the offer stated:

It is further mutually understood and agreed by and between the parties to this agreement that the validity of said proposed agreement is subject and conditioned upon the parties agreeing upon and reducing to writing all terms and conditions necessary and incidental to the validity of said proposed agreement.

This provision could use revision. See Chapter 17, *The Language of Drafting*. Consider the following:

• "It is further mutually understood and agreed by and between the parties to this agreement" is surplus -- a contract is a mutual agreement. Strike it.

• There is only one proposed agreement. Strike "said."

• Why use the twofer "subject and conditioned upon" when one word will do? Use one word expressing a condition.

• When the parties come to an agreement, they will execute a signed writing. Therefore "agreeing upon and reducing to writing" expresses the same thought.

• What do the parties mean by "all terms and conditions necessary and incidental to the validity of said proposed agreement"? If they sign a writing, isn't that their final agreement?

The revised agreement might look like this:

To be enforceable, an agreement between the parties must be written and signed by both parties.

§ 1.4.   Objective manifestation of assent.

On click-wrap agreements, see Christina L. Kunz, Maureen F. Del Duca, Heather Thayer, and Jennifer Debrow, *Click-through Agreements: Strategies for Avoiding Disputes on Validity of Assent*, 57 Bus. Law. 401 (2001). Helpful advice can be found at the Federal Trade Commission web site, http://www.ftc.gov/bcp/conline/pubs/buspubs/dotcom/index.html#II

§ 1.5.   The Battle of the Forms.

Sources include CALAMARI & PERILLO, CONTRACTS § 2.21 (4th ed.); WHITE & SUMMERS, UNIFORM COMMERCIAL CODE § 1-3 (5th ed.); 5A HART & WILLIER, FORMS AND PROCEDURES UNDER THE U.C.C. § 25.07; a bibliography of law review articles appears at 6C BENDER'S UNIFORM COMMERCIAL CODE SERVICE § 2-207, at 2-220.2 to .3. Much of the form language in the text is adapted from 5A HART & WILLIER, FORMS AND PROCEDURES UNDER THE U.C.C. § 25.07.

Many authorities have suggested that § 2-207 is inadequately drafted. See *Roto-Lith v. F.P. Bartlett & Co.*, 297 F.2d 497 (1st Cir. 1962) ("not too happily drafted"); *Southwest Engineering. Co. v. Martin Tractor Co.*, 205 Kan. 684, 473 P.2d 18 (1970) ("a murky bit of prose"). See generally Barron and Dunfee, *Two Decades of 2-207: Review, Reflection and Revision*, 24 Clev. St. L. Rev. 171 (1975).

One of the problems is that the statute reaches a number of logical decision points (i.e., forks in the road) and only pursues one of the alternatives. For example, it states the rule for additional terms but not for different terms and it states the rule for agreements between merchants but does not state the rule for agreements between merchants and non-merchants. The flow chart was designed to supply the missing alternatives.

A number of difficulties arise in drafting under § 2-207:

1. An acceptance is effective in forming a contract even though it states additional or different terms. But to operate as an acceptance, the expression must be "definite." If the terms are substantially different (i.e., differences in description of the goods, price, or quantity), is there a contract?

See WHITE & SUMMERS, UNIFORM COMMERCIAL CODE § 1-3 (5th ed.), Case 8, citing cases holding that a return document containing significantly different material terms is not an acceptance. 3 DEUSENBERG & KING, SALES AND BULK TRANSFERS § 3.04(1) note that "what is necessary to constitute a 'definite and reasonable expression of acceptance' is somewhat cloudy under the Code . . . ." See also authorities cited in CALAMARI & PERILLO, CONTRACTS § 2.21 (4th ed.).

2. The expression is not an acceptance if it is "expressly made conditional on assent to the additional or different terms." If the offeree states that the agreement is "subject to conditions printed on the reverse side of this form," has the offeree made the acceptance conditional?

See WHITE & SUMMERS, UNIFORM COMMERCIAL CODE § 1-3, case 4. This issue arises in the cases of *Roto-Lith, Ltd. v. F.P. Bartlett & Co.* and *Matter of Doughboy Industries, Inc.*, which are included in many casebooks. Neither case seems satisfactory, for the former deems the different term an express condition while the latter assumes it without discussion. It is hoped that the Exercise provides a clearer application of the concept.

3. If a contract is created by conduct, § 2-207(3) controls. This could be detrimental to the offeror, for the terms supplied by the U.C.C. could be more generous than those in offeror's form. If offeror is buyer, the terms of the U.C.C. are probably more advantageous than seller's terms, for the U.C.C. warranty and limitations provisions are more likely to favor buyer.

However, Official Comment 6 views the language "any other provisions of this Act" in Subsection (3) as including § 2-207(2). Under this analysis, between merchants the offeree's terms could become part of the agreement unless buyer complied with one of the exceptions in Subsection (2).

4. When offeror's language does not prevent formation of a contract, but restricts the terms to those of the offer, the offeror takes advantage of Subsection (2)(a), rejecting the additional terms of the acceptance. What becomes of the different terms? Presumably the different terms have already been rejected because the fact that they conflict with offeror's terms constitutes "notice of objection" under (2)(c). See Comment 6. Is a term in the response that differs from a term that is not expressly in the offer but is implied by the Code an additional or a different term? Presumably, it is different. Some states have muddled (or simplified?) any distinction by amending Subsection (2) to read "The additional or different terms ...."

5. If the offeror included the language of Subsection (2)(a) and the offeree included the language of Subsection (1) after the comma, it could be argued that the language of the acceptance was a different term. This analysis is incorrect, for you would drop down to Subsection (3), not Subsection (2). To have a different term in an agreement, there first has to be an acceptance. Under the exception to subsection (1), the language of express condition prevents offeree's response from being an acceptance.

§ 1.6. Ethics in offer and acceptance.

A good case on the issue of whether an illiterate person is bound by a contract is *Ellis v. Mullen*, 238 S.E.2d 187 (N.C. Ct. App. 1977).

The quote is from *Kang v. Harrington*, 587 P.2d 285 (HI 1978) (citing *Cummins v. Cummins*, 24 Haw. 116, 122 (1917) quoting from *Linington v. Strong*, 107 Ill. 295, 302 (1883)). An attorney was found to have committed fraud when he engaged in this practice in *Wright v. Pennamped*, 657 N.E.2d 1223 (Ind. Ct. App. 1995). The court found that the lawyer violated Model Rule 4.1, which provides, "In the course of representing a client a lawyer shall not knowingly make a false statement of fact or law." The court stated at 1231:

> By undertaking the tasks of a drafting attorney, including the distribution of draft loan documents and the solicitation of review and approval of the documents, Pennamped assumed a duty to disclose any changes in the documents prior to execution to the other parties or their respective counsel. [citation omitted] The existence of such as duty is supported by common sense and notions of fair dealing. Thus, Pennamped, as the drafting attorney, had a duty to inform Brown or, in his absence, Wright, of any changes occurring after Brown's review and approval of the loan documents. Were the rule otherwise, pre-closing review of loan documentation would become a futile act, and counsel would be required to scrutinize every term of each document at the moment of execution.

§ 1.7. Exercises.

1. The Click-Wrap Agreement.

This agreement was found at www.gateway.com on 2/3/2003. The user is not compelled to look at the Terms before indicating that he or she has read and agreed to them. Because the bold print terms might be deemed to be beyond the user's reasonable expectations, Company might arrange them for separate assent.

Putting this together, the ordering page might have the user click on:

> Go to Warranty and Terms and Conditions Agreement.

The user might then go to Terms and Conditions which are scrolled through and end with the following:

> I have read and accept the Terms and Conditions.
>
>   YES   NO
>
> I understand that this agreement applies to my purchase unless I notify Company in writing that I do not agree to this agreement within 15 days after I receive this agreement and I return the product or cancel services under company's refund policy.
>
>   YES   NO

I understand that this agreement contains a dispute resolution clause. Please see section 8 above.

YES   NO

Only if the user answered YES to each statement would the user then be enabled to continue to order the goods.

2. The "Battle of the Forms."

These forms are adapted from MANDEL, THE PREPARATION OF COMMERCIAL INSTRUMENTS, Forms 1 and 2.

This dispute involves the classic "Battle of the Forms." Buyer, as offeror, has sent Seller a standard form for the purchase of goods. Seller, as offeree, has responded with its standard form. Both forms coincide on the essential terms of the deal: price, quantity, delivery, and payment. But on other terms, there is a disparity. Because the parties agreed on the essential terms, they performed, and the other terms became significant only after a dispute arose.

Resolution of the disputed substantive terms must wait, for there is initially a procedural dispute. Buyer claims that because of the presence of an arbitration clause in its form, it is entitled to arbitration. Seller claims that because of the prohibition of arbitration in its form, the matter must be resolved in the court.

The issues are whether there is an agreement between Buyer and Seller and, if so, what is its provision with respect to arbitration. At common law an acceptance had to be the mirror image of the offer; if not, the acceptance became a counter-offer. Under this analysis, Seller's divergent acceptance would be a counter-offer. The issue would then be whether Buyer accepted by its conduct. Since Buyer paid for the goods, it probably became bound to Seller's terms when it did not immediately reject the goods. Seller fired the "last shot," so its terms, including the no arbitration clause, would be binding.

The common law has been changed by the enactment of the Uniform Commercial Code, which governs the sale of goods. The relevant section is 2-207. Analysis of the problem under the Code requires application of the statute to the distinctions between Buyer's and Seller's forms.

In analyzing these forms in light of the statute, it is important to work through all the decision points. For example, you can not begin analyzing whether the proposals become part of the contract under subsection (2) until you have first determined that subsection (2) is applicable. The critical decision points are identified in WHITE & SUMMERS, UNIFORM COMMERCIAL CODE § 1-3 (5th ed.), which breaks the combinations of circumstances into eight categories:

(1)   Cases in which the parties send printed forms to one another, and a crucial term is covered one way in one form and the other way in the other form.

(2)   Cases in which a crucial term is found in the first form sent (the offer), but no term on that question appears in the second.

(3)   Cases in which a crucial term is found in the second form (the acceptance), but there is no consistent or conflicting term in the first.

(4)   Cases in which a crucial term is found in the second form but not in the first, and the second form is a counter-offer (because "expressly conditional").

(5)   Cases in which at least one form contains a term that provides that no contract will be formed unless the other party accedes to all of the terms on that form and offers no others.

(6)   Cases in which there is a prior oral agreement. (In cases (1) through (5) we have assumed that there may be prior oral negotiations but that no oral agreement was reached before parties sent their forms.)

(7)   Cases in which the parties do not use forms but send a variety of messages and letters and conduct intermittent oral negotiations that ultimately produce an agreement.

(8)   Cases in which the second form differs so radically from the first that it does not constitute an "acceptance."

This exercise is modeled on case (1). Other sources include the Official Comments to the U.C.C., the U.C.C. Digest, and the many law review articles on this topic.

Buyer is offeror. Is Seller's Acknowledgment an acceptance? Students will claim that ¶7 of Buyer's Purchase Order is sufficient to prevent an acceptance from arising. They probably do not realize that a court would characterize this provision as serving two other functions. First, it is a merger clause. See § 6.4. Second, it is a no-oral-modification clause. See § 11.9. Similarly, students will claim that ¶1 of Seller's Sales Confirmation serves this purpose. Point out to them that clauses relating to *modification* presume that there is first a contract to modify. That step cannot occur until after 2-207 is used to determine what the contract terms are. Review the language that is considered sufficient to satisfy the statutory requirement and emphasize the importance of tracking the statute.

Hypothetically, if there were no acceptance because of the language after the comma, then under subsection (3), the agreement would be found in the UCC. In each of the problem areas, we would read in not the parties' language, but the default provisions of the Code.

Assuming that there is an acceptance, let us analyze the application of subsection (2). I find it helpful to list Buyer's and Seller's terms side by side on the board, then after the analysis cross out one term or the other and see what is left as part of the contract.

Let us examine in turn the hypotheticals in the Exercise:

a. Seller claims it can't fully perform because of a fire.

Buyer's offer is silent on this subject while Seller's acceptance contains an *additional* term in ¶3. This proposed additional term is presumed accepted between merchants, as both parties apparently are. Exception (a) does not apply if Buyer's ¶7 is not considered sufficient for this purpose. Exception (c) doesn't apply. Therefore the issue comes down, as it often does, to exception (b). Because of the widespread acceptance of force majeure clauses (see § 9.4), Seller's term probably does not materially alter the offer. Therefore Seller's term is in the contract.

This example points out the difficulty of distinguishing between *additional* and *different* terms. Although we characterized the term as additional because Buyer's form was silent on it, technically Buyer's form can be said to include it as a default clause. That is, in the absence of a force majeure clause, the law would imply one under § 2-615.

b. Buyer claims the delivered goods are not merchantable.

Buyer's offer states in ¶4 that the goods must be merchantable. Seller's acceptance states in ¶2 that there is no warranty of merchantability. The acceptance clearly contains a different term. Assuming we treat this different term the same way we would treat an additional term, it is clearly excluded under subsection (2)(b). Therefore Buyer's term is in the contract.

c. Twenty days after receipt of the goods, Buyer gives Seller notice that the goods are not merchantable.

Buyer's offer is silent on the time of notice while Seller's acceptance requires 15 days notice in ¶6. This can be viewed as an additional term or as a different term if we take Buyer's silence as incorporating the default provision of reasonable notice found in § 2-607(3)(a). It is difficult to analyze Seller's proposal under subsection (2)(b). It may impose a hardship on Buyer to bar a claim as five days late. On the other hand, under § 1-102(3), the parties are free to determine standards of reasonableness if not manifestly unreasonable. If 15 days is not manifestly unreasonable, then Seller's term is in the contract.

d. Buyer returns the goods to Seller.

In ¶1, Buyer retains the right to return goods while in ¶7 Seller denies Buyer this right. This proposed term probably materially alters the terms of the offer, so Buyer's term is in the contract.

e. Buyer seeks to have the dispute resolved in arbitration.

In ¶6, Buyer's offer contains an arbitration clause while ¶10 of Seller's acceptance contains a no-arbitration clause in ¶10. Because the forum for dispute has been held to be material, Buyer's term would be in the contract. Note that the more common case holds that an arbitration clause proposed in the acceptance is not in the contract.

Under Buyer's view, the common law rule is reversed: the party who fires the *first* shot gets its way when there is a conflict. This may be appropriate, for it accords with the idea that the offeror is master of the offer and it gives the offeree an opportunity to object rather than perform. Under the facts, if Buyer's approach prevails, there would be arbitration and the motion should be granted.

Under Seller's view, if the forms do not make a contract or if neither term is part of the contract, then there is an agreement under § 2-207(3). Under this approach, by creating differences, the party who fires the last shot will get no less than what the U.C.C. provides. The U.C.C. is silent on arbitration. Therefore in the absence of agreement or statute requiring arbitration, arbitration may not be compelled and the parties must resolve the problem in court. (See the many annotations to 9 U.S.C.A. § 2.)

f. Buyer asks that New York law be applied to resolve the dispute.

In ¶8, Buyer chooses New York law while in ¶11 Seller chooses Montana law. Because the law in either event is the UCC, which has few differences, Seller's term does not materially alter the offer and is part of the contract. Curiously, it might make a difference in this case, because Montana has enacted a nonstandard version of 2-207(2), modifying the language to read "The additional or different terms are to be construed ..." When Wisconsin adopted this language, the U.C.C. Permanent Editorial Board objected.

3. Ethics.

Who is your client? If there is a dispute about the terms, who are you going to represent? What happens if one party comes to believe that the other party got more favorable terms? Because you have an obligation of loyalty to your client, it is the best practice to represent only one party to a contract.

Chapter 2
Consideration

§ 2.1. Introduction.

See the examples following RESTATEMENT (SECOND) § 71. In *Hoffmann v. Wausau Concrete Co.*, 58 Wis. 2d 472, 207 N.W.2d 80 (1973), the court held that love and affection between parent and child is not a sufficient consideration.

Students should note that to constitute consideration, a performance does not require the payment of money or the delivery of material goods. RESTATEMENT § 71 states that the performance may consist of (a) an act, (b) a forbearance, or (c) the creation, modification or destruction of a legal relation. For example, a separation agreement between husband and wife may not provide for the payment of money. Nevertheless, the destruction of the legal relation, marriage, is a sufficient consideration. Each party is releasing the other from the claims inherent in that relationship. In some jurisdictions, this point may be made by statute. Cal. Civ. Code § 160 (repealed) provided:

> The mutual consent of the parties is a sufficient consideration for [a separation agreement].

§ 2.2. Statutes dispensing with consideration.

Students may find the prose of § 2-203 a bit murky. Official Comment 1 states in part:

> This section makes it clear [!] that every effect of the seal which relates to "sealed instruments" as such is wiped out insofar as contracts for sale are concerned.

It may be important to distinguish between contracts under seal and other seals required by law. For example, a statute may require that a document be notarized, which may require a notary seal, or that a corporation affix its seal.

§ 2.3. Recital of consideration.

On the issue of whether a court would find an implied promise where the parties clearly intended a bargain, see *Stewart v. Griffith*, 217 U.S. 323 (1910). The seller promised to sell a parcel of land but the buyer did not expressly promise to buy it. The court held that "[t]he tenor of the 'agreement' throughout imports mutual undertakings." Justice Holmes reasoned:

> The $500 is paid as "part purchase price of the total sum to be paid," that is, that the purchaser agrees to pay. The land is described as "being sold." There are words of present conveyance inoperative as such but implying a concluded bargain, like the word 'sold' just quoted.... Here is an absolute promise in terms, which it would be unreasonable to

make except on the footing of a similar promise as to the main parcel that the purchaser desired to get. We are satisfied that Stewart bound himself to take the land.

On the recital of reasons for an imbalance in consideration, the court held against the landlord in *Cardona v. Eden Realty*, discussed in § 4.9, finding the form of a bargain but no substance. Nevertheless, the drafter's effort might be successful in appropriate circumstances.

The drafter should be sure that the agreement *contains* consideration for the mutual promises; it is less important that the agreement recite the consideration as such. The standard practice is simply to express the mutual obligations. Often an agreement will contain language such as:

> In consideration of the mutual promises and agreements herein contained, the parties agree as follows ...

This language is not meaningful if the agreement does not actually contain mutual promises; if it does contain mutual promises, the language is surplusage. Omit it.

§ 2.4. The adequacy of consideration.

Some states have statutory presumptions that "A written instrument is presumptive evidence of a consideration" (Cal. Civ. Code § 1614) or "There was good and sufficient consideration for a written contract" (Cal. Civ. Proc. Code § 1963(39) [repealed]).

Even if paid, the recited consideration may be a sham. In *Fischer v. Union Trust Co.*, 138 Mich. 612, 101 N.W. 852 (1904), a father gave his daughter a deed. Her brother gave her a dollar which she gave to her father. The court stated, "The passing of the dollar by the brother to his sister, and by her to her father, was treated rather as a joke than as any actual consideration."

§ 2.6. Illusory contracts.

The historical background of *Wood v. Lucy, Lady Duff-Gordon* is presented in Pratt, *American Contract Law at the Turn of the Century*, 39 S.C. L. Rev. 415 (1988). Unfortunately, Prof. Wood was unable to discover what happened between the parties after the case was decided.

The court stated of Lady Duff-Gordon that "[h]er favor helps a sale." Suppose one of your students signed a contract with Mr. Wood, granting him the exclusive right to use their name to endorse products. Is the promise good consideration? The contract with Wood would probably be enforceable. Even if the name has little value in selling products, the student has suffered a legal detriment. You have given up the right to have your name used for endorsements.

The standard songwriter's contract is an excellent modern example of an agreement in which one party (the songwriter) promises exclusive rights to a party (the publisher) who does not expressly promise to do anything. See *Clifford Davis Management Ltd. v. WEA Records Ltd.*, 1 All E.R. 237 (C.A. 1974), involving an onerous agreement signed by members of the group "Fleetwood Mac" when they were virtually unknown. See SHEMEL & KRASILOVSKY, THIS BUSINESS OF MUSIC for this form contract.

§ 2.7. Distributorship agreements.

In the absence of a termination provision, clearly the parties are not bound forever. Some courts hold that the agreement is illusory. Others permit a distributorship agreement to be terminated at will by either party; reasonable notice may or may not be required. Others provide that the agreement is terminable at will only after a reasonable time and on reasonable notice. See Annot., *Termination by Principal of Distributorship Contract Containing No Express Provision for Termination*, 19 A.L.R.3d 196 (1968). One of the principal reasons for allowing termination after a reasonable time is the substantial reliance of the distributor. The measure of a reasonable time might be a sufficient time to recover the reliance costs. See *Clausen & Sons v. Theo. Hamm Brewing Co.*, 395 F.2d 388 (8th Cir. 1968).

Because of the acute problem of termination of a franchise, a number of jurisdictions have enacted statutes to protect franchisees. See, *e.g.*, Cal. Bus. & Prof. Code §§ 2000 et seq. See also Annot., *Validity, Construction, and Effect of State Franchising Statute*, 67 A.L.R.3d 1299 (1975).

On the limitation of "good faith," *Bushwick-Decatur Motors, Inc. v. Ford Motor Co.*, 116 F.2d 675 (2d Cir. 1940), may be contrasted with 15 U.S.C. §§ 1221-25, the "Automobile Dealers' Day in Court Act." In *Bushwick-Decatur*, the court stated: "With a power of termination at will here so unmistakably expressed, we certainly cannot assert that a limitation of good faith was anything the parties had in mind."

§ 2.8. Output and requirements contracts.

The output contract example is adapted from *Feld v. Henry S. Levy & Son, Inc.*, 37 N.Y.2d 466, 335 N.E.2d 320, 373 N.Y.S. 102 (1975). An example of a requirements contract would be Buyer's promise to purchase from Seller "all the bread crumbs Buyer requires."

§ 2.10. Exercises.

2. Recital of consideration.

Sure. Students sometimes make the mistake of looking for consideration for each item in a contract. Instead, they should merely look to see whether each side has bargained for a return promise. And, of course, the lack of equivalent value is not a consideration issue.

3. Recital of consideration.

Sure. As provided in RESTATEMENT § 71(3)(c), consideration is found in "the creation, modification, or destruction of a legal relation." The same would work for any mutual rescission of a contract in which each gives up rights against the other.

4. The Family Dispute.

The facts of this exercise are adapted from *Allen v. Allen*, 133 A.2d 116 (D.C. 1957). In most jurisdictions today, the recital of the seal would have no effect. The court reasoned that the copy stated that the agreement was executed under seal. It was therefore a question of fact whether the original was actually executed under seal. The trial court determined that it was not. This reasoning suggests that in the District of Columbia at the time, the presence of a seal was meaningful.

The court stated that while the court will not generally inquire into the adequacy of consideration, there may be exceptions where the exchange is grossly inadequate. This agreement did not fall within the exception, however. Because the brothers were not obligated to sell, an exchange would not necessarily occur. Note also that the fact that the mother did not actually receive anything for her promise is not an impediment to an enforceable contract.

Finally, the court held that the contract was not enforceable if in fact the one dollar was not paid. That consideration would be a pretense.

The case illustrates the point made in Fuller, *Consideration and Form*, 41 Colum. L. Rev. 779 (1941), that the legal formality of the exchange of consideration performs an "evidentiary" function so that the existence and terms of the contract may be proven, and a "cautionary" function so that parties may appreciate the significance of their acts.

5. The Charitable Subscription.

The pledge form used in this exercise comes from *Jordan v. Mount Sinai Hospital of Greater Miami, Inc.*, 276 So. 2d 102 (Fla. Dist. Ct. App. 1973), *aff'd*, 290 So. 2d 484 (Fla. 1974). The District Court of Appeals reviewed the approaches used in other jurisdictions. Those approaches included recognizing that when the hospital used one pledge to induce others to make pledges, the additional contributions were a consideration for the first pledge. Alternatively, the hospital may have relied on the pledge. Finally, as a matter of public policy, consideration might be dispensed with. The court rejected all of those approaches, reasoning that the assertion that a pledge might induce the pledges of others was a fiction, that reliance must be proven, and that public policy was not an adequate reason to do away with consideration.

The Florida Supreme Court stated:

> Therefore, in order for a pledge to survive the death of the donor and be considered a valid claim against the estate, two elements must coincidentally exist. First, the document stating the conditions of the pledge must recite with particularity the specific purpose for which the funds are to be used....Secondly, the donee must affirmatively show actual reliance of a substantial character in furtherance of the specified purpose set forth in the pledge instrument before the claim may be honored by the estate.

The pledge might be rewritten to begin, "To assist in the establishment of a cancer research facility,..." The hospital would then have to demonstrate that it had undertaken work to construct the facility.

Contrast the outcome of this case with RESTATEMENT (SECOND) § 90(2), which suggests that a charitable subscription may be binding without proof of reliance.

6. The Buy-Sell Agreement.

The Special Provisions are examples of "satisfaction" clauses, for the report and the remodeling are subject to Buyer's satisfaction. It appears that Buyer's obligation to go through with the purchase is conditioned by an event entirely within his control. All he has to do is say, "I'm not satisfied," and the deal is off. If one party has the option of performing or not performing, the agreement is illusory. Note that even though Buyer is the one who has this option, Seller may use this principle to escape from the deal. Seller may do so because an agreement that lacks consideration is not enforceable. To put it another way, if both parties are not bound, neither party is bound.

Under the modern view, however, satisfaction clauses do not necessarily make an agreement unenforceable. Satisfaction clauses are of two types: objective and subjective. Objective satisfaction clauses relate to quality, operative fitness, or mechanical utility. Courts apply a reasonable person standard: Would a reasonable person standing in the shoes of the contracting party be satisfied if objective criteria are applied. For example, the clause that states that Buyer must be satisfied with the engineer's report is probably an objective satisfaction clause. It is not enough that Buyer is not personally satisfied. He would have to demonstrate that a reasonable person would not be satisfied.

Subjective satisfaction clauses relate to fancy, taste, or judgment. Courts do not look at whether a reasonable person would be satisfied but whether the party who may exercise the satisfaction clause is satisfied. However, that party must use good faith in exercising his or her judgment. Good faith is defined in U.C.C. § 1-201(19) as "honesty in fact." When this standard is applied, the exercise is no longer a matter of whim. It is open to objective examination of the honesty of the party. For example, the clause that states that Buyer must be satisfied with the remodeling is probably a subjective satisfaction clause. The issue is whether Buyer, not a reasonable person, thinks the drapes match the rug. But Buyer must act honestly. If Seller could show that Buyer had already agreed to purchase another property and therefore had a motive to express dissatisfaction, Buyer would be bound.

Therefore, the buy-sell agreement is probably enforceable in spite of the satisfaction clauses. The agreement is not illusory, for the satisfaction clauses may not be exercised at the whim of Buyer. They are limited in one case by standards of reasonableness and in the other case by standards of good faith. These principles are analyzed in *Mattei v. Hopper*, 51 Cal. 2d 119, 330 P.2d 625 (1958), and *Fursmidt v. Hotel Abbey Holding Corp.*, 10 A.D.2d 447, 200 N.Y.S.2d 256 (1960). See also Annot., *Reasonableness or Personal Judgment of Buyer as Test Where Goods are Sold Subject to Being Satisfactory to the Buyer*, 86 A.L.R.2d 200 (1962).

One way to lessen the problem of allowing the parties to exercise their satisfaction is to provide for the satisfaction of a third party. For example, a contract between an owner and a builder could provide that the owner's obligation to pay is conditioned on his or her satisfaction with the results. See Annot., *Construction and Effect of Provision in Private Building and Construction Contract that Work Must be Done to Satisfaction of Owner*, 44 A.L.R.2d 1114 (1955). Alternatively, the contract could leave the decision up to a third party, an architect, as in American Institute of Architects Document A201. On the good faith requirement, see Annot., *Liability of Architect or Engineer for Improper Issuance of Certificate*, 43 A.L.R.2d 1227 (1955).

Here is an additional Exercise:

7. Termination of a franchise. A client comes to your office with this problem. She had entered into the franchise agreement that follows two years ago and had built the business into a successful operation. Suddenly, pursuant to the termination provision in the contract, the franchisor terminated the agreement. Does she have any remedy?

Notice the dilemma you are faced with. If the agreement is enforceable, your client has no remedy. If you succeed in convincing a court that the agreement is not enforceable, your client may have no remedy either! How can you fashion a solution that will accomplish your objective: enforce the agreement and at the same time lessen the harshness of a sudden termination?

Franchise Agreement — Sale of Food
[Excerpted from 4A Am. Jur. Legal Forms 2d § 50:13]

Franchise agreement made _____, 19__, between _____ [*name of franchisor*], _____ [*if appropriate, add:* a corporation incorporated in the State of _____, and doing business in several states, including the State of _____], herein referred to as franchisor, and _____ [*name of franchisee*], of _____ [*address*], City of _____, County of _____, State of _____, herein referred to as franchisee.

RECITALS

1. Franchisor is the owner of the registered trademark, "_____" [*set out trademark*].

2. Franchisee wishes to establish a business of preparing and selling _____ [*describe type of food*] in conformity with franchisor's recipes, food preparation procedures, and business methods, and desires the benefit of the national goodwill inherent in franchisor's trademark.

3. Franchisor has already franchised a number of competent and qualified individuals and corporations in _____ [*describe area of franchise activities*]. It has given each the right to exploit the trademark, and by close supervision of each such franchisee, as well as by strict enforcement of meticulous standards as to preparation of the food that is sold under the trademark and the sanitary conditions and general appearance of outlets at which such food is sold, endeavors to maintain a nationwide goodwill with respect to products that will benefit all of its licensed franchisees.

4. The franchise fee and royalty that are established in Section Eighteen herein constitute the sole consideration to franchisor for exploitation of its system and trademark. The restrictions and controls on franchisee's operation and acquisition of supplies established herein are intended solely to protect franchisor's rights to its trademark and to discharge franchisor's obligation to other franchisees to maintain a high level of quality of trademarked products.

In consideration of the premises and the mutual covenants herein set forth, it is agreed by and between franchisor and franchisee:

SECTION ONE
LICENSE OF TRADEMARK

Franchisor licenses and grants franchisee the right to sell prepared food products bearing the trademark, "_____", and to generally operate a business in conformity with franchisor's trademarked system of food preparation and service, in accordance with procedures to be made known to franchisee. This license shall continue for a period of __ years from the date of establishment of franchisee's place of business, unless sooner terminated as provided in this agreement.

The parties understand and agree that this license is of franchisor's registered trademark, "_____", and of the related system of preparation and sale of food, which franchisor has developed as this system presently exists or may hereafter be modified, including the right to use all names, symbols, and trademarks associated with franchisor's name and system of operation.

SECTION TWENTY-FIVE
OPTIONAL TERMINATION BY FRANCHISOR

At any time after _____ months from the date of opening of franchisee's unit, franchisor may terminate this agreement and the license granted franchisee hereunder, on _____ days' written notice to franchisee and purchase of or payment for the following:

1. Franchisee's inventory at franchisee's cost;

2. All equipment and fixtures at franchisee's cost less depreciation of ____ per cent (__%) per month for the first ____ months of use of each item of equipment, and ____ per cent (__%) per month for the _____ [*ordinal number*] through _____ months' use of each such item;

3. Reimbursement in full for all amounts spent by franchisee for local advertising within _____ weeks of termination;

4. As full compensation for franchisee's established local goodwill, ____ percent (__%) of franchisee's gross sales for _____ years prior to termination (or for such portion thereof as franchisee has operated the unit);

5. A refund of the franchise fee established herein less ____ percent (__%) per month or fraction of a month of franchisee's operation of the unit together with ____ per cent (__%) simple interest on the portion of the franchise fee refunded.

Franchisor's optional right to terminate this agreement established herein shall be suspended during any period in which franchisor is obligated to manage franchisee's unit pursuant to Section Twenty-Four. _____ [*If desired, add:* Franchisor's optional right to terminate shall further be suspended for ____ months after any ____ month in which franchisee's gross sales, as reported for purposes of payment of royalty, exceed _____ Dollars ($__).]

Consider the following questions. What would be the legal effect of each of these alternatives to § 25 of the agreement:

      a. There is no termination provision.

      b. At any time after the opening of franchisee's unit, franchisor may terminate this agreement and the license granted franchisee hereunder, without notice....

      c. At any time after <u>two</u> months from the date of opening of franchisee's unit, franchisor may terminate this agreement and the license granted franchisee hereunder, on <u>10</u> days' written notice to franchisee....

      d. At any time after <u>120</u> months from the date of opening of franchisee's unit, franchisor may terminate this agreement and the license granted franchisee hereunder, on <u>180</u> days' written notice to franchisee....

7. Termination of a Franchise.

The best result for a client who wishes to continue performance is to have the agreement enforced with the interpretation that the franchisor could only terminate for cause or on reasonable notice. Hopefully this goal was accomplished at the drafting stage rather than in court. Franchise agreements, however, are notoriously contracts of adhesion, allowing for no revisions by the franchisee.

a. The various alternatives when an agreement contains no termination provision are discussed in the text. Note that many of the problems arise when the agreement contains no *term*. Here, Section 1 of the agreement provides for a term of _____ years. Where an agreement is otherwise enforceable and specifies a term, termination would probably require cause sufficient to breach the contract in such a way as to relieve the other party of its obligations under the contract. See *Fursmidt, supra*; *Ard Dr. Pepper Bottling Co. v. Dr. Pepper Co.*, 202 F.2d 372 (5th Cir. 1953).

b. Allowing one party to terminate at any time without notice could make an executory contract unenforceable. If the franchisee had begun performance, the provision would be onerous. The analysis used by courts in this situation varies widely. In *Bushwick-Decatur Motors, Inc., supra*, the provision was enforced as written. In *Richard Bruce & Co., Inc. v. J. Simpson & Co., Inc.*, 243 N.Y.S.2d 503 (Sup. Ct. N.Y. Co. 1963), applying the reasoning of *Wood*, the court held that termination in one party's absolute discretion meant "a discretion based upon fair dealing and good faith--a reasonable discretion."

c. and d. These provisions contrast a very short and a relatively long period before termination becomes effective. The short period may in reality give the franchisee no more protection than termination at will. The longer period may reduce the reliance of the franchisee. Note that even the longer provision would be in violation of Cal. Bus. & Prof. Code § 20020:

> Except as otherwise provided by this chapter, no franchisor may terminate a franchise prior to the expiration of its term, except for good cause. Good cause shall include, but not be limited to, the failure of the franchisee to comply with any lawful requirement of the franchise agreement after being given notice thereof and a reasonable opportunity, which in no event need be more than 30 days, to cure the failure.

A more extensive problem involving various provisions in a franchise agreement may be found in KNAPP, CRYSTAL & PRINCE, PROBLEMS IN CONTRACT LAW Problem 7-2 (4th ed.).

Chapter 3
Indefiniteness

§ 3.1. Introduction.

The fact that routine transactions are often conducted without elaborate provisions is illustrated by many parodies of legalese. This example appears in FELSENFELD & SIEGEL, WRITING CONTRACTS IN PLAIN ENGLISH 1:

> It has been suggested that if a fruit dealer asked for legal advice on how to sell an orange, the lawyer would supply a document in the following form:
>
>> Know all men by these presents, that Joe's Market, a Michigan corporation ("Seller"), in consideration of one dollar and other good and valuable consideration paid by John Smith ("Purchaser"), the receipt whereof is hereby acknowledged, does hereby grant, sell, assign, transfer and deliver unto Purchaser, its successors and assigns, to have and to hold unto Purchaser, its successors and assigns forever, one orange, together with all its rinds, skin, juice, pulp and pits and with all right and advantages therein, with full power to bite, cut, suck and otherwise to eat the same; and Seller hereby covenants with Purchaser that Seller is the true and lawful owner of the said goods and chattels; that they are free from all encumbrances and security interests; that Seller has good right to sell the same as aforesaid; and that Seller will warrant and defend the same against the lawful claims and demands of all persons, anything hereinbefore or hereinafter or in any other means of whatever nature or kind whatsoever to the contrary in any wise notwithstanding.

Of course, in a more sophisticated transaction the attention to detail might be appropriate, even if the particular language is not.

There is a passage in ROBERT BOLT, A MAN FOR ALL SEASONS 72-73 (Vintage, 1962) in which Thomas More demonstrates that while he may ultimately be headed for martyrdom, his concern with the language of an instrument, in this case a statute, shows that he is first of all a *lawyer*:

> ROPER   There's to be a new Act through Parliament, sir!
> MORE   (Half-turning, half-attending) Act?
> ROPER   Yes, sir--about the marriage!
> MORE   (Indifferently) Oh. (Turning back again. ROPER and MARGARET look at one another)
> MARGARET   (Puts a hand on his arm) Father, by this Act, they're going to administer an oath.

MORE	(With instantaneous attention) An oath! (He looks from one to the other) On what compulsion?
ROPER	It's expected to be treason!
MORE	(Very still) What is the oath?
ROPER	(Puzzled) It's about the marriage, sir.
MORE	But what is the wording?
ROPER	We don't need to know the (Contemptuously) wording--we know what it will mean!
MORE	It will mean what the words say! An oath is made of words! It may be possible to take it. Or avoid it. (To Margaret) Have we a copy of the Bill?
MARGARET	There's one coming out from the City.
MORE	Then let's get home and look at it.

§ 3.2. The parties do not intend to enter into a contract.

The question of whether a less-than-final agreement is effective received a great deal of attention in the Pennzoil/Texaco litigation. For representative cases, see *Brause v. Goldman*, 10 A.D.2d 328, 199 N.Y.S.2d 606 (1960), *aff'd*, 9 N.Y.2d 620, 210 N.Y.S.2d 225, 172 N.E.2d 78 (1961); *Smissaert v. Chiodo*, 163 Cal. App. 2d 827, 330 P.2d 98 (1958). The suggested language is adapted from *Smissaert*.

The difference between the general practices of businesses and the exceptional cases that end up in the reporters is a subject that commands greater attention. See FRIEDMAN, CONTRACT IN AMERICA; Macaulay, *The Use and Non-Use of Contracts in the Manufacturing Industry*, 9 Prac. Law. 13 (Nov. 1963); ROSETT, CONTRACT LAW AND ITS APPLICATION 59-62 (4th ed.).

Many agreements are not intended to be enforced through the legal system. Examples are domestic arrangements between husband and wife or other family arrangements, such as the SADD "Contract for Life."

§ 3.3. The parties intend to enter into a contract.

MELLINKOFF, LEGAL WRITING: SENSE & NONSENSE 117-18 refers to a term that the parties fudge in the hope that the circumstances to use it will never arrive as a "calculated ambiguity:"

Both sides to a negotiation may be eager to make a deal--a contract, a treaty, a statute, a majority for an appellate opinion. It is agreement now or maybe never. The alternative is too costly--strike, lockout, loss of tentative accord on some points that have taken months to work out, loss of a coveted property, disruption. The sticking point is substance not form, yet both sides would like to believe that some word magic will solve their problem. Let's not get bogged down in words. Though they may disavow it later, both sides are ready for the *calculated ambiguity*.

Ambiguity is sometimes limited to double meaning, as distinguished from *vagueness*, a general uncertainty. (On this distinction, see DICKERSON, THE INTERPRETATION AND APPLICATION OF STATUTES (1975).) Lawyers commonly ignore the distinction, and use *calculated ambiguity* to refer to "the deliberate use of language which everyone recognizes as being easily misunderstood." In this sense, *ambiguity* is not a "disease of language" but an instrument chosen to avoid an impasse. We may never have to cross that bridge. Maybe others will. Maybe no one ever will. Whatever happens tomorrow, we must get something settled right now.

The example of the citrus crop is adapted from *Bornstein v. Somerson*, 341 So. 2d 1043 (Fla. Dist. Ct. App. 1977). The agreement was held not to be too indefinite to enforce.

§ 3.5. The resources of the law: The U.C.C.

Many cases not arising under the U.C.C. have enforced similar provisions. See, for example, *Krauss v. Kuechler*, 300 Mass. 346, 15 N.E.2d 207 (1938) (shareholder agreement provided that at the death of a shareholder, his shares shall be sold to the corporation at a price agreed upon by the remaining shareholders); *E.B. Kaiser Co. v. Ludlow*, 243 So. 2d 62 (Miss. 1970) (employment agreement provided that a special commission shall be established by the principal for jobs greater than $250,000).

§ 3.6. Other resources to make an agreement definite.

a. The example is adapted from *Haines v. City of New York*, 41 N.Y.2d 769, 364 N.E.2d 820, 396 N.Y.S.2d 155 (1977).

b. The example is adapted from *California Lettuce Growers, Inc. v. Union Sugar Co.*, 45 Cal. 2d 474, 289 P.2d 785 (1955). See also *Bornstein v. Somerson*, 341 So. 2d 1043 (Fla. Dist. Ct. App. 1977), *cert. denied*, 348 So. 2d 944 (Fla. 1977). The Court of Appeal stated, "we would note that substantial evidence was adduced during these proceedings to suggest that this type of sales agreement, with one or more terms left open, is common in the citrus industry and that greater harm would be done by holding this contract void for indefiniteness."

c. The example is adapted from *Bob Robertson, Inc. v. Webster*, 679 S.W.2d 683 (Tex. Civ. App. 1984).

d. The first example is adapted from *Miller v. Bloomberg*, 26 Ill. App. 3d 18, 324 N.E.2d 207 (1975); the second is adapted from *Neiss v. Franze*, 101 Misc. 2d 871, 422 N.Y.S.2d 345 (Sup. Ct. Rensselaer Co. 1979).

§ 3.7. Ethics in Drafting.

Sources on ethics in drafting are scarce. See Schwartz, *The Professionalism and Accountability of Lawyers*, 66 Calif. L. Rev. 669 (1978); Brown & Brown, *What Counsels the Counselor? The Code of Professional Responsibility's Ethical Considerations--A Preventive Law Analysis*, 10 Val. U. L. Rev. 453 (1976); Scott J. Burnham, *Teaching Ethics in the Contracts Class*, 41 J. Legal Educ. 105 (1991).

§ 3.8. Exercises.

1. The Uniform Commercial Code.

a. The quantity is not ascertainable. Under § 2-204(3) there is no reasonably certain basis for giving an appropriate remedy unless the quantity can be ascertained from past dealings or admissible extrinsic evidence.

b. The time of performance can be reasonably determined. § 2-309. Place of delivery and payment are supplied by § 2-308 and § 2-310. The agreement to sell the entire crop is an output contract. At common law this was indefinite, for B did not agree to have an output. Under § 2-306(1) the agreement is valid, for good faith supplies a standard for performance.

c. Where there is no price, § 2-305 provides for a reasonable price, probably the market price. You might use another hypothetical to clear up a common misconception -- the statute does not require that an agreed-upon price be reasonable.

d. Sale of the house is not a U.C.C. transaction. Sec. 2-102. Under the common law, the absence of a basic term is probably fatal. See *Seal v. Polehn*, 284 Or. 259, 586 P.2d 345 (1978). This makes sense, for there is generally a market that provides an objective price for the sale of goods. One would be foolish to buy for more or sell for less than market price. This is less true with the house, a unique property.

2. Commitment.

This agreement lacks specificity and also lacks commitment. The UCC gap-fillers will provide the specifics. Price, for example, will be a reasonable price under § 2-205. Is there a way to supply any commitment on the part of Company and Customer? Yes. Even though the sale is subject to the approval of Company's Board of Directors, the requirement that the Board must act in good faith commits Company to the contract. Similarly, even though the sale is subject to Customer's satisfaction, Customer must act reasonably in exercising its satisfaction. See § 2.9.

3. Ethics in Drafting.

This exercise is taken from BROWN & DAUER, PLANNING BY LAWYERS 929-30. The authority referred to is *United States Steel Corp. v. Fortner Enterprises, Inc.*, 429 U.S. 610 (1977), and *Perma-Life Mufflers, Inc. v. International Parts Corp.*, 392 U.S. 134 (1968).

Brown and Dauer provide the following guidance on advising the franchisee:

The A.B.A. *Code* speaks around some aspects of the issue. DR 4-101(C)(3) provides that a lawyer *may reveal* the intention of his client to commit a crime; EC 7-5 recommends that the lawyer not knowingly assist the client in undertaking illegal conduct, and DR 7-102(A)(7) precludes the lawyer's assisting in illegal *or fraudulent* conduct (cf DR 7-102(B)(1). Thus, one initial query -- would the attorneys' nondisclosure to the franchisor of his (hypothetically firm) conclusion that the agreement is "illegal" be the commission of a "fraud" in the negotiation process? If, under *Perma Life*, the client can maintain an action as plaintiff, is the client (franchisee) performing an illegal act?. . . Who might be injured by such a contract?

The citations to the *Code* correlate with the *Rules* as follows:

Code Section	Rule Section
DR 4-101(C)(3)	1.6(a)&(b)
EC 7-5	1.2(d), 3.1, 3.3(a)(4), 4.1
DR 7-102(A)(7)	1.2(d), 3.3(a)(4), 4.1
DR 7-102(B)(1)	1.6(b)(1), 3.3(b), 4.1

4. The Buy-Sell Agreement.

This exercise reminds me of those children's puzzles with captions like How Many Animals Can You Find Hidden in this Picture? The animals here are probably no better hidden. For drafting classes, a more sophisticated exercise would involve redrafting this form in Plain Language. See Chapter 18, *Plain Language*. The comments that follow are keyed to the clauses identified by number in the left margin of the Agreement.

1. The disparity between the written-out amount and the numerals is a problem of interpretation. It is resolved in favor of the former, presumably because the additional time and trouble required for the expression makes that a more likely expression of intent. Some advocates of plain language suggest using numerals only. See MELLINKOFF, LEGAL WRITING: SENSE AND NONSENSE 130-31.

2. The property sold is indefinite, for it is described by its informal rather than legal designation (the same problem might arise with a street address). This is probably not fatal if the

Seller owns only one Smith Ranch so that the intended property is ascertainable. See *Northern Pacific Railway Co. v. United States*, 70 F. Supp. 836 (D. Minn. 1946) for an intriguing discussion of the meaning of "Grand Coulee Dam" in a construction contract. See also *Werling v. Gross*, 76 Ill. App. 3d 834, 395 N.E.2d 629 (1979).

Note that the definition (hereafter "Property") is not used in the agreement. See DICKERSON, MATERIALS ON LEGAL DRAFTING 221-24, on the use of "Humpty-Dumptyisms" such as this. Note also that "property" in the agreement is sometimes real, sometimes personal, and sometimes both.

3. In the printed form, *venetian blinds* are listed as property included in the sale but they are excluded in writing. Under the principle of interpretation that writing prevails over printing, they would be excluded. The rule makes drafting sense, for the parties probably intended that the language they took the trouble to write out in full should govern.

4. The price is indefinite, for it requires a V.A. appraisal. This provision must be read in conjunction with Paragraph 13. Under Paragraph 13, when the purchase price exceeds the appraised value, purchaser is not in breach for refusing to perform but has the option of performing. Seller has taken a substantial risk by stating the price in this fashion, for the contract is expressly voidable by purchaser. Some cases have held that since the price is ascertainable, the agreement is enforceable. *Bendalin v. Delgado*, 406 S.W.2d 897 (Tex. 1966). But contrary cases include *Conos v. Sullivan*, 250 Mass. 403, 145 N.E. 529 (1924).

It could be argued that the agreement lacks mutuality since the purchaser is not bound. Could the seller use this to escape? Some cases have held that complete concession by the party who is willing to perform cures the indefiniteness. See FARNSWORTH, CONTRACTS § 3.29. On this theory, if purchaser was willing to perform, seller would be bound.

5. The provision calling for a purchase money mortgage requires another contract, a financing agreement between purchaser and seller, to be negotiated in the future. It may appear to be an agreement to agree, unenforceable because there is no basis for ascertaining the terms. But *Hedges v. Hurd*, 47 Wash. 2d 683, 289 P.2d 706 (1955) held otherwise. The court recognized that as a practical matter the earnest money receipt is used widely in the state. At the time it is executed, the parties do not wish to work out all the details of the agreement. "At this state, the parties are interested only in the execution of a simple agreement which will have some effective legal significance as to both." A concurring judge stated that "there is an implied agreement between the seller and the purchaser that they will negotiate in good faith the terms of the executory real-estate contract contemplated by the agreement."

In *Hedges*, the remedy sought was damages. The court distinguished the case from earlier cases in which the remedy sought was specific performance. An agreement may be too indefinite to be specifically enforced but sufficiently definite to permit calculation of money damages. The Montana Supreme Court awarded specific performance of an earnest money agreement where the purchaser and seller had discussed the terms and had reached agreement on the interpretation of the clauses. *Ehly v. Cady*, 212 Mont. 82, 687 P.2d 687 (1984).

In a complex situation, drafters may consider bypassing the earnest money agreement and executing all the documents at closing. If problems turn up as they negotiate, neither party can claim that the other is bound. There may still be an issue as to whether they intended no agreement until a writing was executed or whether they intended the writing to be a memorialization of a binding oral agreement. See, e.g., *Brown v. Finney*, 53 Pa. 373 (1866). The issue is unlikely to arise in real estate transactions, for the oral agreement will generally be unenforceable under the Statute of Frauds. In negotiating contracts outside the Statute of Frauds it might be wise to clarify the understanding.

6. The amount of the payment is indefinite. Courts have held that a payment of this nature is definite enough if both parties to the agreement are familiar with trade practices and there is no evidence that this payment would be insufficient to liquidate the deferred balance within a reasonable number of years. See *Steen v. Rustad*, 132 Mont. 96, 313 P.2d 1014 (1957), and *McCandless v. Schick*, 85 Idaho 509, 380 P.2d 893 (1963).

7. This provision is enforceable according to *Brotman v. Roelofs*, 70 Mich. App. 719, 246 N.W.2d 368 (1976). If the zoning permit is not issued, purchaser may have an out, but may choose to continue with the deal, and seller is still bound.

8. The agreement is indefinite as to date of performance, but time is generally not a material factor which can defeat an agreement. See *Kays v. Brack*, 350 F. Supp. 1243 (D. Idaho 1972) and *Brotman v. Roelofs*, *supra*. Many states have statutes stating that unless otherwise agreed, time is not of the essence; e.g. Cal. Civ. Code § 1658.

9. The terms of the V.A. loan are indefinite, but there is an external standard available. Students are sometimes confused as to whether purchaser gets a refund of earnest money if the agreement is held to be indefinite or if purchaser cannot satisfy a condition such as obtaining financing. The earnest money is liquidated damages for breach (¶ 5), so the issue becomes whether purchaser breached. If held to be indefinite, there is no agreement to breach, so purchaser gets the money back. If a condition does not occur, it is necessary to determine whether it was a promissory condition, that is, whether purchaser promised to bring it about. If so, and it seems so when purchaser was to obtain a V.A. loan, the issue is whether purchaser made reasonable efforts to bring it about, e.g., by seeking financing. If a pure condition never occurred, then the obligation never arose, so purchaser gets the money back. See Chapter 10, *Promise and Condition*.

10. The seller has promised to pay the broker a commission for securing a ready and willing purchaser, as indicated by the purchaser's signature on this agreement, whether or not the sale is concluded. If the purchaser breaches, the earnest money deposit is first used to satisfy the broker's commission. If it is insufficient, the broker has not agreed to look exclusively to the

earnest money deposit and may look to the seller, who may look to the purchaser. The broker's agreement with the seller and case law may affect this result.

5. Negotiation Exercise.

I use this exercise on the first day of class to introduce students to many of the topics in Contracts. See Scott J. Burnham, *Drafting in the Contracts Class*, 44 St. Louis U. L. J. 1535 (2000). After the students have had enough time to negotiate their agreements, I initiate a class discussion by asking the students questions such as the following:

> Did you reach agreement between Buyer and Seller?
> > If not, is there a contract?
> > > If yes, what are its terms?
> > If yes, did you memorialize the agreement in writing? How did you do that?

> Who has to perform first?
> > Is Buyer paying before Seller ships the goods?
> > > What happens if Seller doesn't ship?
> > Is Seller shipping the goods before Buyer pays?
> > > What happens if Buyer doesn't pay?
> > Is the exchange simultaneous?
> > > How did you accomplish that?
> What payment form is Buyer using?
> > Does Seller have any assurance of payment?
> What shipping method is Seller using?
> > Does Buyer have any assurance of receipt?
> What happens if the goods are lost in transit?

> What happens if the goods are not as described by Seller in the auction (dog-eared and soiled)?
> > Who determines what "mint condition" means, anyway?
> What would the terms be in the areas above if the parties did not address them in their agreement?

> What law governs this agreement?
> > Are those rules mandatory or facilitatory?

> Is it practical to bring a law suit against the other party?
> Are there any alternatives to bringing a law suit?
> What is the role of an attorney here?
> Would one of the parties have considered using an attorney to draft the contract?

Chapter 4
Enforceability

§ 4.1. Introduction.

Perhaps because they read so many cases in which court decisions affect contracts, students sometimes forget that intervention is the exception and freedom of contract remains the general rule. The material in the chapter should be seen in that context: given that parties may establish the private law that will govern them, what restrictions do they face and what policies lie behind those restrictions?

§ 4.2. Regulation of form.

Plain language laws have been adopted in a handful of states and are pending in a number of others. A thoughtful analysis of the different statutory approaches is found in MELLINKOFF, LEGAL WRITING: SENSE & NONSENSE 205-18.

In the absence of a general statute, some states may have specific statutes such as the "Life and Disability Insurance Policy Language Simplification Act." For an analysis of the problems of rewriting standard contracts in plain language, see FELSENFELD & SIEGEL, WRITING CONTRACTS IN PLAIN ENGLISH.

Davis, *Revamping Consumer-Credit Contract Law*, 68 Va. L. Rev. 1333, 1398-99 (1982) contains a "laundry list" of unenforceable provisions commonly found in loan agreements. Interestingly, Davis found that these provisions are often eliminated when the agreements are rewritten in "plain language."

Statutes prohibiting specific language are rare. An excellent article, *Note, Preventing the Use of Unenforceable Provisions in Residential Leases*, 64 Cornell L. Rev. 522 (1979), advocates legislation to penalize a party for including certain clauses in a lease. See also the UNIFORM RESIDENTIAL LANDLORD AND TENANT ACT § 1.403 [Prohibited Provisions in Rental Agreements].

Specific language is often required in retail installment sales agreements, insurance policies, and in the names of entities. Statutes dealing with real estate often require language that must be "substantially" complied with. The best known example of required -- and unreadable -- language is 16 C.F.R. §§ 433.1-.3, the FTC Holder in Due Course Rule:

NOTICE

ANY HOLDER OF THIS CONSUMER CREDIT CONTRACT IS SUBJECT TO ALL CLAIMS AND DEFENSES WHICH THE DEBTOR COULD ASSERT AGAINST THE SELLER OF GOODS OR SERVICES OBTAINED PURSUANT HERETO OR WITH

THE PROCEEDS HEREOF. RECOVERY HEREUNDER BY THE DEBTOR SHALL
NOT EXCEED AMOUNTS PAID BY THE DEBTOR HEREUNDER.

The question of sanctions for failure to attach this language is discussed in Banks, *The FTC
Holder in Due Course Rule: A Rule Without a Private Remedy*, 44 Mont. L. Rev. 113 (1983).

Type size and format is often required in installment sales and insurance statutes.
Section 2-316(2) of the U.C.C. requires that certain language be "conspicuous." Consider the
notorious telephone book statute that provided:

> In every telephone directory ... there shall be printed in type not smaller than any
> other type appearing on the same page, a notice preceded by the word 'warning'
> printed in type at least as large as the largest type on the same page ....

Terms that are implied include U.C.C. warranties, the U.C.C. "gap-fillers" and, in some
jurisdictions, reciprocal attorneys' fees.

§ 4.3. Regulation of substance.

A good source on the use of checklists and forms is PARHAM, THE FUNDAMENTALS OF
LEGAL WRITING, chs. 1 and 2.

§ 4.4. Surrendering a right.

The maxim of equity is codified in Cal. Civ. Code § 3514.

The agreement to limit the statute of limitations is adapted from 12 AM. JUR. LEGAL
FORMS 2D, Limitation of Actions 167:14. As a general rule, while the statute of limitations may
be shortened by agreement, it may not be unreasonably short. See Annot., *Validity of
Contractual Time Period, Shorter Than Statute of Limitations, for Bringing Action*, 6 A.L.R.3d
1197 (1966).

The opinion in *Williams v. Walker-Thomas Furniture Co.*, 350 F.2d 445 (D.C. Cir. 1965),
does not recite the clause and other facts of the case, which may be found in Dostert, *Appellate
Restatement of Unconscionability: Civil Legal Aid at Work*, 54 A.B.A.J. 1183 (1968). The lower
court stated:

> We note that were the Maryland Retail Installment Sales Act, Art. 83, §§
> 128-153, or its equivalent, in force in the District of Columbia, we could grant
> appellant appropriate relief. We think Congress should consider corrective
> legislation to protect the public from such exploitative contracts as were utilized
> in the case at bar.

The Circuit Court remanded for a determination as to whether the clause was unconscionable. Some jurisdictions have enacted the Uniform Consumer Credit Code, which prohibits this clause in § 3.303.

It is impossible to assemble a definitive list of clauses that cannot be waived, particularly since enforceability may depend on the circumstances, but some significant examples include:

a. Waiver of constitutional rights. See the standards in *D.H. Overmeyer v. Frick Co.*, 405 U.S. 174 (1972) (cognovit clause); *Fuentes v. Shevin*, 407 U.S. 67 (1972) (replevin).

b. Waiver of all remedies. See U.C.C. § 2-719(2).

c. Limitation of consequential damages for personal injuries in the case of consumer goods. See U.C.C. § 2-719(3).

d. Agreement of purchaser of consumer goods not to assert defenses against assignees. See U.C.C. § 9-403(d) and Official Comment 5. See also any relevant state law and the FTC Holder-In-Due-Course Regulations, 16 C.F.R. §§ 433.1-.3.

e. Agreement that a contract shall be incontestable for fraud or duress.

f. Waiver of statute of limitations.

g. Waiver of defenses created by usury laws.

h. Waiver of statutory exemptions of property from execution for debt.

i. Waiver of discharge of a debt in bankruptcy.

j. Waiver of all rights to counterclaim or set-off.

k. Article 9 provides in § 9-602 a list of Article 9 provisions that may not be waived or varied.

Helpful sources include 6A CORBIN, CONTRACTS § 1515; 17 AM. JUR., CONTRACTS §§ 188-90; Davis, *Revamping Consumer-Credit Contract Law*, 68 Va. L. Rev. 1333 (1982).

§ 4.5. Unconscionability. Suggestions on drafting to prevent unconscionability are found at 5 HART & WILLIER, FORMS AND PROCEDURES UNDER THE U.C.C. § 21.03.

In general, courts are unwilling to define unconscionability. As stated in *Nu Dimensions Figure Salons v. Becerra*, 73 Misc. 2d 140, 340 N.Y.S.2d 268 (N.Y.C. Civ. Ct. 1973) at 272:

The court in its decision has referred to the term unconscionable in its description of the penalty clause. A reading of the Uniform Commercial Code and many cases discussing unconscionability indicates that there never was an intent on the part of the legislature to give a definition to the term unconscionable. If a definition were given, it would only limit the application of the concept. Every set of facts should have to stand on its own regarding the surrounding circumstances and the industry it applies to.

On the other hand, the various practices that may constitute unconscionability were enumerated in *Willie v. Southwestern Bell Telephone Company*, 219 Kan. 755, 549 P.2d 903 (1976) at 906-7:

Although the doctrine of unconscionability is difficult to define precisely courts have identified a number of factors or elements as aids for determining its applicability to a given set of facts. These factors include: (1) The use of printed form or boilerplate contracts drawn skillfully by the party in the strongest economic position, which establish industry wide standards offered on a take it or leave it basis to the party in a weaker economic position (*Henningsen v. Bloomfield Motors, Inc.*, supra; *Campbell Soup Co. v. Wentz*, 3 Cir., 172 F.2d 80); (2) a significant cost-price disparity or excessive price; (3) a denial of basic rights and remedies to a buyer of consumer goods (*Williams v. Walker-Thomas Furniture Company*, 121 U.S.App.D.C. 315, 350 F.2d 445; 18 A.L.R.3d 1305); (4) the inclusion of penalty clauses; (5) the circumstances surrounding the execution of the contract, including its commercial setting, its purpose and actual effect (*In re Elkins-Dell Manufacturing Company*, 253 F.Supp. 864, [E.D.Pa.]); (6) the hiding of clauses which are disadvantageous to one party in a mass of fine print trivia or in places which are inconspicuous to the party signing the contract (*Henningsen v. Bloomfield Motors, Inc.* supra); (7) phrasing clauses in language that is incomprehensible to a layman or that divert his attention from the problems raised by them or the rights given up through them; (8) an overall imbalance in the obligations and rights imposed by the bargain; (9) exploitation of the underprivileged, unsophisticated, uneducated and the illiterate (*Williams v. Walker-Thomas Furniture Company*, supra); and (10) inequality of bargaining of economic power. (See also Ellinghaus, *"In Defense of Unconscionability"*, 78 Yale L.J. 757; 1 ANDERSON ON THE U.C.C., § 2-302, and cases cited therein.)

§ 4.7. Consumer Protection Acts.

For an example of use of a Consumer Protection Act, see *Leardi v. Brown*, 394 Mass. 151, 474 N.E.2d 1094 (1985). A Massachusetts landlord included unenforceable provisions in a lease. One paragraph stated:

THERE IS NO IMPLIED WARRANTY THE PREMISES ARE FIT FOR HUMAN OCCUPATION (HABITABILITY) except so far as government regulation, legislation or judicial enactment otherwise requires.

In fact, in Massachusetts an implied warranty of habitability is found in leases. The tenants claimed that the landlord violated the Consumer Protection Act, even though they had not read the provisions of the lease and had not been damaged by them. The court agreed, finding that the language of the lease had the tendency to deceive. The court upheld an award of minimum damages for each tenant who signed the lease and attorney's fees for plaintiffs' counsel.

The language from an act is taken from Tenn. Code Ann. § 47-18-104(b)(12) (1988).

§ 4.8. Ethics in drafting.

Ethical responsibilities in drafting agreements have received little consideration from the bar, for ethical standards are directed almost entirely toward the adversarial context. See BROWN & DAUER, PLANNING BY LAWYERS 1-27. Schwartz, *The Professionalism and Accountability of Lawyers*, 66 Calif. L. Rev. 669, 685-86 (1978), suggests the following Professional Rule for the Nonadvocate:

(A)   When acting in a professional capacity other than that of advocate, a lawyer shall not render assistance to a client when the lawyer knows or it is obvious that such assistance is intended or will be used:

   (1)   to facilitate the client in entering into an agreement with another person if the other person is unaware

      (a)   of facts known to the lawyer such that under the law the agreement would be unenforceable or could be avoided by the other person, or

      (b)   that the agreement is unenforceable or could be avoided under the policy of the law governing such agreements; or

   (2)   to aid the client in committing a tort upon another person, provided that this rule applies in business or commercial transactions only to torts as to which it is probable that the other person will in the circumstances be unable to obtain the remedy provided by the law; or

   (3)   to allow the client to obtain an unconscionable advantage over another person.

(B)   For the purpose of this rule, "assistance" does not include advice to a client that a particular course of action is not unlawful.

It could be argued that the adversarial/non-adversarial distinction is not apt. Since a consumer is free to consult an attorney before entering the agreement, thereby equalizing the parties, the consumer takes the risk of foregoing that opportunity. The suggestion seems specious, for while the attorney might help the consumer better understand the agreement, there would be no increase in the consumer's bargaining power. Furthermore, consumers may not look at the transaction as one where the presence of an attorney would be helpful. While lawyers have been taught in their Contracts courses to look at contracts with skepticism if not with disrespect, are lay persons to be faulted for thinking that a solemn agreement is meaningful? The *in terrorem* effect of the clause may cause the person who takes it literally to forego a legal right. It is a perhaps ironic result of the movement to have contracts written in plain language that greater accessibility to the contract may also dissuade a consumer from consulting an attorney prior to entering it.

In an article analyzing the terms of consumer credit contracts, Davis, *supra*, 1369 n. 142 notes:

> In fairness, the motives of the drafters who include these clauses cover a broad range. Some drafters include them inadvertently; some drafters are unsure of their enforceability and choose to err on the side of the creditor; and some know full well that they are unenforceable. Regardless of the drafter's motive, however, these clauses do not belong in the form.

The zealous service extended by an attorney seeking every advantage for the client may be appropriate in an adversary situation but less so in planning. In planning, there may also be more opportunity to persuade the client that the consequences of drafting to the brink of legal unenforceability are not worth the risks. Karl Llewellyn often made the point that the lawyer's formal view of contract obligations conflicts with the business person's less formal view. See, for example, *What Price Contract?--An Essay in Perspective*, 40 Yale L.J. 704 (1983); *The Modern Approach to Counselling and Advocacy--Especially in Commercial Transactions*, 46 Colum. L. Rev. 167 (1946).

In *Cooper v. Fortney*, 703 S.W. 2d 217 (Tex. Ct. App. 1985), an attorney included provisions in a sales contract that violated Texas antitrust laws. The court held that "a contract that violates Texas antitrust laws is an illegal contract," barring the parties from any remedy based on the agreement. On the issue of whether the attorney had committed malpractice, the court remanded to the trial court to determine the extent to which the attorney caused his client to lose money.

§ 4.9. Application: exculpatory clauses.

On exculpatory clauses, see Kuklin, *On the Knowing Inclusion of Unenforceable Contract and Lease Terms*, 56 U. Cin. L. Rev. 845 (1988) and Annot., *Validity of Exculpatory Clause in Lease Exempting Lessor from Liability*, 49 A.L.R.3d 321 (1973).

Additional examples of issues other than exculpatory clauses are indemnity clauses and restrictive covenants in employment contracts. See, e.g., *Weaver v. Am. Oil Co.*, 257 Ind. 458, 276 N.E.2d 144 (1971) (indemnity clause), RESTATEMENT (SECOND) § 188 (Ancillary Restraints on Competition).

On whether drafters may draft around laws making persons responsible for their negligent acts, see, e.g., Cal. Civ. Code § 1714. See, also *Henrioulle v. Marin Ventures, Inc.*, 20 Cal. 3d 512, 143 Cal. Rptr. 247, 573 P.2d 465 (1978), applying to residential leases the criteria for invalidating exculpatory clauses established in *Tunkl v. Regents of the Univ. of Cal.*, 60 Cal. 2d 92, 32 Cal. Rptr. 33, 383 P.2d 441 (1963).

Many examples of possible ethical dialogues with clients are found in THOMAS SHAFFER, ON BEING A CHRISTIAN AND A LAWYER (1981).

§ 4.10. Exercises.

1. Research. With the help of the Montana Legislative Council, I was able to locate the Montana statutes that follow. An index is often little help in finding statutes affecting language, but using computerized legal research, it may be useful to search for these words: *conspicuous*, *folio*, *type size*, *language*, *English*, *must contain*, and *recite*.

Prohibited Terms:

28-2-702, -703, -706, -707, -708, -709. Illegal terms in contracts.
70-24-202. Prohibited provisions in landlord-tenant agreements.
70-24-403. Penalty for purposeful use of prohibited provisions.

Required Language:

30-6-107. Bulk Transfer notice ("shall state").
30-7-703. Warehouse receipt must have the word *duplicate* on a copy.
30-8-408(a). Securities statement "must bear a conspicuous legend reading substantially as follows."
30-9-402(3). Filing finance statement ("a form substantially as follows is sufficient to comply").
30-11-110. Covenants on sale of real property ("must be in substance as follows").
31-1-231. Retail installment contract ("shall contain the following notice").
32-2-201. Articles of incorporation of a Building and Loan. The words *building and loan association* or *savings and loan association*" shall form a part of the name."
32-5-303. Consumer loan contract must show certain items "in clear and distinct terms."
32-5-304. On repayment, a loan shall be marked *paid* or *canceled*.
Title 33, ch. 22, Part 2. Policy requirements for disability insurance.
35-1-301. Corporate name must contain the words *corporation*, *company*, *incorporated*, or *limited* or their abbreviation.

35-2-301. Corporate name--nonprofit corporation.
35-2-805. Corporate name--foreign corporation.
35-4-206. Professional Corporation name must contain the words *professional corporation* or the abbreviation *P.C.*
35-12-505. Limited partnership name must contain the words *limited partnership* in full.
35-12-1304. Foreign limited partnership.
35-18-201. Rural electric cooperatives. Each co-op shall include the words *electric* or *telephone* and *cooperative* and the abbreviation *Inc..* The words *electric* or *telephone* and *cooperative* shall not be used in the name of any other corporation.
70-20-103. Form of grant of an estate in real property ("may be made in substance as follows").
71-1-204. Form of mortgage ("may be made in substantially the following form").
71-3-605. Form of logger's lien ("shall be substantially in the following form").

Required Design or Format:

30-2-316(2). Language excluding or modifying the implied warranty of merchantability must be "conspicuous."
31-1-231, -232. Retail Installment Contract--type size.
33-14-301. Insurance premium finance agreement--type size.
33-15-321 to -329. Life and Disability Insurance Policy Language Simplification Act; Note 33-15-325, Life Insurance Policy Language Simplification Standards.
33-22-201. Disability Insurance--format and captions.

Implied Terms:

28-3-601. Time of performance is reasonable when not expressed.
28-3-701 to -704. Provisions Implied by Law. (Note 28-3-702: all things incidental to a contract or necessary to carry it into effect are implied. See also 1-3-213).
28-3-704. Reciprocal attorneys' fees.
30-2-305- to -311. Under the U.C.C. "gap filler" provisions, terms such as price, place of delivery, time of delivery or time of payment may be implied.
30-2-312 to -315. Warranties.

2. Representing an Unsavory Client. The language of the exculpatory clause is adapted from *Kuzmiak v. Brookchester, Inc.*, 33 N.J. Super. 575, 111 A.2d 425 (1955), which held that it was unenforceable.

In preparing the lease, the attorney is probably assisting the client in evading laws making persons responsible for their negligent acts (see, e.g., Cal. Civ. Code § 1714). It could be argued that this law can be contravened by private agreement. Many jurisdictions have adopted standards for determining the extent of public interest. See, for example, *Henrioulle v. Marin Ventures, Inc.*, 20 Cal. 3d 512, 143 Cal. Rptr. 247, 573 P.2d 465 (1978), applying to residential leases the criteria for invalidating exculpatory clauses established in *Tunkl v. Regents of the University of California*, 60 Cal. 2d 92, 32 Cal. Rptr. 33, 383 P.2d 441 (1963). In fact, research indicates that exculpatory clauses do mislead parties by discouraging them from bringing suit. See Dennis P. Stolle & Andrew J. Slain, *Standard Form Contracts and Contract Schemas: A Preliminary Investigation of the Effects of Exculpatory Clauses on Consumers' Propensity to Sue*, 15 Behavioral Sciences and the Law 83 (1997).

In preparing the letter, the attorney may be assisting in misleading the tenant, yet, as discussed above, an element of fraud may be missing. At present, the question of the attorney's liability is indeterminate. In an excellent article, *The Lawyer's Role in Contract Drafting*, 43 Cal. St. B.J. 362, 367 n.6 (1968), Professor Justin Sweet states:

> The problem of professional responsibility of the lawyer in the drafting process is largely ignored by the Canons of Professional Ethics.
> What should an attorney do when asked to draft a clause restricting competition by an employee after he leaves employment when the attorney believes the clause to be unenforceable because it is unreasonable?
> Would his professional opinion or responsibility be altered if the employee were represented by counsel? What about drafting an exculpatory clause in a form presented to a patient upon entering the hospital, when such clauses have been declared unenforceable? See *Tunkl v. Regents of University of California*, 60 Cal. 2d 92, 32 Cal. Rptr. 33, 383 P.2d 441 (1963).

Even if the conduct is not unethical based on analysis of the Rules, an attorney may still refuse to draft the clause. The Comment to Rule 1.16 states that "[t]he lawyer also may withdraw where the client insists on a repugnant or imprudent objective." More positively, it may be possible to engage in an ethical dialogue with the client. Many examples are found in SHAFFER, ON BEING A CHRISTIAN AND A LAWYER. Little may be changed, however, if these matters are left to the conscience of the individual client or lawyer, for the pull of the adversary system may be too strong. An ethical restriction such as that proposed by Schwartz should be explored.

3. Thinking Like a Lawyer. This case, *Cardona v. Eden Realty Co., Inc.*, 118 N.J. Super. 381, 288 A.2d 34 (1972), nicely illustrates the point that even a tightly drafted document may not be enforced if it elevates form over substance. The opinion continues:

> We are uninformed as to the circumstances under which the lease was signed, except that the record indicated the tenant was not represented by counsel and that the landlord's manager was an attorney. However, the lease in its entirety reveals that the landlord was in an eminently superior bargaining position. The lease included provisions which clearly support this conclusion: no interest was to be paid on security deposits; the tenant (as well as the landlord) waived trial by jury in any action brought by either against the other on any matters arising out of or in any way connected with the tenant's

use or occupancy of the premises or the common stairways, halls, sidewalks, etc.; the tenant waived any exemptions the law gave him on a distress for nonpayment of rent, and the lease attempted to release defendant from the responsibility of maintaining the building in good repair, contrary to N.J.S.A. 55:13A-1 et seq.

While it is conceivable that even in some noncommercial transactions a landlord and tenant might properly negotiate a lease to rent property "as is" and in consideration of a reduced rental the tenant assume all liability for repairs and insurance coverage, it is clear that in this multiple-tenant tenement house lease, the provisions thereof were oppressively for the benefit of the landlord and against public policy.

The tenant's option as to the landlord's liability did not convert their obviously unequal bargaining positions into equal positions, and the exculpatory agreement, despite the method made available to remove it, is against public policy and should not be enforced. The lease represents a legalistic effort to circumvent the positive public policy of this State, and the clauses in issue must be held to be invalid.

The summary judgment in favor of defendant dismissing the complaint is reversed and the matter remanded for trial on the merits.

It might be noted that the only consequence of the circumvention of the law was that the clause was not enforced.

Chapter 5
Capacity

§ 5.2. Behavior.

In Nash, *A Videowill: Safe and Sure*, 70 A.B.A. J. 86 (Oct. 1984), the author advocates using a videotape to preserve evidence of both the testator's state of mind and intentions. On very rare occasions, the parties to a contract might wish to preserve evidence of mental capacity. While that evidence might be straightforward in a jurisdiction applying the *cognitive* test of capacity, it would be particularly cumbersome in a jurisdiction applying the *volitional* test. Compare the tests applied in *Smalley v. Baker*, 262 Cal. App. 2d 824, 69 Cal. Rptr. 521 (1968), and *Ortelere v. Teachers' Retirement Board*, 25 N.Y.2d 196, 250 N.E.2d 460, 303 N.Y.S.2d 362 (1969).

§ 5.3. Fraud.

The case cited is *Danann Realty Corp. v. Harris*, 5 N.Y.2d 317, 157 N.E.2d 597, 602 (1959) (Fuld, J., dissenting) (quoting *Arnold v. Nat'l Aniline & Chem. Co.*, 20 F.2d 364 (2d Cir. 1927)).

As an example of a merger clause that might bar evidence of fraud, consider this agreement between a contractor and a subcontractor:

Subcontractor has, by examination, satisfied itself as to the nature and location of the work; the character, quantity and kind of materials to be encountered; the character, quantity and kind of equipment needed during the prosecution of the work; and the location, conditions and other matters which can in any manner affect the work under the subcontract. No oral agreement with Contractor or its agents either before or after the execution of this subcontract shall affect or modify any term herein contained and this contract is conclusively considered as containing and expressing all the terms agreed upon by the parties.

This language is adapted from *Sherrodd, Inc. v. Morrison-Knudsen Co.*, 249 Mont. 282, 815 P.2d 1135 (1991) (excluding evidence of actual fraud). See also *Danann Realty Corp. v. Harris*, 5 N.Y.2d 317, 157 N.E.2d 597, 602 (1959) (excluding evidence of tort fraud); *Wilkinson v. Carpenter*, 276 Or. 311, 554 P.2d 512 (1976) (excluding evidence of innocent misrepresentations).

§ 5.6. Authority.

The corporate power of attorney is adapted from 1 AM. JUR. LEGAL FORMS 2D §§ 14:96 and 14:132.

§ 5.7. Exercise.

1. Dealing with a minor. This form is found at 9 AM. JUR. LEGAL FORMS 2D § 144:19. In 9B AM. JUR. LEGAL FORMS 2D § 144:4, the form was revised to provide for the feminine gender and to eliminate *herein*.

a. This would seem to be an opportune clause to draft in plain language, for the ability of the minor to understand the clause may be in issue. Advice on redrafting would include:

• Use of the first person would contribute to clarity and would eliminate sexist language.

• The phrase "not subject to any known disability to enter this agreement" is not meaningful. If the only issue is whether the person is a minor, this clause is superfluous.

• What does "as recited herein" modify? The preceding language recites that the person has read, understood, and accepted the terms, so it would be redundant to reiterate that. If it refers to "the terms of the agreement," it is also redundant--where else would the terms be found other than "herein?"

• Have the person initial the provision to indicate that he or she has read it.

A redraft might look like this:

I declare that I am over the age of 18. I am _____ years old. I have read all the terms of this agreement. I understand and accept them. Initial here: _____.

b. One issue that may arise is whether the minor in fact read the agreement and the relevant provision. For this reason, the redraft should include blanks to be filled in by the minor, indicating a knowing acknowledgment of the provision. Some courts have held that the provision is not probative if buried in a contract of adhesion where it is not likely to be read by the purchaser. In *Kiefer v. Fred Howe Motors, Inc.*, 39 Wis. 2d 20, 158 N.W.2d 288 (1968), the court did not give effect to this statement: "I represent that I am 21 years of age or over and recognize that the dealer sells the above vehicle upon this representation." On the other hand, in *Martin v. Stewart Motor Sales*, 247 Iowa 204, 73 N.W.2d 1 (1955), the court gave effect to this statement: "I certify that I am 21 years of age or over ..." See also *Woodall v. Grant & Co.*, 62 Ga. App. 581, 9 S.E.2d 95 (1940); *Rutherford v. Hughes*, 228 S.W.2d 909 (Tex. Civ. App. 1950).

    c. The merchant would be well advised to use caution in dealing with minors. A merchant cannot rely on the representation as a substitute for reasonable inquiry into the purchaser's age. Nor is the representation a guarantee that the minor will be denied disaffirmance. But a number of cases have held that where the minor seeks return of the consideration paid, the misrepresentation may demonstrate "unclean hands," barring recovery by the minor. See, *e.g.*, *Tuck v. Payne*, 159 Tenn. 192, 17 S.W.2d 8 (1929); *Lubin v. Cowell*, 25 Wash. 2d 171, 170 P.2d 301 (1946).

Chapter 6
Parol Evidence

§ 6.2. Is the agreement final?

Whether an instrument contains the final and complete agreement of the parties is a question of intent. In suggesting that the drafter make clear that the agreement appears on its face to be final, I do not intend to advocate the "Willistonian" view of parol evidence. Most courts will admit evidence on the subject of finality beyond the "four corners" of the instrument. Care in drafting may, however, win over those judges who do adopt the Willistonian view and will assist in marshaling proof for those who do not.

§ 6.3. Is the agreement complete?

Similarly, while it is imperative to include a merger clause to indicate completeness, the merger clause is by no means foolproof. As indicated in Childres & Spitz, *Status in the Law of Contract*, 47 N.Y.U. L. Rev. 1 (1972), a court is more likely to give weight to a merger clause in a negotiated agreement than in an informal contract or a contract of adhesion.

The provision in the sale of a medical instrument is adapted from *Computerized Radiological Services, Inc. v. Syntex Corp.*, 595 F. Supp. 1495 (E.D.N.Y. 1984), *rev'd on other grounds*, 786 F.2d 72 (2d Cir. 1986).

The example of the gas station lease is from *State v. Frederick*, 208 Mont. 112, 676 P.2d 213 (1984).

§ 6.4. Merger clause.

The examples of merger clauses are adapted from WHITE & SUMMERS, UNIFORM COMMERCIAL CODE §§ 2-12, 12-4 (5th ed.). The FTC Used Car Trade Regulation Rule is intended to make clear that representations outside of the contract are of no effect. See Chapter 12, *Warranties*.

The delivery date example is adapted from *Bob Robertson, Inc. v. Webster*, 679 S.W.2d 683 (Tex. Civ. App. 1984).

The franchise agreement example is adapted from *Mobil Oil Corp. v. Handley*, 76 Cal. App. 3d 956, 143 Cal. Rptr. 321 (1978). Note, however, that courts will give additional scrutiny to adhesion contracts and may disregard a merger clause where it was not part of a negotiated agreement. See Childres & Spitz, *supra*.

§ 6.7. The U.C.C. parol evidence rule.

The example of the sale of steel slabs is from *Associated Metals & Minerals Corp. v. Sharon Steel Corp.*, 590 F. Supp. 18 (S.D.N.Y. 1983), *aff'd*, 742 F.2d 1431 (2d Cir. 1983). Compare *Nanakuli Paving and Rock Co. v. Shell Oil Co., Inc.*, 664 F.2d 772 (9th Cir. 1981).

The examples of clauses to circumvent trade usage are adapted from 5 HART & WILLIER, FORMS AND PROCEDURES UNDER THE U.C.C. § 21.06.

§ 6.8. Collateral agreement.

The eyesore example is, of course, from *Mitchill v. Lath*, 247 N.Y. 377, 160 N.E. 646 (1928). See the discussion at FARNSWORTH, CONTRACTS § 7.3 (3d ed.).

§ 6.11. Exercises.

1. Separation Agreement. A light should go on in the lawyer's head and the words PAROL EVIDENCE should pop up. If the Wife, recalling the Husband's promise, later requests more money, the Husband will probably say, "HA HA, it's not in the contract." At this point the Wife would have to get around the parol evidence rule in order to enforce the Husband's promise. The agreement is probably the parties' final and complete understanding. Therefore the Husband's promise is not part of the agreement. The promise would probably fail as a collateral agreement as well, for there is no consideration for it and it does not appear to be definite enough to be enforceable.

As the Wife's attorney, you should say, "Hold everything! Let's put that in the agreement." At that point the Husband may balk. If he does not, you may have difficulty drafting the provision to everyone's satisfaction. For example, questions such as what kind of need triggers the supplementary payment and how much the Husband must pay may be difficult to answer. But you have nothing to lose. The attempt to get the provision into the agreement at the time of signing will be more productive than the attempt to later circumvent the parol evidence rule.

2. Sale of goods. The statement as to gas mileage should be included in the agreement. It may be possible to circumvent the parol evidence rule by showing that the statement fraudulently induced Barney to enter the contract, but you have an opportunity at the time the transaction is entered to prevent that need from arising. The statement could be included as a representation and warranty:

> Seller warrants and represents that the auto gets at least 25 miles per gallon around town.

The attorney might want to word the statement to make clear that Buyer has the right of avoid the contract in the event the statement is not true rather than only the right to damages. See Chapter 10, *Promise and Condition*.

3. Distribution agreement. This problem is based on *Gianelli Distributing Co. v. Beck & Co.*, 172 Cal. App. 3d 1020, 219 Cal. Rptr. 203 (1985). According to the view of Corbin and RESTATEMENT § 209(1), evidence may always be admitted to show that a writing was not intended as a complete integration of the parties' agreement. Even under the Williston view, this agreement does not contain a merger clause and does not appear to contain all the terms of a distributorship agreement. Therefore the evidence should be allowed.

The extrinsic evidence was offered to show that in the industry distributorship agreements were terminated only for cause. The court analogized to the U.C.C. and allowed the evidence to explain or supplement the agreement. The evidence was held not to contradict the agreement, for the agreement "could reasonably be interpreted as referring only to the duration of the agreement and not the permissible reasons for its termination."

The drafter could have added additional terms and a merger clause to better indicate that the agreement was complete. The specific point could have been covered by adding "Either party may terminate this agreement for any cause or for no cause."

4. Settlement agreement. This problem is based on *Zim v. Western Publishing Co.*, 573 F.2d 1318 (5th Cir. 1978), a case that delightfully echoes *Genesis*.

In Paragraphs 8 and 9, Western promises to pay the royalty and the bonus for each Guide "published by Western." The author claims that *Insect Pests* was published by Western as the company that acquired Eastern. The publisher claims that *Insect Pests* was published by Eastern, the publisher whose imprint is found on the book. It argues that it would have to pay the additional royalty and the bonus only if the book had been re-issued under the imprint of Western.

The issue is the meaning of *Western*. The author offered as evidence the testimony of the attorney who represented him during the contract negotiations to show that *Western* meant not only Western Publishing Co. but its affiliates and subsidiaries as well. Expert testimony as to trade custom and usage might also have been offered.

The appellate court sustained the trial court's exclusion of this evidence. The court found the agreement was not ambiguous. *Western* is defined in the caption as "Western Publishing Co., Inc., a Wisconsin Corporation, its successors and assigns (referred to as `Western')." When the parties meant *Western* to mean something other than that corporate entity, they specified that meaning as indicated in definition 1.2:

1.2. "Individual Contract" as used herein means a contract between Western (including Western's predecessors in interest) and the Author.

The agreement could have been clarified by defining Western:

1.3. "Western" as used herein means Western Publishing Co., Inc. and its predecessors in interest.

Alternatively, each provision could have been more specific:

8. Western shall pay to the Author with respect to each Guide published or to be published or distributed *under the imprint of Western or its predecessors in interest*, a royalty on the retail price of every copy sold, less returns, of ten percent (10%). For example, if under an Individual Contract the Author was entitled to a royalty of 7%, Western shall pay an additional 3%, so that the total royalty is 10%.

9. In addition to the foregoing, Western shall pay the Author a bonus of $10,000 for each Guide published *under the imprint of Western or its predecessors in interest*.

While the correctness of the outcome is debatable, the case illustrates the process used by a court when parol evidence is offered on a question of interpretation. The court correctly admitted the extrinsic evidence on the issue rather than relying on the "four corners" test. But it was strongly persuaded by the fact that the parties had supplied their own "dictionary" as to the meaning. It may be especially significant that the contract was negotiated fairly and in detail.

Chapter 7
Interpretation

§ 7.1. Introduction.

Judges and other writers often wax eloquent on the subject of interpretation. "This is the kind of case that has been described as 'one where no principle of law is involved, but only the meaning of careless and slovenly documents.'" *Robinhorne Construction Corp. v. Snyder*, 47 Ill. 2d 349, 265 N.E.2d 670 (1970). "Glaziers should glaze and lawyers should scriven; and neither ought to do the other, for, when glaziers write and lawyers glaze, they are apt to make porous contracts and drafty windows." *Schauerman v. Haag*, 68 Wash. 2d 868, 416 P.2d 88 (1966). "In short, lawyers are supposed to be wordsmiths; stevedores are not." *Atlantic & Gulf Stevedores, Inc. v. Kominers*, 456 F.2d 1146 (2d Cir. 1972) (interpreting contingency fee contract in favor of stevedores and against lawyers).

There are many good sources of guidance for interpretation. See MELLINKOFF, LEGAL WRITING: SENSE AND NONSENSE; DICKERSON, THE FUNDAMENTALS OF LEGAL DRAFTING; DICK, LEGAL DRAFTING; AITKEN & PIESSE: THE ELEMENTS OF DRAFTING. The usefulness of talking back to your draft is discussed in Dickerson, *Legal Drafting: Writing as Thinking, or, Talk-Back from Your Draft and How to Exploit It*, 29 J. Legal Educ. 373 (1978).

Advanced students may wish to consult Allen, *Symbolic Logic: A Razor-Edged Tool for Drafting and Interpreting Legal Documents*, 66 Yale L.J. 833 (1957), and Allen and Engholm, *Normalized Legal Drafting and the Query Method*, 29 J. Legal Educ. 380 (1978).

It is hard to find humor in the poor drafting of attorneys. The results achieved by lay persons may allow us to laugh, for not only are the mistakes not ours, but we can take comfort in thinking we can do better. My favorites include *Baldwin v. Stuber*, 182 Mont. 501, 597 P.2d 1135 (1979), in which the parties' agreement began:

On this date 3-8-77, I, Terry L. Baldwin, here-to-fore known as sellor, and Alan D. Stuber, here-to-fore known as sellee, enter into a selling agreement, which is here-to-fore known as The Natural Look Barber Salon, ...

and went downhill from there.

There are a number of good sources for examples of interpretation. A number of instructive examples are found in the illustrations to RESTATEMENT (SECOND) §§ 200-203.

JACKSON & BOLLINGER, CONTRACT LAW 1005 (2d ed. 1980) lists these cases as examples where better drafting might have avoided the litigation:

Groves v. John Wunder Co., 205 Minn. 163, 286 N.W. 235 (1939).

Evergreen Amusement Corp. v. Milstead, 206 Md. 610, 112 A.2d 901 (1955).

Duckwall v. Rees, 119 Ind. App. 474, 86 N.E.2d 460 (1949).

Freedman v. Rector, Wardens & Vestrymen of St. Mathias Parish, 37 Cal. 2d 16, 230 P.2d 629 (1951).

Tilbert v. Eagle Lock Co., 116 Conn. 357, 165 A. 205 (1933).

Marchiondo v. Scheck, 78 N.M. 440, 432 P.2d 405 (1967).

Sherwood v. Walker, 66 Mich. 568, 33 N.W. 919 (1887).

Masterson v. Sine, 68 Cal. 2d 222, 436 P.2d 561, 65 Cal. Rptr. 545 (1968).

Macke Company v. Pizza of Gaithersburg, Inc., 259 Md. 479, 270 A.2d 645 (1970).

Crawford v. Peabody Coal Co., 34 Ill. App. 2d 388, 181 N.E.2d 369 (1962).

Wood v. Lucy, Lady Duff-Gordon, 222 N.Y. 88, 118 N.E. 214 (1917).

Allegheny College v. National Chautauqua County Bank of Jamestown, 225 A.D. 778, 246 N.Y. 369, 159 N.E. 173 (1927).

Drennan v. Star Paving Co., 51 Cal. 2d 409, 333 P.2d 757 (1958).

House of Vision, Inc. v. Hiyane, 37 Ill. 2d 32, 225 N.E.2d 21 (1967).

O'Brien v. Atlas Finance Co., 223 Ark. 176, 264 S.W.2d 839 (1954).

and at 1028 these cases that illustrate principles of interpretation:

Mantell v. International Plastic Harmonica Corp., 141 N.J. Eq. 379, 55 A.2d 250 (1947) (interpret as a whole).

Zelle v. Chicago & N.W.R. Co., 242 Minn. 439, 65 N.W.2d 583 (1954) (arbitration clause).

Metts v. Central Standard Life Ins. Co. of Ill., 142 Cal. App. 2d 445, 298 P.2d 621 (1956) (resolve ambiguities against insurer-draftsman).

Davis v. Nelson-Deppe, Inc., 91 Idaho 463, 424 P.2d 733 (1967) (intent to benefit third party).

Wood v. Lucy, Lady Duff-Gordon, 222 N.Y. 88, 118 N.E. 214 (1917) (implied counter promise).

Mattei v. Hopper, 51 Cal. 2d 119, 330 P.2d 625 (1958) (satisfaction clause).

Jones v. Star Credit Corp., 59 Misc. 2d 189, 298 N.Y.S.2d 264 (1969).

Pacific Allied v. Century Steel Products, Inc., 162 Cal. App. 2d 70, 327 P.2d 547 (1958).

Kantrowitz v. Perlman, 156 Conn. 224, 240 A.2d 891 (1968).

Mignot v. Parkhill, 237 Or. 450, 391 P.2d 755 (1964).

Mereminsky v. Mereminsky, 20 Misc. 2d 21, 188 N.Y.S.2d 771 (1959).

Aetna Insurance Co. v. Maryland Cast Stone Co., 254 Md. 109, 253 A.2d 872 (1969).

Arizona Land Title & Trust Co. v. Safeway Stores, Inc., 6 Ariz. App. 52, 429 P.2d 686 (1967).

Butterfield v. Byron, 153 Mass. 517, 27 N.E. 667 (1891).

VERNON, CONTRACTS: THEORY AND PRACTICE Problem 2-21 at 43-44 (2d ed.) asks students how they would have redrafted the contract in these cases:

Sherwood v. Walker, 66 Mich. 568, 33 N.W. 919 (1887),
Raffles v. Wichelhaus, 2 H. & C. 906, 159 Eng. Rep. 375 (1864),
Frigaliment Importing Co. v. B.N.S. International Sales Corp., 190 F. Supp. 116
       (S.D.N.Y. 1960), and
Flower City Painting Contractors, Inc. v. Gumina Construction Co., 591 F.2d 162 (2d
       Cir. 1979).

In his teachers' guide, Vernon makes the following comments:

       1. *Sherwood*: Since the contract price was only $80, it would be uneconomical
for the parties to have used an individually designed lawyer-drafted contract. The
Walkers, in the business of buying and selling cattle, well might employ a lawyer to
prepare a general form contract for them. If the form is too favorable to the Walkers,
enforceability problems will haunt them. (Students tend to draft clauses in which their
client prevails in all situations, without regard to breach or wrongdoing.) We spend a
few minutes of class time discussing drafting techniques in the preparation of forms.
Since students are unfamiliar with the doctrine of unconscionability, I present a simplistic
view of it as background for discussing the pros and cons of drafting a one-sided
contract. Since contracts are read against the drafting party, a well-balanced form read
against the drafter may be converted into one favoring the other party. On balance,
however, the preferable route seems to call for a balanced form aimed at protecting the
client only to the extent necessary to meet the client's needs, with those needs identified
with restraint.

       2. *Raffles*: A contract clause could identify the ship relatively easily by
identifying its registry or its owner. If time of shipment is the real issue, as it seems to
be, the contract probably should not name the ship, but should concentrate on describing
when it will be under way or when it will arrive.

       3. *Frigaliment*: Clarification of the nature of the goods sold is relatively easy.
Such clarification would pinpoint the area of dispute and permit the parties to negotiate a
contract they both understood or to agree to go their separate ways.

       4. *Flower City*: The extent of the painter's obligation obviously could be
established by a contract clause within the form used in Flower City.

       While this book emphasizes the substance of contracts in drafting, it is impossible not to
discuss expression. However, I have emphasized only some topics that are of particular
importance to the drafter, particularly a drafter who is a beginning law student. I recommend
ROBERT DICK, LEGAL DRAFTING (2d ed.), and DAVID MELLINKOFF, LEGAL WRITING: SENSE AND
NONSENSE as the most accessible student texts covering additional matters relating to
expression. Swisher, *Techniques of Legal Drafting: A Survival Manual*, 15 U. Rich. L. Rev. 873
(1981) is a good concise summary.

§ 7.2. Recitals. See Chapter 15, *The Framework of a Contract* for additional examples.

§ 7.3. General and particular. One writer on *ejusdem generis* suggests: "To make it clear that the specific examples cited are not intended to limit the inclusiveness of the general word, draftsmen frequently employ some saving phrase, such as 'without limitation or restriction of the generality of the foregoing.'" COOPER, WRITING IN LAW PRACTICE 278.

§ 7.4. Ambiguity. The useful distinction between vagueness and ambiguity is explained in DICKERSON ch. 3.

§ 7.4.1. Connectives.

The problem of "and" and "or" has captured the attention of many writers. See, for example, DICKERSON, THE FUNDAMENTALS OF LEGAL DRAFTING § 6.2 (2d ed.); DICK, LEGAL DRAFTING Rule 9 at 100-04 (2d ed.); Kirk, *Legal Drafting: The Ambiguity of "And" and "Or,"* 2 Tex. Tech L.R. 235 (1971), AITKEN & PIESSE, THE ELEMENTS OF DRAFTING, ch. 9; Note, *Avoiding Inadvertent Syntactic Ambiguity in Legal Draftsmanship*, 20 Drake L. Rev. 137 (1970). Kirk concludes at 253:

> There is no solution which provides euclidean comfort; rather, there are techniques and forms which sometimes help to keep the risk of ambiguity at a minimum. Or, one can say "or both" or "but not both"; or, where the structure is in the singular, he can *define* "and" to be "joint" (A or B, jointly but not individually) and "or" to be inclusive (A or B, or both). Ultimately, however, the greatest benefit will be found in a self-discipline in which "and" or "or" gives one "great pause"--because *every* use of "and" or "or" as a conjunction involves *some* risk of ambiguity.

Allen and Engholm's distinction between *and* as "full-sentence connecting" and "sentence-part connecting" is a useful way to describe the problem of the several and joint sense of *and* when classes or characteristics overlap. *And* is full-sentence connecting when "The corporation shall pay a bonus to directors and shareholders" means "The corporation shall pay a bonus to directors and the corporation shall pay a bonus to shareholders." See Allen & Engholm, *Normalized Legal Drafting and the Query Method*, 29 J. Legal Educ. 380, 385-86 (1978).

Another helpful distinction may be between mandatory and permissive sentences. DICKERSON, FUNDAMENTALS OF LEGAL DRAFTING § 6.2 (2d ed.), points out that if a sentence is permissive, the inclusive *or* means the same as the several *and*. "Seller may ship broilers or fryers" is the equivalent of "Seller may ship broilers and fryers." However, beware of using the permissive verb *may* rather than the mandatory verb *shall* in an attempt to cure this ambiguity. By using the permissive, the drafter intends to state that seller complies by shipping broilers or fryers or both. The drafter has created another ambiguity, however, for the discretion may relate not to the choice between broilers and fryers but between shipping and not shipping.

§ 7.4.2. And/or.

Sources on *and/or* include DICKERSON, THE FUNDAMENTALS OF LEGAL DRAFTING § 6.2 (2d ed.); DICK, LEGAL DRAFTING Rule 10 at 104-08 (2d ed.); AITKEN & PIESSE, THE ELEMENTS OF DRAFTING 81-85. On the response of courts to and/or, the following colorful comments are representative:

> In the matter of the use of the alternative, conjunctive phrase "and/or," it is sufficient to say that we do not hold this to be reversible error, but we take our position with that distinguished company of lawyers who have condemned its use. It is one of those inexcusable barbarisms which was sired by indolence and damned by indifference, and has no more place in legal terminology than the vernacular of Uncle Remus has in Holy Writ. I am unable to divine how such senseless jargon becomes current. The coiner of it certainly had no appreciation for terse and concise law English.

Cochrane v. Florida East Coast Railway Co., 107 Fla. 431, 435, 145 So. 217, 218-19 (1932).

> It is manifest that we are confronted with the task of first construing "and/or," that befuddling, nameless thing, that Janus-faced verbal monstrosity, neither word nor phrase, the child of a brain of some one too lazy or too dull to express his precise meaning, or too dull to know what he did mean, now commonly used by lawyers in drafting legal documents, through carelessness or ignorance or as a cunning device to conceal rather than express meaning with view to furthering the interest of their clients. We have even observed the "thing" in statutes, in the opinions of courts, and in statements in briefs of counsel, some learned and some not.

Employers' Mutual Liability Insurance Co. of Wisconsin v. Tollefsen, 219 Wis. 434, 263 N.W. 376, 377 (1935).

A number of cases and other historical sources are discussed in MELLINKOFF, THE LANGUAGE OF THE LAW 150-52, 306-10. Other cites are found in COOPER, WRITING IN LAW PRACTICE 29-30.

§ 7.4.5. Modifiers.
The case described is *Business Men's Assurance Ass'n v. Read*, 48 S.W.2d 678 (Tex. Civ. App. 1932).

§ 7.5.1. Definitions.

Among the pitfalls of users of definitions are the "Humpty-Dumptyism," whereby a term is defined to mean anything the parties want it to mean, and the one-shot definition, whereby a term is defined to be used only once. For example, in Chapter 3, *Indefiniteness*, in the Buy-Sell agreement after the legal description, the agreement states "(hereinafter `property')" but the definition is never used.

Helpful sources are DICKERSON ch. 7 (2d ed.) and CHILD ch. 10 (2d ed.).

§ 7.5.2. Tabulation. See DICKERSON § 6.3 (2d ed.), DICK 116-23 (2d ed.). The Texas case is *Sears v. Bayoud*, 786 S.W.2d 248 (Tex. 1990). The other example is from the IRS VOLUNTEER ASSISTOR'S GUIDE (1987).

§ 7.5.3. Application of tabulation.

The Magnuson-Moss definition of "written warranty" is at 15 U.S.C. § 2301(6). The Regulation is at 16 C.F.R. § 700.3. The explanation of the definition in the regulation seems unreasonable to me. If a seller's affirmation of fact states "100% Cotton," either it is all cotton or it isn't; specifying a period of time has nothing to do with it. A period of time is relevant only to a level of performance.

The Flesch test of Plain Language measures two factors: syllables per word and sentence length. See FLESCH, HOW TO WRITE PLAIN ENGLISH (1979); Wydick, *Lawyers' Writing* (a review of the Flesch book), 78 Mich. L. Rev. 711 (1980); FELSENFELD & SIEGEL, WRITING CONTRACTS IN PLAIN ENGLISH ch. 9 (1981). The Flesch Test has been codified in many states in the Uniform Life and Disability Insurance Policy Language Simplification Act. The three drafts of Magnuson-Moss (original statute, tabulation, and draft from tabulation) received almost identical scores on syllables per word. The divergence in scores is entirely due to the sentence length. The original statute consists of one sentence. In the tabulation, the use of semicolons broke it down into five sentences. The draft from the tabulation retained some of the semicolons and hence counted as three sentences.

§ 7.5.4. Normalized drafting.

This material was developed by Prof. Grayfred Gray of the University of Tennessee College of Law.

The following provision, normalized by Layman Allen, illustrates this diagnostic technique. Here is the provision in non-normalized form:

REINSTATEMENT: If any renewal premium be not paid within the time granted the Insured for payment, a subsequent acceptance of premium by the Company or by any agent duly authorized by the Company to accept such premium, without requiring in connection therewith an application for reinstatement, shall reinstate the policy; provided, however, that if the Company or such agent requires an application for reinstatement and issues a conditional receipt for the premium tendered, the policy will be reinstated upon approval of such application by the Company or, lacking such approval, upon the 45th day (30th day in New Mexico) following the date of such conditional receipt unless the Company has previously notified the Insured in writing of its disapproval of such application. The reinstated policy shall cover only loss resulting from such accidental injury as may be sustained after the date of reinstatement and loss due to such sickness as may begin more than 10 days after such date. In all other respects the Insured and the Company shall have the same rights thereunder as they had under the policy immediately before the due date of the defaulted premium, subject to any provisions endorsed hereon or attached hereto in connection with the reinstatement. Any premium accepted in connection with a reinstatement shall be applied to a period for which premium has not been previously paid, but not to any period more than 60 days prior to the date of reinstatement

In this normalized scheme, the syntax terms are not capitalized and bullets are used to list items that follow the preceding tabulated item. The normalized provision looks like this:

If

1.   any renewal premium is not paid within the time granted the Insured for payment, and

2.   (A)   there is a subsequent acceptance of premium by the Company or by any agent duly authorized by the Company to accept such premium, without requiring in connection therewith an application for reinstatement, or

        (B)   1. the Company or such agent
                •   requires an application for reinstatement, and
                •   issues a conditional receipt for the premium tendered, and

                2.   (A)   such application is approved by the Company, or

                        (B)   the Company has not before the 45th day (30th day in New Mexico) following the date of such conditional receipt notified the Insured in writing of its disapproval of such application,

then

3.   the policy shall be reinstated, and

4.   the reinstated policy shall cover only loss resulting from such accidental injury as may be sustained after the date of reinstatement and loss due to such sickness as may begin more than 10 days after such date, and

5.   in all other respects the Insured and the Company shall have the same rights thereunder as they had under the policy immediately before the due date of the defaulted premium, subject to any provisions endorsed hereon or attached hereto in connection with the reinstatement, and

6.   any premium accepted in connection with a reinstatement shall be applied to a period for which premium has not been previously paid, but not to any period more than 60 days prior to the date of reinstatement.

§ 7.6. Vagueness.

I like to emphasize UCC § 1-102(3) [§ 1-302 in the Revision], the freedom of contract provision of the UCC, which states that the rules are default rules that can be changed by the parties. It then goes on to say that the obligations of "good faith, diligence, reasonableness and care" may not be disclaimed, but the parties may "determine the standards by which the performance of such obligations is to be measured if such standards are not manifestly unreasonable." For example, if you are providing for the time that a buyer must give notice of defects (§ 2-607(3)(b)), instead of the statutory or express "reasonable time," you are probably free to prescribe that the party has 60 days, if that is a reasonable standard, but you are probably not free to prescribe that the party has 3 days, for that may be "manifestly unreasonable."

CHARLES M. FOX, WORKING WITH CONTRACTS 82-100 contains excellent advice and examples of vague language that can be used to "soften the edges."

§ 7.7. Exercises.

1. Research. The rules are stated in slightly different form in RESTATEMENT (SECOND) §§ 201-03. Many additional examples may be found there. SWEET, LEGAL ASPECTS OF ARCHITECTURE, ENGINEERING, AND THE CONSTRUCTION PROCESS ch. 19 (West, 1977), contains many examples from this particular area of law. Note also the importance of U.C.C. §§ 2-202, 1-205, and 2-208, dealing with course of dealing, usage of trade, and course of performance. Similar provisions are found in RESTATEMENT (SECOND) §§ 219-23.

Simpson's rules of interpretation are illustrated by the following cases:

The three primary rules of interpretation are:

   1. Words are to be given their plain and normal meaning; except

       (a) Usage may vary the normal meaning of words.

In *Hurst v. W.J. Lake & Co.*, 141 Or. 306, 16 P.2d 627 (1932), a contract for the delivery of horse meat scraps specified "minimum 50% protein," and provided for discounts for shipments that did not meet the specifications. In rejecting the buyer's claim for a discount, the court held that in the business of buying and selling horse meat scraps, 49.5% or more is considered 50%. The case contains an instructive list of other trade usages.

In *Eskimo Pie Corp. v. Whitelawn Dairies, Inc.*, 284 F. Supp. 987 (S.D.N.Y. 1968), defendant offered evidence that when the parties used the term "non-exclusive" in their agreement, they meant "exclusive." The court allowed the evidence not to show "a secret code meaning given to it by the parties but whether it might objectively be recognized by a reasonably intelligent person acquainted with applicable customs, usages and the surrounding circumstances as having such a special meaning."

       (b) Technical words are to be given their technical meaning.

In *Robin v. Sun Oil Co.*, 548 F.2d 554 (5th Cir. 1977), the court stated that "Counsel in this case were competent maritime lawyers. They knew the difference between liability and negligence. They knew how to use other words if they chose to do so."

       (c) Where possible, words will be given the meaning which best effectuates the intention of the parties.

In *Reed v. Merchants Mutual Insurance Co.*, 95 U.S. 23 (1877), an insurance policy contained the clause "the risk to be suspended while vessel is at Baker's Island loading." The ship was destroyed while moored at Baker's Island but before loading. Under the circumstances, the intention was to suspend the risk while the ship was at that particular place. Therefore, the court held that the risk was suspended when the vessel was at Baker's Island for the purpose of loading, whether loading had commenced or not.

Sometimes the parties expressly state their intentions, often in the form of recitals at the beginning of the instrument. Recitals are discussed in Chapter 15, *The Framework of a Contract*. Courts sometimes state as rules of interpretation that "If the recitals are clear and the operative part is ambiguous, the recitals govern the construction. If the recitals are ambiguous, and the operative part is clear, the operative part must prevail. If both the recitals and the operative part are clear, but they are inconsistent with each other, the operative part is to be preferred." *Ex Parte Dawes*, 17 Q.B.D. 275 (1886).

2. Every part of a contract is to be interpreted, if possible, so as to carry out its general purpose.

In *Spaulding v. Morse*, 322 Mass. 149, 76 N.E.2d 137 (1947), a husband promised his wife that he would pay $1200 per year for the support of their minor child until the child's entrance into college and thereafter $2200. The child was drafted after graduating from high school. Because the general purpose of the agreement was to provide for the child's maintenance and education, the husband was not required to make the payments while the child was in the military.

3. The circumstances under which the contract was made may always be shown.

In *United States ex rel. White Masonry, Inc. v. F.D. Rich Co.*, 434 F.2d 855 (9th Cir. 1970), a subcontractor did not perform work according to specifications. The court found that the subcontractor had met with the contractor prior to submitting its bid and had made clear that its bid was based on its not doing the work. The court held that the additional work did not fall within the subcontract.

If after applying the primary rules the meaning of the contract is yet not clear, there are secondary rules tending to the same end--to ascertain and effectuate the intention of the parties. They are:

1. Obvious mistakes of writing, grammar or punctuation will be corrected.

In *Newbern Banking & Trust Co. v. Duffy*, 153 N.C. 62, 68 S.E. 915 (1910), a promissory note stated "If any instalment of interest is not paid when due or within ten days after demand, then the principal of said note shall become due and payable." When the obligor claimed that demand had not been made, the obligee claimed demand was not required by the terms of the note since default occurred on the happening of one of two events. The court held that since demand was of the essence of the contract, the phrase "or within ten days after demand" meant "*nor* within ten days after demand."

2. The meaning of general words or terms will be restricted by more specific descriptions of the subject matter or terms of performance.

In *United States v. The Agioi Victores*, 227 F.2d 571 (9th Cir. 1955), a statute made it unlawful to "impair the usefulness of any sea wall, bulkhead, jetty, dike, levee, wharf, pier, or other work built by the United States ..." The court held that the ship was not liable for injuring a dredged channel, which did not resemble the particulars specified in the statute.

In *Warner Bros. Pictures v. Columbia Broadcasting System*, 216 F.2d 945 (9th Cir. 1954), *cert. denied*, 348 U.S. 971 (1955), the court held that where the contract specified the transfer of certain items but failed to mention another, the item not mentioned was not transferred. The agreement was for rights in the book *The Maltese Falcon*; it did not transfer the right to use the character name "Sam Spade" in other works.

In *Detsch & Co. v. American Products Co.*, 152 F.2d 473 (9th Cir. 1945), a sales agreement stated that "Second Party shall cooperate with First Party to further the sales of said products, and towards this end Second Party shall furnish to First Party, without recourse and free of any charge, any and all price lists, advertising matter and samples." The court held that this list did not exhaustively enumerate the forms of cooperation that the Second Party was required to extend to the First Party.

In *Detsch & Co.*, it might be noted that the Second Party contended that the doctrine of *ejusdem generis* applied to restrict the duties owed, but *expressio unius* would be more appropriate.

> 3. A contract susceptible of two meanings will be given the meaning which will render it valid.

In *Ballard v. MacCallum*, 15 Cal. 2d 439, 101 P.2d 692 (1940), a trust agreement could be read as providing for two effects of the beneficiary's failure to make monthly payments. Under one, the beneficiary's rights were forfeited; under the other, the forfeiture was not automatic but occurred only after notice and failure to cure. The court held that the interpretation which avoids forfeiture is favored.

> 4. Between repugnant clauses, a possible interpretation which removes the conflict will be adopted.

In *Unicon Management Corp. v. United States*, 375 F.2d 804 (Ct. Cl. 1967), a contractor claimed that specifications called for a concrete floor while the government claimed that drawings indicated a steel-reinforced floor. The court held that the parts of the agreement did not conflict, for the drawings could be seen as complementing the specifications.

Often courts invoke the rule that a particular provision governs over a general one. A specific clause better indicates the parties' intentions.

Sometimes the parties include language intended to resolve a conflict. In *William F. Klingensmith, Inc. v. United States*, 505 F.2d 1257 (Ct. Cl. 1974), a contractor claimed that it was required to use gravel while the government claimed it was required to use macadam. The drawings supported the contractor while the specifications supported the government. However, the contract expressly provided that "in case of difference between drawings and specifications, the specifications shall govern."

> 5. A contract will, if possible, be interpreted so as to render it reasonable rather than unreasonable.

In *Elite, Inc. v. S.S. Mullen, Inc.*, 469 F.2d 1127 (9th Cir. 1972), a construction contract called for the contractor to provide the quarry site from which the subcontractor would obtain rock. When the site proved unproductive, the subcontractor sought to obtain its additional expenses. The court held that "The crux of the agreement ... was the obtaining of suitable riprap in a reasonably economical manner from a quarry selected by Mullen. To interpret this contract as not requiring Mullen to provide a quarry where riprap could be produced would render the entire contract meaningless."

6. Words will generally be construed most strongly against the party using them.

In *State Farm Mutual Automobile Insurance Companies v. Queen*, 212 Mont. 62, 685 P.2d 935 (1984), an insurance company provided coverage for the use of "non-owned automobiles" to "the first person named in the declaration." The declaration listed the following: "Queen, Gary A. and Rhonda R." Under this rule of interpretation, the court held that Rhonda was covered while driving a non-owned automobile. The insurer subsequently redrafted the policy to state, "The 'first **person** named' is that **person** whose surname followed by a given name or initial is printed first in the 'insured' section of the Declarations Page."

This rule was also cited by the court in *Business Men's Assurance Ass'n v. Read*, 48 S.W.2d 678 (Tex. Civ. App. 1932), discussed in § 7.4.5.

7. In case of doubt, the interpretation given by the parties is the best evidence of their intention.

In *Sunbury Textile Mills, Inc. v. Commissioner*, 585 F.2d 1190 (3d Cir. 1978), the interpretation given by the parties to a contract prevailed over the interpretation urged by the I.R.S.

The parties often indicate their interpretation through their performance. In *Hanson v. P.A. Peterson Home Ass'n*, 35 Ill. App. 2d 134, 182 N.E.2d 237 (1962), the court stated that "there is no more convincing evidence of what the parties intended by their contract than to see what they did in carrying out its provisions."

Note that in many cases, an issue of the admissibility of parol evidence to support an interpretation arises. See Chapter 6, *Parol Evidence*.

The oft-quoted observation of Learned Hand that an objective interpretation obtains even if the parties did not share the interpretation is found in *Eustis Mining Co. v. Beer, Sondheimer & Co.*, 239 F. 976, 984-85 (S.D.N.Y. 1917).

8. Where conflict between printed and written words, the writing governs.

In *Hagan v. Scottish Union & National Insurance Co.*, 186 U.S. 423 (1902), a printed insurance policy stated that the policy was void if the insured transferred title to the ship. The owner did transfer title, but claimed that the provision did not apply because the handwritten portion of the policy insured "Peter Hagan and Company for account of whom it may concern." The court held that the handwritten portion governed and contemplated a transfer of title.

The same principle applies to typewritten words. In *Preugschat v. Hedges*, 41 Wash. 2d 660, 251 P.2d 166 (1952), the court stated this principle but did not apply it when the typewritten words could be construed as consistent with the printed words.

2. Ambiguity.

a. The phrase "in trust for the maintenance and education of my son" is ambiguous in that the *and* may be read as either joint or several. The joint sense could be clearly expressed as "in trust for both the maintenance and education of my son." The several could be clearly expressed as "in trust for either the maintenance or education, or both, of my son."

b. There are a number of problems with this provision. The word *school* is vague, for it covers a spectrum of institutions. The word *tuition* is not vague, but it may be overly particular. Did the drafter intend to include other costs of attending the institution, such as registration fees, activity fees, etc.? The phrase "in the state system" is an ambiguous modifier. These are possible redrafts:

---

1. Husband shall pay the tuition of the children at any post-secondary school, any college, or any university in the state system.

---

2. Husband shall pay the tuition of the children at any of the following in the state system: post-secondary schools, colleges, and universities.

---

3. Husband shall pay the tuition of the children at any:
    1) post-secondary school;
    2) college; or
    3) university in the state system.

---

4. Husband shall pay the tuition of the children at any:
    1) post-secondary school;
    2) college; or
    3) university
in the state system.

The phrase "post-secondary school" replaces "school" to clear up the vagueness. Example 1 clarifies that only *university* is modified by "in the state system" while Example 2 clarifies that all the words are. Examples 3 and 4 use tabulation, 3 to make clear that only *university* is modified by "in the state system" while 4 makes clear that all the words are.

      c. Did the drafter mean this: Never include in a contract a provision which you do not understand.

      d. Does "by the Company" modify *termination* or *employment*? If the former, then she does not get benefits because she was not terminated by the Company. If the latter, then she gets benefits because her employment by the Company was terminated. This might be one of those cases where the ambiguity will be construed against the drafter, which is probably the Company.

      e. Whose expenses -- Company's or Customer's?

Additional problems dealing with ambiguity may be found in DICKERSON, MATERIALS ON LEGAL DRAFTING 239-41.

3. Tabulation.

      a. The passage from a homeowner's insurance policy is from *Payne v. Safeco Ins. Co.*, 222 Mont. 198, 720 P.2d 1197 (1986).

> This coverage excludes: ... 2. motorized vehicles, except such vehicles pertaining to the service of the premises and not licensed for road use.

In a fire, the homeowners lost an antique car that was not licensed. The insurer claimed that the *and* was joint, indicating that vehicles excepted from the exclusion had to have two characteristics: they had to pertain to the service of the premises and they had to be not licensed for road use. The insured claimed that the *and* was several, with the policy excepting two classes of vehicles from the exclusion: those pertaining to the service of the premises and those not licensed for road use. Under this interpretation, the insured's vehicle fell within one of the classes even though it did not have both characteristics.

      After the ambiguity is detected, the drafter can redraft the sentence to express the intended meaning. The provision might be redrafted to read, for the insurer: "except such vehicles both pertaining to the service of the premises and not licensed for road use" and for the insured: "except such vehicles pertaining to the service of the premises or not licensed for road use, or both."

      The provision could be stated in this tabulation form:

> This coverage excludes:
>
> ....
>
> 2. Motorized vehicles, except vehicles that
>
>> a. pertain to the service of the premises; [*and* or *or*]
>> b. are not licensed for road use.

The appropriate connective under the insurer's interpretation that the conditions are cumulative would be *and*; under the insured's interpretation that the conditions are alternative, it would be *or*.

       b. This example is from the IRS VOLUNTEER ASSISTOR'S GUIDE (1987). The Guide tabulates the provision as follows:

> 1. A person is permanently and totally disabled when:
>
>> 1.   The person cannot engage in any substantial gainful activity because of a physical or mental condition, and
>>
>> 2.   A physician determines that the disability has lasted or can be expected to last continuously for at least a year, or can be expected to lead to death.

      This tabulation follows Rules 1, 2, and 4. The enumeration is part of the sentence that precedes it. The tabulation illustrates Rule 5, with the next-to-last item of the enumeration ending with *and*. The final provision could be further broken down.

      Additional example. The Tax Code and IRS Publications provide numerous examples of tabulation. The following is a tabulation in which the enumerated items comprise a list. The tabulation illustrates Rule 6, with the list following a complete sentence:

> 2. If a taxpayer is under age 65, all of the following tests must be met:
>
>> 1.   The taxpayer retired on permanent and total disability on the date he or she retired, or if the taxpayer retired before January 1, 1977, he or she was permanently and totally disabled on January 1, 1976, or January 1, 1977.
>>
>> 2.   The taxpayer received taxable disability income for 1986.
>>
>> 3.   On January 1, 1986, the taxpayer had not reached the mandatory retirement age required by his or her employer.

c. The section broken down:

If

Company does not have another use at the site for such facilities to serve other Company customers, and

the Customer makes an offer to purchase such facilities for the unamortized investment in the facilities as determined pursuant to Exhibit F plus the appraised value of the property on which the facilities are located, and

Company rejects the offer,

then the Customer shall not be required to reimburse Company for any unrecoverable costs pursuant to Exhibit F.

The section in tabulated form:

If :

     1. Company does not have another use at the site for such facilities to serve other Company customers, and

     2. the Customer makes an offer to purchase such facilities for the unamortized investment in the facilities as determined pursuant to Exhibit F plus the appraised value of the property on which the facilities are located, and

     3. Company rejects the offer,

then the Customer shall not be required to reimburse Company for any unrecoverable costs pursuant to Exhibit F.

The section back-formed:

If 1) Company does not have another use at the site for such facilities to serve other Company customers, and 2) the Customer makes an offer to purchase such facilities for the unamortized investment in the facilities as determined pursuant to Exhibit F plus the appraised value of the property on which the facilities are located, and 3) Company rejects the offer, then the Customer shall not be required to reimburse Company for any unrecoverable costs pursuant to Exhibit F.

---

d. Additional Exercise. As additional exercise in tabulation, ask students to tabulate Paragraph (B) of the Magnuson-Moss definition. It can be analyzed as follows:

(B) any undertaking in writing

(in connection with the sale by a supplier of a consumer product)

to refund, repair, replace, *or* take other remedial action with respect to such product in the event that such product fails to meet the specifications set forth in the undertaking,

(which written affirmation, promise, *or* undertaking becomes part of the basis of the bargain between a supplier *and* a buyer for purposes other than resale of such product).

After analysis, it is clear that the language that ends Paragraph (B) (which written affirmation, promise, *or* undertaking ...) must modify both Paragraphs (A) and (B), for Paragraph (A) refers to an affirmation of fact or a promise and Paragraph (B) refers to an undertaking. In accordance with Dick's rule #2, this item should respond to the words in refers to in (A) as well as in (B).

Note that the language in (B) (in connection with the sale by a supplier of a consumer product) is virtually the same as that in (A) (made in connection with the sale of a consumer product by a supplier to a buyer). According to the Golden Rule of Drafting, never change your language unless you wish to change your meaning. Instead of being repeated, this item can be rearranged to respond to both (A) and (B).

Paragraph (B) can be combined with (A) as follows:

The term "written warranty" means --

any written

    1. affirmation of fact;
    2. promise; or
    3. undertaking

which

    1. is made in connection with the sale of a consumer product by a supplier to a buyer; and
    2. becomes part of the basis of the bargain between a supplier *and* a buyer for purposes other than resale of such product.

An affirmation of fact or promise must

     1. relate to the nature of the material *or* workmanship; *and*
     2. affirm *or* promise that such material *or* workmanship

          a. is defect free; *or*
          b. will meet a specified level of performance

over a specified period of time.

An undertaking must offer to

     1. refund;
     2. repair;
     3. replace; *or*
     4. take other remedial action with respect to such product

in the event that such product fails to meet the specifications set forth in the undertaking.

The draft would be further improved by replacing *such* with *the*.

    e. Additonal Exercise. Here is another provision to tabulate:

5. EXCEPTIONS TO CONFIDENTIAL INFORMATION

The Receiving Party shall have no obligation with respect to information which (i) was rightfully in possession of or known to the Receiving Party without any obligation of confidentiality prior to receiving it from Company; (ii) is, or subsequently becomes, legally and publicly available without breach of this Agreement; (iii) is rightfully obtained by the Receiving Party from a source other than Company without any obligation of confidentiality; (iv) is developed by or for the Receiving Party without use of the Confidential Information and such independent development can be shown by documentary evidence; (v) becomes available to the Receiving Party by wholly lawful inspection or analysis of products offered for sale; (vi) is transmitted by a party after receiving written notification from the other party that it does not desire to receive any further Confidential Information; (vii) is disclosed by the Receiving Party under a valid order issued by a court or government agency, provided that the Receiving Party provides Company (a) prior written notice of such obligation and (b) the opportunity to oppose such disclosure or obtain a protective order.

This is easily done by following the numbered divisions:

5. EXCEPTIONS TO CONFIDENTIAL INFORMATION

The Receiving Party shall have no obligation with respect to information which

(i) was rightfully in possession of or known to the Receiving Party without any obligation of confidentiality prior to receiving it from Company;

(ii) is, or subsequently becomes, legally and publicly available without breach of this Agreement;

(iii) is rightfully obtained by the Receiving Party from a source other than Company without any obligation of confidentiality;

(iv) is developed by or for the Receiving Party without use of the Confidential Information and such independent development can be shown by documentary evidence;

(v) becomes available to the Receiving Party by wholly lawful inspection or analysis of products offered for sale;

(vi) is transmitted by a party after receiving written notification from the other party that it does not desire to receive any further Confidential Information;

(vii) is disclosed by the Receiving Party under a valid order issued by a court or government agency, provided that the Receiving Party provides Company

(a) prior written notice of such obligation and

(b) the opportunity to oppose such disclosure or obtain a protective order.

While this draft is already clearer, we now see that (vi) is not parallel because it applies to "a party" while the others enumerate information in the hands of the Receiving Party. We also need a connective for the next to last item, which should probably be an *or*.

4. Definition.

In this definition, "base alimony" is $100. Plugging this definition into the provision, in the second year Husband pays Wife $100 + (10% x $100), or $110. In the third year, Husband pays Wife $100 + (10% x $100), or $110. Wife will claim (probably correctly) that this was not the intended result. The problem would have been avoided if the definition had been more precisely drafted. Perhaps this was intended:

Cost of living increase. In the first calendar year, Husband shall pay Wife $100 per week. In each week of the subsequent calendar year, Husband shall pay Wife the amount payable in the prior year plus a cost of living increase. The cost of living increase is the amount payable in the prior year multiplied by the inflation rate for the prior year as determined by the Department of Labor.

5. General and particular. This example is adopted from DICK, LEGAL DRAFTING 124 (2d ed.).

> If either trustee is at any time unable to act by reason of death, disability, or absence from the country, the other may act alone.

This provision overlooks the possibility that one trustee may have resigned and perhaps other possibilities, such as incompetence. It could be redrafted as:

> If either trustee is at any time unable to act for any reason, including but not limited to death, disability, or absence from the country, the other may act alone.

Alternatively, there may be no reason to include any particulars. The provision could be redrafted as this general statement :

> If either trustee is at any time unable to act, the other may act alone.

6. Vagueness. I think the following phrases are vague:
> the manufacturer's installation specifications
> the standard practices of the telecommunications industry
> reasonable access
> timely and adequate
> other [environmental requirements]

These seem to me to be usefully vague terms. Perhaps there is a question about what those other environmental requirements are. In fact, I edited out the original end of that sentence, which contained some examples:

> telecommunications connections and other environmental requirements, including but not limited to HVAC systems, specified in Seller's instructions, including those connections required for Customer's choice of local and long distance telecommunications services.

7. Connectives.

a. The Company may terminate this Agreement upon 7 days' notice to Customer if <u>one or more of</u> the following events occur: A, B, [or] C.

b. The Company may terminate this Agreement upon 7 days' notice to Customer if <u>one and only one of</u> the following events occur: A, B, [or] C.

c.   The Company may terminate this Agreement upon 7 days' notice to Customer if <u>all of</u> the following events occur: A, B, <u>and</u> C.

8. Ethics. This example is from GEOFFREY HAZARD, THE LAW OF LAWYERING § 37.3. This is Hazard's analysis:

> It is not improper for a lawyer to draft a contract containing deliberately ambiguous terms. Competent representation requires L to warn the company, however, that even if it wins the potential litigation over its other game, it will incur litigation expenses and possible loss of reputation in the industry. However, that is the extent of his obligation to the company. He has no obligation to flag the ambiguity for the inventor; instead he has a duty not to do so unless otherwise authorized by his client.

Chapter 8
Mistake

§ 8.3. Assuming the risk.

The land sale problem is discussed in FARNSWORTH, CONTRACTS § 9.3 (3d ed.). A warranty that facts were as promised was found in *Hoffa v. Fitzsimmons*, 499 F. Supp. 357 (D.C. 1980), aff'd in part and vacated in part, 673 F.2d 1345 (D.C. Cir. 1982). The example of an absolute promise to perform irrespective of the actual conditions existing is *Flippin Materials Co. v. United States*, 312 F.2d 408 (Ct. Cl. 1963). The omitted footnote containing the promise states in part:

11. "GC-2 SITE INVESTIGATION AND REPRESENTATIONS.

"The contractor acknowledges that he has satisfied himself as to the nature and location of the work, the general and local conditions, particularly those bearing upon transportation, disposal, handling and storage of materials, availability of labor, water, electric power, and roads, uncertainties of weather, river stages, tides or similar physical conditions at the site, the conformation and condition of the ground, the character, quality and quantity of surface and subsurface materials to be encountered, the character and equipment and facilities needed preliminary to and during the prosecution of the work and all other matters which can in any way affect the work or the cost thereof under this contract. Any failure by the contractor to acquaint himself with all the available information concerning these conditions will not relieve him from responsibility for estimating properly the difficulty or cost of successfully performing the work ...."

§ 8.4. Releases.

RESTATEMENT (SECOND) § 152 Comment f states:

Releases. Releases of claims have afforded particularly fertile ground for the invocation of the rule stated in this Section. It is, of course, a traditional policy of the law to favor compromises as a means of settling claims without resort to litigation. See Comment a to § 74. Nevertheless, a claimant who has executed such a release may later wish to attack it. The situation may arise with respect to any claim, but a particularly common example involves claims for personal injury, where the claimant may have executed the release without full knowledge of the extent or, perhaps, even of the nature of his injuries. Such a claimant has a variety of possible grounds for attacking the release on discovering that his injuries are more serious than he had initially supposed. He may seek to have the release interpreted against the draftsman so as to be inapplicable to the newly discovered injuries (§ 206). He may seek to have the release reformed on the ground that it does not correctly express the prior agreement of the parties (§ 155). He may seek to avoid the release on the ground that it was unfairly obtained through misrepresentation, duress or undue influence (Chapter 7). He may seek to have the release, or at least that part purporting to cover the newly discovered injuries, held unenforceable as unconscionable (§ 208). Or he may seek to avoid the release on the ground that both he and the other party were mistaken as to the nature or extent of his injuries. Assuming that the release is properly interpreted to cover unknown injuries and that it was not unfairly obtained or unconscionable, his case will turn on the application of the rule stated in this Section to his claim of mistake. In dealing with such attacks on releases, a court should be particularly sensitive to obscure or misleading language and especially alert to the possibility of unfairness or unconscionability. However, the same rules relating to mistake apply to such releases as apply to other contracts, and if the results sometimes seem at variance with those rules, the variance can usually be attributed to the presence of one of the alternative grounds listed above.

A claimant's attempt at avoidance based on mistake of both parties, therefore, will frequently turn on a determination, in the light of all the circumstances, of the basic assumptions of the parties at the time of the release. These circumstances may include the fair amount that would be required to compensate the claimant for his known injuries, the probability that the other party would be held liable on that claim, the amount received by the claimant in settlement of his claim, and the relationship between the known injuries and the newly discovered injuries. If, for example, the amount received by the claimant is reasonable in comparison with the fair amount required to compensate him for his known injuries and the probability of the other party being held liable on that claim, this suggests that the parties assumed that his injuries were only those known. Furthermore, even if the parties do not assume that his injuries are only those known, they may assume that any unknown injuries are of the same general nature as the known ones, while differing in extent. Although the parties may fix the assumptions on which the contract is based by an express provision, fairly bargained for, the common recital that the release covers all injuries, known or unknown and of whatever nature or extent, may be disregarded as unconscionable if, in view of the circumstances of the parties, their legal representation, and the setting of the negotiations, it flies in the face of what would otherwise be regarded as a basic assumption of the parties. What has been said here with respect to releases of claims for personal injury is generally true for releases executed in other contexts.

The examples are from 16 AM. JUR. LEGAL FORMS 2D Releases 223:27, 54, and 70 respectively. The seaman's "red release," so called because the boldface language is printed in red, is a classic for hammering home the meaning of the release. It is found at 16 AM. JUR. LEGAL FORMS 2D Releases 223:70:

Read Carefully--By signing this you give up every right you have.

I, ___1___, Age ___2___ ___3___ (Write here whether you are married or single)

Address ___4___; in exchange for ___5___ Dollars ($____) which I have received, do hereby ___6___ (Write the word "release" to show that you know what you are doing) and forever discharge ___7___ and their heirs, executors, administrators, successors and assigns, and their several vessels and in particular the ss. ___8___ and the owners, agents, operators, charterers, masters, officers, and crews, of such vessels from each and every right and claim which I now have, or may hereafter have on account of injuries and illnesses suffered by me as follows: ___9___, and, in addition to that, I ___10___ (Write the word "release" to show that you know what you are doing) them from each and every right and claim which I now have or may hereafter have because of any matter or thing which happened before the signing of this paper, it being my intention by the signing of this paper to wipe the slate clean as between myself and the parties released, even as respects injuries, illnesses, rights and claims not mentioned herein or not known to me.

(1)   I know that this paper is much more than a receipt. **It is a release. I am giving up every right I have.**

(2)   I know that in signing this release I am, among other things, now settling in full for all injuries, illnesses and disabilities which I have had already, which I have now, and which I may have in the future, either because of the particular occurrence mentioned above or because of any other occurrence in the past, or because of both, even though I do not know that I have had already, have now or may have in the future such injuries, illnesses and disabilities, and even though they are not mentioned particularly in this release; and I do all this regardless of what anyone may have told me about my injuries, illnesses and disabilities or about anything else.

(3)   **I know that doctors and other persons make mistakes, and I am taking the risk that what they may have told me is wrong. If that should be the case, it is my loss, and I cannot back out of the settlement.**

(4)   I realize that the payment of the money mentioned above is not an admission that anyone is liable to me for anything.

(5)   I am signing this release because I am getting the money. I have not been promised anything else.

(6)   I am satisfied.

THE FOLLOWING IS TO BE FILLED IN BY THE CLAIMANT HIMSELF IN HIS OWN HANDWRITING.

A.   Have you read this paper from beginning to end? __11__

B.   Do you know what this paper is that you are signing? __12__

C.   What is this paper which you are signing? __13__ (Write here "release of everything")

D.   Do you make the six numbered statements printed above and do you intend that the parties whom you are releasing shall rely on the statements as the truth? _ __14__

E.   Do you know that signing this paper settles and ends every right or claim you have for damages as well as for past and future maintenance, cure, and wages? ___ 15__

F.   In order to show that you know what you are doing please copy in your own handwriting, in the space immediately following, the third numbered statement above: __16__

Therefore, I am signing my name on the words "This is a Release" and alongside the seal, which is printed below and which is adopted by me as my own, to show that I mean everything that is said on this paper.

Dated __17__, 19_18_

Sign Here   **This is a Release**   **(Seal)**

Claimant, if he wishes to sign and seal this paper, should write his name on the words "This is a Release" immediately above and alongside the printed seal.

[Certificate of Witnesses omitted]

§ 8.5. Ethical issues.

The disclosure problem is based on *Spaulding v. Zimmerman*, 263 Minn. 346, 116 N.W.2d 704 (1962).

The quote on reformation is from CALAMARI & PERILLO, CONTRACTS § 9.31 (4th ed.). The separation agreement problem is based on *Stare v. Tate*, 21 Cal. App. 3d 432, 98 Cal. Rptr.

264 (1971). According to Cal. Civ. Code § 3399, a court may reform a contract if there has been "a mutual mistake of the parties or a mistake of one party which the other at the time knew or suspected."

§ 8.6. Exercises.

1. Disclosure. In this case, B and S are on equal footing as far as knowledge of competition is concerned. S would not be obligated to make up for the lack of B's information. S and S's attorney were careful not to make any false representation to B, saying only that B would have to find out for himself. B made a unilateral mistake about the facts existing at the time of the transaction. If the assumption that there was no competition was significant to B, B should have asked S to make a representation that there would be no competition for a particular period of time. The contract could then have provided for rescission of the contract if the event occurred. Of course, S would probably not have agreed to this concession. Had B's attorney raised it, however, it would have made B more aware of the risk he was taking based on his inadequate knowledge.

A more complex disclosure problem is discussed in Kaplan, *Legal Ethics Forum*, 62 A.B.A.J. 1049 (1976), based on the facts of *Kardon v. National Gypsum Co.*, 69 F. Supp. 512 (E.D. Pa. 1946), 73 F. Supp. 798 (E.D. Pa. 1947).

2. Taking advantage of a mistake. This question was answered in ABA Committee on Ethics and Professional Responsibility, Informal Opinion 86-1518, February 9, 1986:

Obligations to Third Persons

TRUTHFULNESS IN STATEMENTS TO OTHERS --

Lawyer whose client would be advantaged by inadvertent omission of important provision from contract to which client had previously agreed should bring error to attention of other party's lawyer and may do so without consulting his own client.

Digest of Opinion: A and B, with the help of their lawyers, negotiate a commercial contract. At the end of negotiations, A agrees to a provision that had been in dispute and without which B would not have agreed to the contract. However, the final version of the contract, which was typed in the office of B's lawyer, does not contain this provision. The committee has been asked its opinion of the ethical duty of A's lawyer.

This situation involves a mere scrivener's error, not an intentional change in position. A meeting of the minds occurred. The committee concludes the error is appropriate for correction between the lawyers without client consultation. (Assuming for purposes of discussion that the error is "information relating to [the] representation," under Model Rule 1.6 disclosure would be "impliedly authorized in order to carry out the representation.")

A's lawyer does not have a duty to advise A of the error pursuant to any obligation of communication under Model Rule 1.4. There is no "informed decision," in the words of the rule, that A needs to make; the client has already made the decision on the contract. Furthermore, the comment to Model Rule 1.2 points out that a lawyer may decide, without consultation with the client, the "technical" means to employ to carry out the objective of a representation.

The client does not have a right to take unfair advantage of the error. The client's right under Model Rule 1.2 to expect committed and dedicated representation is not unlimited. Indeed, any suggestion by the lawyer that A capitalize on the clerical error might raise a serious question that the lawyer violated his Model Rule 1.2(d) duty not to counsel the client to engage in, or assist the client in, conduct the lawyer knows is fraudulent. In addition, Model Rule 4.1(b) admonishes the lawyer to disclose a material fact to a third person when disclosure is necessary to avoid assisting his client's fraudulent act, and 8.4(c) prohibits the lawyer from engaging in conduct involving dishonesty, fraud, deceit, or misrepresentation.

The result is the same under the Model Code. While EC 7-8 teaches that a lawyer should use best efforts to ensure that a client's decisions are made after the client has been informed of relevant consideration, and EC 9-2 charges the lawyer with fully and promptly informing the client of material developments, the scrivener's error is neither a relevant consideration nor a material development. (The delivery of the erroneous document is not a "material development" of which the client should be informed under EC 9-2, but the omission of the provision from the document is a "material fact," which under Model Rule 4.1(b) must be disclosed to B's lawyer.) DR 7-101's duty of zealous representation is limited to lawful objectives. DR 7-102(A)(7) prohibits a lawyer from counseling or assisting the client in conduct known to be fraudulent, and DR 1-102(A)(4) prohibits the lawyer from engaging in conduct involving dishonesty, fraud, deceit, or misrepresentation.

3. Drafting a release. Most casebooks use the case method profitably to contrast cases involving releases. From these cases, a number of factors emerge that courts examine in determining whether to uphold a release. This exercise demonstrates the application of these considerations in practicing preventive law.

For example, the court enforced the release in *Randolph v. Ottenstein*, 238 F. Supp. 1011 (D.C. 1965), and avoided it in *Reed v. Harvey*, 253 Iowa 10, 110 N.W.2d 442 (1961). A comparison of these cases illuminates these factors:

Background of parties:
    Randolph: well-educated attorney accustomed to dealing with insurance company. Reed: poorly educated claimant dealing with experienced adjuster.

Origin of mistake:
    Randolph: defendant's doctor accepted plaintiff's doctor's evaluation without checking.
    Reed: defendant personally checked evaluation with plaintiff's doctor.

Preparation of agreement:
>Randolph: plaintiff initiated the settlement and apparently drafted the release. Reed: defendant initiated settlement and drafted the release.

Amount paid:
>Randolph: consideration was $150 more than known expenses. Reed: consideration was for known expenses and $6.41 for "trouble."

Injuries specified:
>Randolph: release was general, covering all injuries. Reed: release specified "dog bite" while actual injury was from fall.

Some of the drafting factors mentioned in RESTATEMENT (SECOND) § 152 include 1) whether the release can be interpreted against the drafter, 2) whether it expresses the prior agreement of the parties, 3) whether it contains misleading language, and 4) whether it correctly expresses the assumptions of the parties as to the extent of injuries.

If we apply these factors to the Kraft/Turner release, we see the following possibilities for revision:

1. Consideration. Kraft received payment only for his actual expenses. Benevolent might include consideration for possible future expenses. Under the doctrine of "conscious ignorance," Kraft would then be assuming the risk of further unknown expenses.

2. Background of parties. Kraft entered the agreement immediately after the accident without an opportunity to evaluate the situation. Benevolent might at least wait and might suggest that Kraft consult with counsel if he wishes.

3. Injuries specified. By specifying "neck injuries," the agreement would not exclude claims for other injuries. The specific injury should be omitted from the draft.

4. Preparation of agreement. While the insurance company will always prepare the agreement, a court is more likely to enforce an agreement that is clearly written so that the other party understands it. Benevolent might consider reflecting in the agreement that Kraft knows what he is doing and expressing that knowledge in plain language. This would prevent Kraft from claiming that he thought he simply signed a receipt. Recall Examples 2 and 3 in § 8.4.

Chapter 9
Force Majeure

§ 9.2. Qualifying an obligation.

a. Examples of option contracts for the purchase of a business and for the purchase of real property may be found in 15B and 16 AM. JUR. LEGAL FORMS 2D.

b. See Chapter 10, *Promise and Condition*.

c. See Chapter 2, *Consideration*.

d. See Chapter 2, *Consideration*. A public policy consideration might arise with a franchise.

e. See Chapter 12, *Warranties*. Note that the limitation of consequential damages for personal injury in the case of consumer goods is prima facie unconscionable. U.C.C. § 2-719.

§ 9.3. Absolute performance.

Comment 8 to U.C.C. § 2-615 states that the parties may assume greater liability by agreement, which may be found "not only in the expressed terms of the contract but in the circumstances surrounding the contracting, in trade usage and the like." An absolute obligation to perform was enforced in *United States v. Huff*, 165 F.2d 720 (5th Cir. 1948); *Wills v. Shockley*, 52 Del. 295, 157 A.2d 252 (1960); *Broderick Wood Products Co. v. United States*, 195 F.2d 433 (10th Cir. 1952).

The clause providing that destruction of the goods is not an excuse is adapted from 5A HART & WILLIER, FORMS AND PROCEDURES UNDER THE U.C.C. § 24.21, Clause 573.

The first example of language interpreted as an absolute obligation is from *Gulf Oil Corporation v. Federal Power Commission*, 563 F.2d 588 (3d Cir. 1977). The second example is from *Broderick Wood Products Co. v. United States*, 195 F.2d 433 (10th Cir. 1952). In *Broderick*, 195 F.2d 433, 437, the court explained:

The deduction from the contract price involved here was made under [the second] provision of the contract. It is to be noted that in substantial difference from the other provision, this one failed to contain any language indicating an intent or purpose on the part of the contracting parties to absolve the company from the rigors of the deduction if the failure to deliver the material within the specified period was due to severe weather conditions or other act of God. Under this provision, the right of the Government to make the deduction was absolute and positive without regard to whether the default in performance was due to an act of God, or otherwise. It is the general rule that where an obligation or duty is imposed upon a person by law, he will be absolved from liability for nonperformance if his performance is rendered impossible without fault on his part, by an act of God. But with certain exceptions and qualifications having no material bearing here, it is well settled that where one voluntarily enters into a positive agreement binding himself absolutely to perform a lawful and possible act within a specified time, he is not relieved of that duty or absolved from liability for failure to fulfill the covenant by a subsequent impossibility of performance caused by an act of God. Berg v. Erickson, 10 Cir., 234 F. 817, L.R.A. 1917a, 648; United States v. Lewis, 8 Cir., 237 F. 80. The time of performance of this contract was fixed. The second provision without condition or qualification authorized the deduction for delay of performance. And having bound itself by absolute provision to make delivery of the material within a specified time, the company assumed the risk of failure of performance and cannot complain that on settlement the deduction was withheld in strict accord with the provision of the contract authorizing the Government to withhold the amount.

A court often regards a *force majeure* clause as an omitted term. The fact that the parties included a *force majeure* clause with several obligations but omitted the clause with another may have created the negative inference that the parties intentionally omitted it. The expression of the Golden Rule is from AITKEN & PIESSE THE ELEMENTS OF DRAFTING 58.

§ 9.4. *Force majeure.*

Example *1* is from the Mississippi enactment of U.C.C. § 2-617, which is not a part of the Official Text. Example *2* is from 5A HART & WILLIER, FORMS AND PROCEDURES UNDER THE U.C.C. § 24.22[1], Clause 575. The concepts of *ejusdem generis* and *exclusio unius est exclusio alterius*, discussed in Chapter 7, *Interpretation*, should be reviewed in connection with their application to drafting *force majeure* clauses.

MELLINKOFF, LEGAL WRITING: SENSE & NONSENSE 120-21 discusses the problem of whether the agreement should be drafted broadly or narrowly:

[2]   A lawyer's vision of the future

Given adequate time to plan and write, the writer's natural inclination is to visualize all the possibilities of fact and law that can affect durability. All to the good. But the farsighted lawyer's vision of the future should not immediately loose a flood of detail. The precious leisure to plan gives opportunity to consider not only what can be put in but also what can be left out.

How far can one's vision reach? If I make the writing more precise, as things appear to me now, will it have the same crispness 10 years from now? Is it better to build in some looseness in the joints? The Constitution of the United States is a classic example of built-in durability, through the use of flexible words--*due process, equal protection, freedom of speech,* etc. Similar considerations affect less monumental writings.

For example:

The *force majeure* (French, irresistible force) clause. Do you spell out all of the events you can think of that are "beyond control," that should extend a period fixed in a contract? War, piracy, riot, fire, flood, strikes, etc. Do you make it precise, tight; these events and no others.

Or do you make it flexible? "*including but not limited to*" the listed events.

Do you want some flexibility, but not too much? The listed events "*or other events similar to those named.*"

Or do you want it very flexible, concentrating not on crystal ball gazing but on the general nature of things that are "beyond control"? The listed events "*or other events beyond control, whether the events are similar or dissimilar to those named.*"

Maybe short, maybe long; maybe precise, maybe not. Maybe clear, maybe not. Durability stands on its own merits. Pattern is not the answer.

Similarly, Alphonse M. Squillante & Felice M. Congalton, *Force Majeure*, Commercial Law Journal, January, 1975, p. 4, express various ways of stating a *force majeure* clause to accomplish different purposes:

Variations on Clause Construction

Variation 1

The promisor may assume absolute liability for non-performance with a contract statement that specifically delineates those factors which will not excuse his performance:

The seller hereby assumes absolute liability for performance of the above mentioned obligations and may not employ as grounds for excuse of non-performance the following . . .

With this particular clause the parties may add specific circumstances under which the promisor gives assurance of his performance regardless of the supervening happening that would otherwise render his performance impossible or impracticable.

Variation 2

A second variation other than one for absolute liability might be drafted as follows:

The seller is excluded from the right to claim excuse for non-performance by any supervening circumstances whatsoever. However, the Uniform Commercial Code § 2-613 shall govern the parties' obligations as to delayed delivery.

Variation 3

The promisor in this particular variation may provide for excuse only in certain stated circumstances. Thus, such a clause can be drafted as follows:

The seller shall not be liable for failure to deliver any (or all) of the above mentioned goods should the failure to deliver result from (1) strikes, (2) floods, (3) et cetera.

Variation 4

Should the parties to the contract wish to avoid the somewhat harsh clauses as set forth in the first three variations, there is a liberal clause which could be drafted as follows:

The promisor is excused from non-performance of any and all contractual obligations in the event that his performance is hindered by some supervening force not procured by his own hand and not foreseeable at the time of the making of the contract.

§ 9.5. Drafting for specific situations.

WINCOR, CONTRACTS IN PLAIN ENGLISH, contains excellent sections on drafting international agreements. At 43-44, he suggests that the over-enumeration of events is peculiarly American:

American contracts generally are more elaborate than others. That puts the case in a nutshell. The Americans try to cover all of the plausible eventualities, and they consume more space in doing so. The British generally go the opposite way; they like their contracts short, matter-of-fact, and confined to setting down the main points. The Americans dislike leaving things up in the air. As soon as one point is settled they raise the question, "But what happens if . . . ?"

The larger part of the world follows the British style in these matters. Reasons for the difference in approach very likely include the relative complexity of the American industrial structure, the magnitude of its stakes, and the large role played by lawyers in the United States. Whatever the reasons, the results are what count. Which is better?

Ideally a clear and concise short form written without lawyers has a surface attraction. Most of the troublesome possibilities never will arise; if they do, goodwill solves everything. We trust each other; besides, if we try spelling everything out, the legal fees will be higher. This is how many Europeans see it.

The best American counterargument is that anything worth doing is worth doing well. They have a point. Sometimes prolix, occasionally guilty of "overkill," American contracts in the main are more sophisticated than others. Perhaps it all depends on whether one prefers Beethoven or plainsong.

The gas price escalation clause is from 4 WILLIAMS & MEYERS, OIL AND GAS LAW § 726. See *Texas Gas Transmission Corp. v. Shell Oil Co.*, 363 U.S. 263 (1960). Details of other provisions that excuse nonperformance are found in 4 WILLIAMS & MEYERS § 733.

§ 9.6. Exercises.

1. Technological change. Manufacturers who contract to produce a product that requires a technological breakthrough have generally assumed the risk that performance may be impracticable. This case is based on *Austin Co. v. United States*, 314 F.2d 518 (Ct. Cl. 1963), *cert. denied*, 375 U.S. 830 (1963). Here the contractor promised to perform according to specifications that it established. It therefore apparently promised absolute performance. Nevertheless, nonperformance may be excused under a *force majeure* clause. In this case, however, the court applied the principle of *ejusdem generis* and found that the contractor's failure was due to the "impossibility of performance inherent in the subject matter of the contract itself," and event that differed from the enumerated events. See also *Excelsior Motor Mfg. & Supply Co. v. Sound Equip., Inc.*, 73 F.2d 725 (7th Cir. 1934), *cert. denied*, 294 U.S. 706 (1934).

2. Endorsement contract. I am grateful to Prof. Robert M. Lloyd of the University of Tennessee, who provided the materials for this exercise.

a. Injury is one of the events enumerated in Clause 16(b). Under that clause, however, Company may terminate the agreement only at the conclusion of a Contract Year. Therefore it would have to pay Consultant for the year in which the injury occurred.

b. The drug charges are not enumerated, nor is there any general language to cover non-enumerated events. Company could probably not terminate on the basis of *force majeure*. Under the doctrine of constructive conditions of exchange, it might claim that it was an implied condition of the contract that Consultant remain fit to make endorsements. The Pittsburgh Pirates apparently relied on the doctrine of constructive conditions when terminating a contract with Dave Parker after the star's drug use was revealed. See Chapter 10, *Promise and Condition*. Note that the promised performance of Consultant emphasizes his ability to play tennis and not his moral character.

c. This question is based on the career of Mary Bacon, an attractive and colorful jockey whose career in endorsements came to an end when she was filmed at a Klan rally. The reasoning would be similar to that in Question b, with Company perhaps in a worse position if the act committed was not illegal.

d. The drafter need not consider every possibility, but must consider what events would cause the most harm to Company. The Company is paying for the use of a name and an image. The value of Consultant's name on its products is clearly a function of his performance both on and off the court. It would therefore be appropriate for the drafter to consider his manners and his morals, for these factors can destroy the "property" purchased just as Acts of God can destroy the value of goods subject to a standard *force majeure* clause.

The extent to which a contract can control the physical appearance and lifestyle of a person who renders personal services is illustrated by the following contract between Calvin Klein Industries, Inc. and the personal corporation of Jose Borain, the "Calvin Klein Girl." Ms. Borain appears in advertisements for the designer's fragrance *Obsession*. These extracts were reprinted in the August, 1985 issue of *Harper's* 24-25:

AGREEMENT made as of the 25th day of September 1984 between CALVIN KLEIN INDUSTRIES, INC., a New York corporation (hereinafter called "CK"), and BORAIN ENTERPRISES, LTD., a New York corporation (hereinafter called "Consultant").

1. A. CK hereby retains Consultant and Consultant hereby agrees to be retained by CK and to provide to and for CK the "Services" of its employee, Jose Borain ("Borain"), as a model in all respects which services shall be deemed to include, without limitation, all broadcast advertising, promotion and exploitation (e.g., network, local, cable and closed circuit television, AM & FM radio and cinema), print advertising, promotion and exploitation (e.g., printed hang-tags, labels, containers, packaging, display materials, sales brochures, covers, pictorial, editorial, corporate reports and all other types of promotional print material contained in the media including magazines, newspapers, periodicals and other publications of all kinds), including but not by way of limitation, fashion shows, run-way modeling, retail store trunk shows, individual modeling and other areas of product promotion and exploitation which are or may be considered to be embraced within the concept . . . of fashion modeling.

4. Consultant shall, and where applicable shall cause Borain to:

A. Keep CK informed of Borain's schedule in the event she travels outside the metropolitan New York area for periods of more than two (2) days consecutively;

B. Maintain Borain's weight, hair style and color and all other features of Borain's physiognomy and physical appearance as they are now or in such other form as CK may, from time to time, reasonably request. Consultant and Borain represent that Borain's current weight level is between 120 and 125 lbs. and CK agrees that Borain's weight up to 130 lbs. will be an acceptable weight pursuant to the provisions hereunder. Illustratively, Borain shall wear hair styles, utilize such make-up and wear such apparel and accessories as CK requests from time to time; use such hair stylists as CK engages or approves; maintain such reasonable physical regimen (including exercise, diet and nutritional programs) as will best enable Borain to perform her Services hereunder; and when requested by CK, consult and comply with the reasonable advice and reasonable recommendations of such physician, exercise coach, hair and make-up stylists and others, etc.;

C. Maintain a personal lifestyle which will, in CK's sole subjective judgment reasonably exercised, be appropriate and most suitable to project an image and persona that reflect the high standards and dignity of the trademark "Calvin Klein" and that do not diminish, impair or in any manner detract from the prestige and reputation of such trademark.

7. A. CK shall pay or cause Consultant to be paid the aggregate sum of one million dollars ($1,000,000) for all of Borain's Services during the three (3) year term hereunder, i.e., the sum of $333,333 per year for each employment year during the term of this Agreement . . .

13. CK may . . . terminate this Agreement forthwith by written notice to Consultant upon the occurrence, or upon CK's becoming aware of the occurrence, of any one or more of the following events:

A. In the event of Borain's disfigurement or disability, which shall be deemed to mean any illness, accident or other physical or mental impairment which renders her, in the sole subjective judgment of CK reasonably exercised (except with respect to disfigurement or other change in physical appearance which may be exercised solely based on Mr. Klein's sole aesthetic subjective standards), incapable of performing or unqualified to perform her Services whenever required under this Agreement . . .

B. . . . If by reason of [Borain's] deliberate or inadvertent action or conduct she shall come into disrepute or her public reputation shall become degraded or discredited so that the Services she is to provide pursuant hereunder shall, in CK's sole subjective judgment reasonably exercised, have become less valuable to CK in projecting the desired image consistent with the dignity and high standards of the CK tradition . . .

G. Notwithstanding anything to the contrary herein contained, this Agreement shall terminate automatically and forthwith upon the death of Borain, the bankruptcy or insolvency of Consultant, or the dissolution, liquidation, merger or consolidation of Consultant.

e. The drafter might consider a happy medium between the amount of control in the Calvin Klein contract and the absence of control in the Company/Consultant contract. The drafter must not simply take language from a formbook, but must consider whether it serves the needs of a client in a particular situation. Language that is appropriate for one purpose may not be appropriate for another. When the contract is for hundreds of thousands of dollars worth of personal services, attention to detail is probably meaningful.

Whatever the value of the contract, attention to *language* is always meaningful. See Chapter 17, *The Language of Drafting*. The form of the Calvin Klein contract is an abomination. Some of the imaginative thought that went into the substance of the terms should have gone into their expression.

3. Fair clause. This exercise might be postponed until students are familiar with the concepts in Chapters 16 and 17. See particularly §§ 16.4 and 17.11. The original provision:

> § 15.5 If either party hereto shall believe that a new situation described in § 15.2 shall have arisen, then, at the request of either party hereto, the parties shall promptly consult with a view toward reaching a mutually acceptable agreement dealing with such situation. In the event that within six months after the date of such request the parties shall not reach agreement with respect to such situation, either party shall have the right, exercisable within three months after the expiration of such six-month period, to refer the matter to arbitration pursuant to § 19.1. The arbitrator or arbitrators shall determine whether the particular situation is a "new situation" described in § 15.2(a) or in § 15.2(b) and, if so, shall, in any award entered, specify the section involved and unless the parties come to a prompt solution themselves, thereafter on the request of either party also establish a solution in conformity with § 15.4. Such arbitrator or arbitrators may obtain, for the purpose of establishing such solution, the opinion of an impartial expert of recognized standing in the international copper business, who shall not be domiciled in either the United States or Germany unless the parties hereto shall otherwise consent. Promptly after the entering of such award the parties hereto shall enter into a written agreement incorporating the terms of such award and making such changes or modifications in this Agreement as may be required in order to give effect to such award.

Step 1. Underline the legally operative words:

> § 15.5 If either party <u>hereto shall believe</u> that a new situation described in § 15.2 <u>shall have arisen</u>, then, at the request of either party <u>hereto</u>, the parties <u>shall promptly consult</u> with a view toward reaching a mutually acceptable agreement dealing with <u>such</u> situation. <u>In the event</u> that within six months after the date of <u>such</u> request the parties <u>shall not reach agreement</u> with respect to <u>such</u> situation, either party <u>shall have the right</u>, exercisable within three months after the expiration of <u>such</u> six-month period, to refer the matter to arbitration pursuant to § 19.1. The arbitrator or arbitrators <u>shall determine</u>

whether the particular situation is a "new situation" described in § 15.2(a) or in § 15.2(b) and, if so, <u>shall</u>, in any award entered, specify the section involved and unless the parties come to a prompt solution themselves, thereafter on the request of either party also establish a solution in conformity with § 15.4. <u>Such</u> arbitrator or arbitrators may obtain, for the purpose of establishing <u>such</u> solution, the opinion of an impartial expert of recognized standing in the international copper business, who <u>shall not be domiciled</u> in either the United States or Germany unless the parties <u>hereto</u> <u>shall otherwise consent</u>. Promptly after the entering of <u>such</u> award the parties <u>hereto</u> <u>shall enter</u> into a written agreement incorporating the terms of <u>such</u> award and making <u>such</u> changes or modifications in this Agreement as may be required in order to give effect to <u>such</u> award.

Steps 2 and 3: Analyze the intended legal consequences and provide for them with precise language:

shall -- this provision gets into a lot of trouble by switching between *shall* to mean the future and *shall* to mean *has a duty to*.

> shall believe -- make it present
> shall have arisen -- make it past
> shall consult -- this is correct, for the parties have a duty
> shall not reach agreement -- make it present
> shall have the right -- make it the permissive *may*
> The arbitrator or arbitrators shall determine -- the arbitrators are not parties to the
> > agreement, so cannot have duties under it. Make *the parties* the subject of the
> > sentence.
> shall not be domiciled -- make it present
> shall otherwise consent -- make it present
> shall enter -- this is correct, for the parties have a duty

Step 4. Write the provision in plain language. See Chapter 18.

> hereto -- delete. Could the agreement be referring to any other party?

> such -- use *the*. Note, however, that the next to the last use of such means *such*!

> in the event that -- make it *if*

We now have a much clearer agreement. Perhaps it would be helpful to tabulate the arbitrators' duties (see § 7.5.2):

The parties shall direct the arbitrator or arbitrators:

(1) *to determine* whether the particular situation is a "new situation" described in § 15.2(a) or in § 15.2(b) and, if so,

(2) in any award entered, *to specify* the section involved and

(3) unless the parties come to a prompt solution themselves, thereafter on the request of either party also to establish a solution in conformity with § 15.4. *The* arbitrator or arbitrators may obtain, for the purpose of establishing *the* solution, the opinion of an impartial expert of recognized standing in the international copper business, who *is not domiciled* in either the United States or Germany unless the parties *otherwise consent*.

The entire agreement now looks like this:

§ 15.5 If either party *believes* that a new situation described in § 15.2 *has arisen*, then, at the request of either party, the parties *shall promptly consult* with a view toward reaching a mutually acceptable agreement dealing with *the* situation. *If* within six months after the date of *the* request the parties *do not reach agreement* with respect to *the* situation, either party *may*, within three months after the expiration of *the* six-month period, refer the matter to arbitration pursuant to § 19.1. The parties shall direct the arbitrator or arbitrators:

(1) *to determine* whether the particular situation is a "new situation" described in § 15.2(a) or in § 15.2(b) and, if so,

(2) in any award entered, *to specify* the section involved and

(3) unless the parties come to a prompt solution themselves, thereafter on the request of either party also to establish a solution in conformity with § 15.4. *The* arbitrator or arbitrators may obtain, for the purpose of establishing *the* solution, the opinion of an impartial expert of recognized standing in the international copper business, who *is not domiciled* in either the United States or Germany unless the parties *otherwise consent*.

Promptly after the entering of *the* award the parties *shall enter* into a written agreement incorporating the terms of *the* award and making *such* changes or modifications in this Agreement as may be required in order to give effect to *the* award.

Chapter 10
Promise and Condition

§ 10.1. Introduction.

The Role of the Lawyer. In the first and second editions of the Lon Fuller CONTRACTS text, the chapter in which this material was discussed was titled "Conditions in Contracts -- Problems in Draftsmanship." I think that title says it all. It is hard to either understand or correct these problems without seeing how they arise in drafting. On the other hand, I am aware that drafting cannot solve all the problems. In two articles, Robert Childres has pointed out that courts may not honor the black letter rule that express conditions will be strictly enforced. See Childres, *Conditions in the Law of Contracts*, 45 N.Y.U. L. Rev. 33 (1969); Childres & Sales, *Restatement (Second) and the Law of Conditions in Contracts*, 44 Miss. L.J. 591 (1973). If this is so, then stating express conditions in contracts more clearly may not bring about the preventive law goal of preventing conflicts from going to court. But if preventive law also means assisting lawyers in thinking about why they are doing what they are doing and strengthening the clarity with which they express their agreement, then the chapter will not have been in vain.

In the contract for sale of the horse, note the problem created by use of the passive voice. The horse is not the actor. If A was obligated to do something, that duty could be more clearly stated by making A the subject of the sentence. If the duty is worded as an obligation of A, the drafter is more likely to ask what happens if A does not do as promised.

The Louis M. Brown quote is from *Specifying Remedies in Contract Documents*, 38 Cal. St. B.J. 293, 294 (1963).

§ 10.3. Condition.

In stating that a term is a condition, be wary of the language used. Often drafters refer to "covenants and conditions" to distinguish between promises and conditions. On the other hand, drafters often use "conditions" to refer to all the terms of the contract. For example, the standard American Institute of Architects contract is entitled "General Conditions of the Contract for Construction" and the Broker's Listing Agreement in § 10.8 refers to the "terms and conditions" of the agreement. These inconsistent usages underline the importance of spelling out the remedy rather than relying on the language.

In Example 2, note that the Insured has not undertaken the duty to furnish proof of loss. It would not make sense to provide:

The Insured shall furnish proof of loss. The Insurer shall pay for any loss within 30 days of receiving proof of loss from the Insured.

If this were merely a promise on the part of the Insured, the Insurer's claim for damages would not be meaningful. It wants to make the Insured's furnishing proof of loss a condition of its obligation to pay for the loss.

§ 10.4. Conditions precedent and conditions subsequent.

See RESTATEMENT (SECOND) §§ 224 and 230. In explaining the disuse of the terms condition precedent and condition subsequent in the Restatement, FARNSWORTH, CONTRACTS § 8.2 (3d ed.) states:

> It is surely preferable to allocate procedural burdens according to factors that are relevant to the policies that underlie them. If the owner of a house conditions the duty to pay for painting the house on the owner's "satisfaction" with the job, it may make more sense to put the burden of proving that the owner is not satisfied on the painter, since the relevant facts are peculiarly within the knowledge of the owner. Some courts have done this, ignoring both the form of expression of the provision and the analytical distinction drawn in contract law. But the terms *precedent* and *subsequent* have not proved well suited to this end.
>
> The Restatement Second has abandoned the term *condition subsequent* and refers more fully to an event that "terminate[s] an obligor's duty of immediate performance or one to pay damages for breach." What has been called a *condition precedent* is called simply a *condition*. The Reporter's Note recognizes that the traditional terminology "has long been criticized and has caused confusion when used in an attempt to answer questions relating to the burdens of pleading and proof." It is too early to tell whether the new terminology will help to clear up the confusion by divorcing those questions from substantive contract law.

On the procedural requirements, FULLER & EISENBERG, BASIC CONTRACT LAW 912-14 (5th ed. 1990) state:

> Looking more closely at the considerations which have actually determined the distribution of these burdens, it is apparent that neither the "form" nor the "substance" of the distinction between conditions precedent and conditions subsequent is necessarily controlling. The problem is one of forensic fairness and convenience, and factors unrelated to any of those thus far discussed are frequently and properly given consideration by the courts and legislatures.
>
> So far as the burden of pleading or allegation is concerned, statutes or rules of court have very commonly relieved the plaintiff from the substance of this burden without respect to the question whether the condition is described as precedent or subsequent. For example, Rule 3015(a) of the New York Civil Practice Law and Rules provides:

"The performance or occurrence of a condition precedent in a contract need not be pleaded. A denial of performance or occurrence shall be made specifically and with particularity. In case of such denial, the party relying on the performance or occurrence shall be required to prove on the trial only such performance or occurrence as shall have been so specified."

The effect of this provision is to place the burden of allegation on the defendant. If he wishes to raise the issue of the plaintiff's performance of a particular condition precedent, he must allege that it was not performed.

Enactments like New York Rule 3015(a) owe their existence chiefly to the fact that contract suits are now typically based on long, printed, standardized documents, the terms of which are not in fact negotiated but are imposed by one party on the other, the most familiar example being the insurance policy. Such contracts customarily contain a long list of conditions limiting the liability of the party drafting them. To require the plaintiff to allege in detail a performance of all of these conditions not only incumbers the record needlessly, but imposes on the plaintiff's attorney the difficult task of seeing to it that every allegation corresponds to the terms of the contract concerning each separate condition.

As to the burden of proof (as distinguished from the burden of allegation or pleading), reforms through statutes or rules of court are less common and the situation is more complicated. However, applying the principles that have generally been developed for the allocation of this burden, it is safe to say that the following factors would influence the determination of this question in the case of conditions in contracts: (1) The form of the condition; whether it is phrased in terms of an event relieving a party from a duty or in terms of an event that must occur before a duty arises. (2) If placing the burden on one party will require him to prove a negative fact (something did *not* happen), the burden of proof may be placed on the other party, who will be asked to prove that it *did* happen. This conclusion is often grounded on the theory that an affirmative is easier to prove than a negative. (3) Where the fact is peculiarly within the knowledge of one party, the burden of proof may for that reason be placed on him. (4) Where the contract is a standardized form, not really negotiated but dictated by one party to the other, this may itself furnish a reason for imposing procedural burdens on the party who drafted the agreement. (5) There is also a consideration of symmetry, according to which the burden of proof ought to follow the burden of allegation, unless there is some reason for allocating the two burdens differently. (6) There is finally, perhaps, the question whether the condition was "in fact" precedent or subsequent, that is, whether the case is one where no suit could be brought until the event was determined, or a case where suit was once possible and the question is whether an event has occurred which extinguished a duty the defendant once had.

As Wigmore has stated, none of these considerations is in any sense controlling; "there is not and cannot be any general solvent" for the problem of allocating the burdens of allegation and proof. When all of these factors are taken into account, the distinction between conditions precedent and conditions subsequent may not entirely disappear, but it certainly diminishes greatly in significance.

FEDERAL RULES OF CIVIL PROCEDURE, Rule 9(c):

Conditions Precedent. In pleading the performance or occurrence of conditions precedent, it is sufficient to aver generally that all conditions precedent have been performed or have occurred. A denial of performance or occurrence shall be made specifically and with particularity.

§ 10.5. Drafting promises and conditions.

The example of making a performance a condition may be more theoretical than real, for as the chapter later explains, courts will not always enforce express conditions. Contrast, for example, the sale of goods. The provisions could read:

> 1. A shall deliver the goods on or before October 1, 1987.

or

> 2. B shall accept and pay for the goods only if they are delivered on or before October 1, 1987.

or

> 3. A shall deliver the goods on or before October 1, 1987. B shall accept and pay for the goods only if they are delivered on or before October 1, 1987.

Alternatively, this example could read:

> 3. Time is of the essence of this agreement.

If A delivered the goods on October 2, would B have the right to reject? WHITE & SUMMERS, UNIFORM COMMERCIAL CODE (5th ed.) suggest in § 8-3 at 314:

We conclude, and the cases decided to date suggest, that the Code changes and the courts' manipulation have so eroded the perfect tender rule that the law would beg little changed if 2-601 gave the right to reject only upon "substantial" non-conformity. Of the reported Code cases on rejection, none that we have found actually grants rejection on what could fairly be called an insubstantial nonconformity, despite language in some cases allowing such rejection.

Similarly, in the construction example in the text, realistically the owner is probably more concerned with the completion date than the starting date. Suppose the owner were able to bargain for a condition that stated:

> B shall accept and pay for the construction only if it is completed on or before October 1, 1987.

This provision would cause a forfeiture and would probably not be enforced as a condition.

In dealing with this material, therefore, it may be necessary to explain that (1) the examples indicate the doctrinal differences and will not necessarily be enforced, and (2) the fact that the provisions will not necessarily be enforced indicates the burdens on the drafter. For example, if some provision, such as a starting time or a completion time are essential, that fact must be drafted with particular care. See § 10.7.

§ 10.6.1. Who is supposed to go first?

The retainer agreement is adapted from a model Attorney Employment Contract first published in HALT, INC., SHOPPING FOR A LAWYER, and now in OSTBERG, USING A LAWYER.

The provision for progress payments is from an older version of the American Institute of Architects, Standard Form of Agreement Between Owner and Contractor. The provision is found in Article 5 of the present agreement.

§ 10.6.2. If one party doesn't perform, must the other party perform anyway?

a. Statute. Another statutory example is discussed in § 10.8, Exercise 1. Perhaps another is the wage protection statute common in many states that provides that the employer must pay all wages due a terminated employee. That is, the employer's promise to pay is independent of any claim for the employee's breach.

b. Court decision. RESTATEMENT (SECOND) § 232 states:

When It Is Presumed That Performances Are to Be Exchanged Under an Exchange of Promises

Where the consideration given by each party to a contract consists in whole or in part of promises, all the performances to be rendered by each party taken collectively are treated as performances to be exchanged under an exchange of promises, unless a contrary intention is clearly manifested.

c. Agreement by the parties. It may cause confusion to state that on the one hand the court will treat obligations as constructive conditions of each other and that on the other hand the court prefers an interpretation that a provision is a promise rather than a condition. RESTATEMENT (SECOND) § 226 Comment c states:

> When the parties have omitted a term that is essential to a determination of their rights and duties, the court may supply a term which is reasonable in the circumstances. Where that term makes an event a condition, it is often described as a "constructive" (or "implied in law") condition. This serves to distinguish it from events which are made conditions by the agreement of the parties, either by their words or by other conduct, and which are described as "express" and as "implied in fact" (inferred from fact) conditions... It is useful to distinguish "constructive" conditions, even though the distinction is necessarily somewhat arbitrary.

The case involving the restrictive covenant is *Orkin Exterminating Co. v. Gill*, 222 Ga. 760, 152 S.E.2d 411 (1966).

On the interpretation of a contract between owner and subcontractor where the owner has not paid the contractor, see *Byler v. Great American Insurance Co.*, 395 F.2d 273 (10th Cir. 1968). For an example of a suit by a broker where the title did not pass, see *Amies v. Wesnofske*, 255 N.Y. 156, 174 N.E. 436 (1931). If the seller prevents title from passing, the seller has breached an implied promise to cause the title to pass. The breach would excuse the condition. *Tarbell v. Bomes*, 48 R.I. 86, 135 A. 604 (1927).

Asking students to redraft the provision in *Southern Surety* to more clearly express the condition could be a productive exercise. Whitmore Gray in his HANDBOOK OF CONTRACT LAW AND PRACTICE suggests the following:

> The court in *MacMillan* (in accord with much case law) said that it would have been possible to draft the notice provision so as to operate as a true condition. In other words, the contract could have said something like:

> > "Provided further, that if the notices of default described in paragraph (x) above are not postmarked within 5 days of the occurrence of such default, then no liability to protect against any loss occasioned by such default shall arise on the part of the Company."

> > or

> > "Provided further, however, that a condition precedent to any liability on the part of the Company to protect against losses resulting from a default shall be the receipt by the Company of written notice of such default within 5 days of its occurrence."

While this makes the intended result clear, it seems likely that MacMillan would have felt that it did not have sufficient protection under such a clause, and might have gone elsewhere for insurance. (The kind of default which might result in injury to MacMillan, for example, could well be one of which they would not learn until more than 5 days after it occurred.)

In drafting express conditions, be wary of the phrase "provided that." DICK, LEGAL DRAFTING 92 (2d ed.) states that this phrase "defies grammatical analysis." Often it means not a condition but an exception. MELLINKOFF, LEGAL WRITING AND NONSENSE, 176-80 devotes a chapter of "Blunders and Cures" to "Provided, provided, provided." He says, "Of all the law words in the specimen, this is the prime troublemaker and the most unnecessary." Find another way to say exactly what you mean.

§ 10.7. Drafting clear conditions.

Of course, preventive law goes only so far. Even if the condition is clearly expressed, it is still subject to legal attack. WILLISTON, CONTRACTS § 827 at 67 states, "The courts have frequently disregarded plainly expressed conditions, because of their unwillingness to deprive a promisee of all rights on account of some trivial breach of condition." Nevertheless, the agreement will exhibit clearer thinking and will more forcefully express the parties intentions. In the event of litigation, summary judgment is more likely when an agreement expressly states a condition; implied conditions raise issues of interpretation.

§ 10.8. Exercises.

1. Lease. The statute is Montana Code Annotated § 70-25-202, based on Uniform Residential Landlord and Tenant Act § 2.101.(b).

The statute uses language of obligation ("Every landlord ... shall provide the departing tenant with a written list ...."). It makes no sense to impose this obligation on the landlord. If it is merely a promise, then if the Landlord does not do it, the Tenant is still bound to pay for the damages. Providing the list should be a condition, an event that must occur before the landlord may withhold the damages. Perhaps something like this was intended:

A landlord who wishes to deduct charges from the tenant's security deposit must, within 30 days subsequent to the termination of a tenancy, provide the departing tenant with a written list of any damage and cleaning charges. The landlord shall submit the list to the tenant with the balance of the security deposit.

The event, the provision of the list, is now a *condition* of the landlord's right to withhold damages from the security deposit. Because it must occur at the same time, it is a *condition concurrent*. Note that there is no need to make this a promissory condition. A landlord is perfectly free not to provide a list, but may not deduct damages if it does not. We could even make this consequence clear in the draft. Add to the end:

> A landlord who does not provide a tenant with a list of damages and charges within 30 days may not deduct any amount from the security deposit.

2. Construction contract. This problem is based on *K & G Construction Co. v. Harris*, 223 Md. 305, 164 A.2d 451 (1960). The contract contains promises by both parties to perform in a workmanlike manner. The Contractor promises to make progress payments to the Subcontractor, but it is a condition of Contractor's obligation that Subcontractor submit the requisition. Note that Subcontractor does not promise to bring about that event.

The Contractor claims: on August 9, you breached your obligation to perform in a workmanlike manner. Performance of that promise was a condition of my performance of the obligation to pay you. Since you did not perform, I did not have to perform.

The Subcontractor claims: My breach was only breach of promise, not condition. Therefore, while you had a right to claim damages for breach of that promise, you had no right to withhold your own performance. Furthermore, you promised to pay me on the 10th of the month. Performance of that promise was a condition of my performance of the obligation to work for you. Since you did not perform, I did not have to perform.

The court noted that the contract does not state whether the promises are also conditions. It determined that, in the absence of express language in the contract, the court must look to the intention of the parties in determining whether promises are dependent or independent. There is also a presumption that the promises are dependent. Here, the court followed the rule of constructive conditions of exchange, holding that the promises were dependent. Therefore the breach by the Subcontractor relieved the Contractor of its obligation.

Promise and condition are closely related to damages, for the issue is what happens if a party doesn't do what it promised to do. Consider the consequences of nonperformance in this case. On August 9, Subcontractor owed Contractor $3400 for the bulldozer damage. On September 12, Contractor owed Subcontractor $1484 for work completed.

The trial court held that the Contractor was entitled to $3400 and the Subcontractor was entitled to $2824. This follows from the premise that the promises are *independent*. Subcontractor breached its promise and caused damage of $3400. If this promise is independent of Contractor's promise to pay, the Contractor should have paid. Since Contractor did not pay, it breached, and owes Subcontractor $2824 in damage for breach of its promise.

The appeals court held that the promises were *dependent*. The breach by the Subcontractor permitted the Contractor to suspend its obligation to pay. Since the Contractor was justified in suspending its performance, the Subcontractor was in breach when it terminated the contract by walking off the job. Contractor recovered its damages for this breach, the $450 greater cost of hiring a replacement to finish the job.

Given the court's conclusion that the promises were dependent, what happens to the $1484 claimed by the Subcontractor for its performance before the breach? Because the Subcontractor did not substantially perform the contract, it cannot claim this amount on a contract theory. The Subcontractor must claim this amount in *restitution*, as a benefit conferred on another party. Authorities are split on whether a party in breach may recover in restitution; in this case, the court did not award recovery. The arguments for and against are presented in *Britton v. Turner*, 6 N.H. 481 (1834). See also RESTATEMENT (SECOND) § 374, which favors restitution for a party in breach.

Note that to reach its conclusion, the court must also have found that the Subcontractor's initial breach was material. Contractor took a chance in treating the contract as terminated, for a fact-finder may later determine either that the breach was not material enough to justify the suspension of performance or that the breach did not continue long enough to justify termination. Because a party takes a risk when it engages in precipitous action, communication between the parties during performance is essential. See Rosett, *Contract Performance: Promises, Conditions and the Obligation to Communicate*, 22 U.C.L.A. L. Rev. 1083 (1975).

3. Sale of goods. This problem is based on *Alan D. Nicholson, Inc. v. Cannon*, 207 Mont. 476, 674 P.2d 506 (1984). Seller promised to sell goods. Buyer promised to make monthly payments. Seller also promised to repair latent defects. Under the rule of constructive conditions, if Seller was in breach, Seller would not have a claim against Buyer for Buyer's nonperformance. However, the agreement specifically provided that if Seller breached the promise to repair, Buyer could have the goods repaired at Seller's expense. By providing this specific remedy, the parties apparently intended that Buyer would not have the remedy of withholding its performance. In other words, Seller's failure to repair the goods was not an event that excused Buyer's performance of its obligation to make monthly payments. The promises were independent.

Nicholson taught Buyer an expensive lesson in promise and condition, for under the agreement the prevailing party was entitled to recover attorneys' fees. The Montana Supreme Court upheld $18,000 in fees awarded by the trial court and awarded additional fees for the appeal.

4. Drafting clear conditions.

a. This example appears in CHARLES M. FOX, WORKING WITH CONTRACTS § 4.2. There are three events that must occur before Owner may terminate. These three events appear more clearly if we enumerate them:

Owner may terminate this agreement, if
1) Owner asserts a breach by Manager of the terms and conditions hereof;
2) Owner gives notice to Manager; and
3) Manager is given a reasonable time to cure such breach.

We might then ask if the terms are too vague: How much of a breach? What kind of notice? What is a reasonable time? See § 7.6. Fox elaborates:

Owner and manager have had a series of increasingly heated conversations over several months regarding a problem in the property's plumbing system that has damaged some furnishings. Owner refers to a section of their contract that requires manager to make all necessary repairs promptly. Manager hires a contractor to repair the plumbing, but the contractor has some other priorities and the repair work is not completed. To manager's surprise, owner sends manager a written notice terminating the management contract. Each party calls its lawyer. Each lawyer separately advises its client that the following arguments may credibly be asserted by owner and would probably survive a motion for summary judgment:

• The phone conversations in which owner asserted that manager failed to comply with the contractual requirement to promptly make the repairs constituted the required notice of termination.

• Manager is not entitled under the contract to the defense that it promptly hired a responsible third party to make the repairs and that the delay was attributable to the third party and not within manager's control.

• The period of time commencing on the date that owner first complained about the failure of manager to make the repairs and ending on the date that owner sent the notice of termination constitutes a reasonable cure period.

Although manager justifiably feels misused by owner, his lawyer advises him that a judge or jury could very well determine that the contract supports the action taken by owner. The result would have been different had the provision been drafted with more care:

If (a) Manager breaches any of its obligations hereunder, (b) Owner delivers a written notice to Manager stating that it is a "Notice of Termination" which identifies such breach, and (c) Manager fails to cure such breach within 30 days after the date of such notice, this Agreement shall terminate, <u>provided, however,</u> that if the cure of such breach reasonably requires the action or cooperation of a third party, no termination shall occur so long as Manager is using its diligent efforts to cause such third party to act or cooperate.

This improved language demonstrates two important lessons. First, it is always possible to make contract language more precise and thus more resistant to the attempts of a party to assert aggressive or spurious interpretations. Second, it is often difficult to craft language so precise that some "gray area" doesn't exist: under the improved language owner can still argue that manager has not employed its diligent efforts to make the third-party contractor perform.

b. I recommend first breaking this provision down using your word processor without changing any of the language:

Seller will make reasonable accommodations if Buyer requests a delay in the originally scheduled In-Service Date, if Buyer gives Seller written notice prior to the CCD.

If Buyer gives notice of a request for delay in the originally scheduled In-Service Date after the Change Control Date ("CCD"), requests more than one delay in the In-Service Date prior to the CCD, or causes a delay in the In-Service Date as a result of Buyer's failure to meet Buyer's under this Agreement, Seller may:

(i) deliver the Products and commence billing as of the originally scheduled In-Service Date for the Order, in which case installation will be scheduled at a mutually agreeable time and additional installation charges may apply; or

(ii) cancel the order and bill Buyer for cancellation charges as set forth in Section XX.

Now make clear the conditions and state them using parallel construction:

If Buyer 1) requests a delay in the originally scheduled In-Service Date, and 2) gives Seller written notice prior to the Change Control Date ("CCD"), Seller shall make reasonable accommodations

If Buyer 1) gives notice of a request for delay in the originally scheduled In-Service Date after the CCD, 2) requests more than one delay in the In-Service Date prior to the CCD, or 3) causes a delay in the In-Service Date as a result of Buyer's failure to meet Buyer's under this Agreement, Seller may:

(i) deliver the Products and commence billing as of the originally scheduled In-Service Date for the Order, in which case installation will be scheduled at a mutually agreeable time and additional installation charges may apply; or

(ii) cancel the order and bill Buyer for cancellation charges as set forth in Section XX.

      c. I recommend first breaking this provision down using your word processor without changing any of the language:

> Company grants Service Provider a non-exclusive, nontransferable right to purchase the Products for use in the Territory in creating and providing Network Services to End Users. Service Provider may resell Products to End Users who purchase Network Services, provided that
>
> > the Products at the time of sale to the End User are intended to be used primarily in connection with access to Network Services,
> >
> > provided further that Service Provider shall indicate on its Purchase Order any Product units which are to be resold to third parties and
> >
> > shall report such sales as required in this Agreement.

You now see that there are three conditions that can be stated using parallel construction:

> Company grants Service Provider a non-exclusive, nontransferable right to purchase the Products for use in the Territory in creating and providing Network Services to End Users. Service Provider may resell Products to End Users who purchase Network Services, if Service Provider:
>
> > determines that, at the time of sale to the End User, the Products are intended to be used primarily in connection with access to Network Services,
> >
> > indicates on its Purchase Order any Product units which are to be resold to third parties, and
> >
> > reports such sales as required in this Agreement.

Some questions I would ask are where the Agreement requires that the sales be reported, and, most importantly, what does the Company expect to happen if these conditions are not satisfied.

      5. Broker's listing agreement. The Broker promises to use reasonable efforts to procure a buyer (¶ I.a.). Note that the Broker does not promise to procure a buyer. If the Broker promised to procure a buyer, he would be in breach if he did not procure one.

      The Broker also promises to use reasonable efforts to find a buyer "on the terms and conditions herein set forth." Here the word *conditions* does not mean events, but terms of the contract. The sentence would mean exactly the same thing if it said "on the terms herein set forth." The principal term is the price of $45,000. Additional terms could have been set forth in ¶ V.

Paragraph II does not contain language of obligation but language of discretion: The Broker *may*. The Broker is not obligated to do these things but is permitted to do these things. The Seller probably impliedly promises to cooperate with the Broker's attempts to do these things.

The Seller gives the Broker an *exclusive* right to sell, which is a promise to refrain from giving the right to anyone else. The Seller promises to refer inquires and to cooperate (¶ III.a. & b.). The Seller also promises to pay the Broker, but this is not an immediately performable duty. The promise to pay is conditional upon the occurrence of the events enumerated in ¶ III.c. Note the use of the word *if* to express this condition.

Those events include (1) A buyer is procured. Who has control over the occurrence of this event? Note the use of the passive voice. This is intentional. The parties are agreeing that the duty to pay is performable if a buyer is procured by anyone, not just by the Broker. This meaning is clarified by (2) which states that payment is due if the property is "sold or exchanged through the efforts of *anyone including the Seller*." Under (3), payment is due if the property is sold six months after the agreement expires. The duty to pay is performable not only on the condition that the property is sold during that time but on the additional condition that the buyer was introduced to the property through the efforts of the Broker during the original term.

If the Broker did not use reasonable efforts to procure a buyer and after a few months the Seller found a buyer on his own, would the Seller have to pay the commission? Note the factual difficulty of proving that the Broker did not use reasonable efforts. If the Seller could prove that, then the Seller would be claiming that the Broker's performance is a condition of the Seller's obligation to perform. This condition is not expressed by the parties. The Seller would be invoking the rule of "constructive conditions of exchange." Because the parties contemplated an exchange of performances, the Seller's claim would probably be upheld. Again, note that this conclusion is premised on the Broker's *material* breach of his promise.

As drafted, the Broker must perform before the Seller is responsible for payment. The drafter could provide for the Broker to be paid out of the Buyer's payments. Any deposit or down payment could be held in escrow for that purpose. The escrow agent could be instructed to accept the balance of the payment on closing and to pay the Broker before turning the balance of the funds over to Seller.

Chapter 11
Modification and Discharge

§ 11.1. Introduction.

If a party is sued for breach, that party might defend by saying, "It may be true that I didn't do what I promised to do in our modified agreement. However, that modification was not legal. I did what I promised to do in our *original* agreement, so I'm not in breach."

§ 11.2. Common law modification of executory agreements.

RESTATEMENT (SECOND) § 89 recognizes the distinction between modifications that are coerced and those entered in good faith:

> 89. Modification of Executory Contract
>
> A promise modifying a duty under a contract not fully performed on either side is binding
>
> > (a)   if the modification is fair and equitable in view of circumstances not anticipated by the parties when the contract was made; or
> >
> > (b)   to the extent provided by statute; or
> >
> > (c)   to the extent that justice requires enforcement in view of material change of position in reliance on the promise.

The pre-existing duty rule has been repealed with respect to the sale of goods by U.C.C. § 2-209(1). How does the Code deal with the problem of a modification extracted by an extortionist? WHITE & SUMMERS, UNIFORM COMMERCIAL CODE § 1-6 at 57-59 (5th ed.), address this question:

> [J]udges can use Code sections 1-203 and 2-302 on bad faith and unconscionability to police those who unjustly demand modifications or waivers....
>
> The case of Roth Steel Products v. Sharon Steel Corp. [705 F.2d 134 (6th Cir. 1983)] suggests that the party seeking to uphold a modification must demonstrate two things. First, he must show that a modification was consistent with commercial standards of fair dealing in the trade. To do this the would-be modifier must demonstrate that he was motivated by factors that would motivate an ordinary merchant in the trade to seek a similar modification. Second, the modifier must have a legitimate commercial reason for seeking the modification.

The example of the modification agreement is adapted from 5 HART & WILLIER, FORMS AND PROCEDURES UNDER THE U.C.C. § 21.07. The drafter might explain the factors identified by White and Summers in *Roth*.

Note the other subsections of U.C.C. § 2-209. An agreement requires that all modifications be in writing. Buyer orally requests an "extra" and Seller supplies it. Buyer refuses to pay, citing the writing. Will Seller be able to obtain a judgment? This question is discussed in § 11.9.

§ 11.4. Settlement of claims.

RESTATEMENT (SECOND) § 282 provides:

282. Account Stated

(1)   An account stated is a manifestation of assent by debtor and creditor to a stated sum as an accurate computation of an amount due the creditor. A party's retention without objection for an unreasonably long time of a statement of account rendered by the other party is a manifestation of assent.

(2)   The account stated does not itself discharge any duty but is an admission by each party of the facts asserted and a promise by the debtor to pay according to its terms.

The following are examples of the concept of account stated:

1. An agreement between *A,* Insurance Company, and *B,* Agent, provides that on termination, *A* will compensate *B* for policies *B* has written. *A* terminates the agreement in February, 1981. Between February, 1981 and April, 1982, *A* sends accounting statements to *B*. *B* makes no objection to the statements. In 1984, *B* seeks an accounting between the parties.

2. An agreement between *A,* Insurance Company, and *B,* Agent, provides that on termination, *A* will compensate *B* for policies *B* has written. The agreement also provides that if *B* does not object to a statement within 30 days, *B* has accepted the statement. *A* terminates the agreement in February, 1981 and sends an accounting statement to *B*. *B* objects to the statement 60 days after receipt. In 1984, *B* seeks an accounting between the parties.

3. An agreement between *A,* Insurance Company, and *B,* Agent, provides that on termination, *A* will compensate *B* for policies *B* has written. *A* terminates the agreement in February, 1981 and sends an accounting statement to *B*. The statement states that if *B*

does not object within 30 days, *B* has accepted the statement. *B* objects to the statement 60 days after receipt. In 1984, *B* seeks an accounting between the parties.

In Example 1, the statement has become an account stated, liquidating the amount due. An unreasonable period of time passed before *B* objected. In Example 2, the parties have determined in their agreement how long a time is reasonable. As long as the agreement is not unconscionable or part of a contract of adhesion, it probably has weight in determining that the statement has become an account stated. In Example 3, the 30-day period has been unilaterally fixed by *A* and would carry no weight. The issue would be whether *B*'s retention of the statement for 60 days without objection was an unreasonable period of time under the circumstances.

These examples are adapted from *Erickson v. General United Life Insurance Co.*, 256 N.W.2d 255 (Minn. 1977). In *Erickson*, the contract provided:

> All payments and accounting given by Company to Agent shall be deemed final and conclusive for the accounting or payment period unless Agent shall, on or before the next monthly accounting is due by the Company to the Agent as stated above, give notice in writing of any error in accounting or payment. If no such objection is made, the Company shall not be obligated to provide a further accounting or payment. Agent shall also state in writing within said period any failure of Company in fulfilling its obligations under the terms of this Contract. Agent waives any claims or actions against Company for the period of the accounting unless Agent objects in writing within said period.

By this provision, the parties established the time in which objection to a statement had to be made. While this provision gives greater weight in establishing that the statement had become an account stated, it would probably not be meaningful in a contract of adhesion or in the statement itself.

The concept of account stated is also useful in computing interest, for interest is due only on a liquidated account.

§ 11.9. Provisions barring modification and waiver.

An example of a statute implying "no oral modification" is Cal. Civ. Code § 1698, which provides:

> A contract in writing may be altered by a contract in writing or by an executed oral agreement, and not otherwise.

The first example of waiver is adapted from 5 HART & WILLIER, FORMS AND PROCEDURES UNDER THE U.C.C. §§ 21.07[3] and [4], clauses 3 and 4. The second is adapted from Note, *Contract Draftsmanship Under Article Two of the Uniform Commercial Code*, 112 U. Pa. L. Rev. 564, 579. Suggesting that the "no waiver" clause is unenforceable, the Note states:

> But subsection 2-209(4) allows "waivers" to override commercial contractual provisions prohibiting oral modification, and it seems contrary to the purposes of that subsection to suppose that a "no waiver" term can prevent waivers although a "no oral modification" clause cannot.

UNIFORM COMMERCIAL CODE CASE DIGEST § 2209.2 collects the relevant cases. See, e.g., *Linear Corp. v. Standard Hardware Co.*, 423 So. 2d 966 (Fla. Dist. Ct. App. 1982) (enforcing the modification); *U.S. Fibres, Inc. v. Proctor & Schwartz, Inc.*, 358 F. Supp. 449 (E.D. Mich. 1972), *aff'd*, 509 F.2d 1043 (6th Cir. 1975) (not enforcing the modification).

The delightful quote from Corbin is found at 6 CORBIN, CONTRACTS § 1295 at 212.

§ 11.10. Exercises.

1. Research. See, e.g., Cal. Civ. Code §§ 1526 and 1524, providing schemes for resolving, respectively, unliquidated or disputed debts, and liquidated and undisputed debts. See Burnham, *Accord and Satisfaction in California: A Trap for the Unwary*, 30 Santa Clara L. Rev. 473 (1990).

2. The unpaid bill. Because the original agreement was to perform services with no mention of a fee, the obligation is unliquidated. When the doctor sent the bill without any objection by the patient for a substantial period of time, the obligation became liquidated in the amount of $1000 according to the doctrine of account stated.

Note that the demand for interest was not part of the contract between doctor and patient. Nor can it become accepted by the inaction of the patient. I conclude that the demand is not enforceable. However, once the obligation has become liquidated, most jurisdictions provide for a statutory rate of interest on liquidated obligations. You should be able to collect this amount beginning a reasonable time from the date the bill was rendered, perhaps 30 days.

3. Settling a case. This problem points out that obligations arising from tort as well as from contract are subject to settlement. P's claim for $5000 was disputed. Therefore there was consideration when P exchanged that claim for a promise to pay $3000. P released D from any obligation and D agreed to pay an amount that P was not previously obligated to pay.

When D did not pay as promised, the issue arises whether the parties entered into an accord or a substituted contract. This appears to be a substituted contract. P settled for the promise to pay $3000. Sometimes a party will settle for a promissory note which the other party fails to pay. Unless otherwise agreed, this is a clear example of a substituted contract. The original claim is lost and P can sue only on the promise.

If the suit had been on a debt, there would be no consideration for D's promise to pay $3000 to satisfy the $5000 obligation. Therefore, unless a statute provided otherwise, you could revive the $5000 claim.

To draft around this problem, the stipulation might have provided:

If D fails to fully make any payment under this stipulation when due, P may enter judgment against D for the full amount of the claim ($5000) less payments made.

4. The disputed bill. The $1000 bill is unliquidated because it was not agreed upon and is disputed because you think it is too high. When I sent you a bill for $600, I probably liquidated the bill in that amount. Alternatively, there was consideration in your giving up the dispute and promising to pay the liquidated amount of $600. Therefore, because we have entered into a substituted contract, I can sue you only for the $600.

If we had agreed on a $1000 fee, the obligation would have been liquidated and undisputed at $1000. However, my bill for $600 might be a substituted contract. Under the common law, we might have rescinded the old contract and entered a new one. If I claim that there was no consideration for the new agreement, why did I reduce the bill? The circumstances suggest a dispute.

To draft around this problem, I should have sent you a bill for $1000 with language stating: "This obligation may be satisfied by payment of $600 within 30 days." Then I could have revived the $1000 bill if you did not comply with the condition.

5. The conditional check. Megawatt Power has no notice that you are offering an accord, so the obligation is not discharged by accord and satisfaction. If your jurisdiction has a statute allowing liquidated and undisputed debts to be satisfied by a writing signed by the creditor, the endorsement is probably not sufficient as a signed writing. As a practical matter, Megawatt endorses by machine and cannot be expected to read all endorsements.

However, if you communicate a good faith dispute in a separate writing, you have communicated an offer to enter into an accord. Megawatt's acceptance of the check then operates as a satisfaction, discharging your obligation. See *Consolidated Edison Co. v. Arroll*, 66 Misc. 2d 816, 322 N.Y.S.2d 420 (Civ. Ct. N.Y. Co. 1971).

It would make no difference if Megawatt crossed off your indorsement. Writing "accepted without prejudice," makes no difference under U.C.C. § 1-207(2).

Chapter 12
Warranties

§ 12.1. Introduction.

The best source for warranty law is the statutes, which I have tried to track. The old saw is that the first rule of statutory interpretation is to read the statute. The second rule is read the statute.... WHITE & SUMMERS, UNIFORM COMMERCIAL CODE is an invaluable source. 5 and 5A HART & WILLIER, FORMS AND PROCEDURES UNDER THE U.C.C., contains excellent forms as well as helpful text. Students desiring a short overview may find useful GENE A. MARSH, CONSUMER PROTECTION LAW IN A NUTSHELL (West 3d ed.).

§ 12.2. Express warranty. The examples are adapted from the Official Comments and from the discussion in WHITE & SUMMERS, UNIFORM COMMERCIAL CODE ch. 9.

§ 12.3. Implied warranty of merchantability. The weed killer example is based on *Vandalia Ranch, Inc. v. Farmers Union Oil & Supply Company of Hinsdale*, 221 Mont. 253, 718 P.2d 647 (1986). The pork chop example is based on *Hollinger v. Shoppers Paradise of New Jersey*, 134 N.J. Super. Ct. Law Div. 328, 340 A.2d 687 (1975), *aff'd*, 142 N.J. Super. Ct. App. Div. 356, 361 A.2d 578 (1975).

§ 12.4. Implied warranty of fitness for a particular purpose. The examples are adapted from the Official Comments.

§ 12.5. Disclaimer of warranties.

§ 12.5.1. Disclaimer of express warranties. The written disclaimer is from 5 HART & WILLIER § 22.33[3] Form 2-1. The first example is adapted from *Leveridge v. Notaras*, 433 P.2d 935 (Okla. 1967). The language of the third example is from WHITE & SUMMERS, UNIFORM COMMERCIAL CODE § 12-4 (5th ed.). The possibility that express warranties can never be entirely disclaimed is discussed in Burnham, *Remedies Available to the Purchaser of a Defective Used Car*, 47 Mont. L. Rev. 273 (1986).

§ 12.5.2. Disclaimer of implied warranties. The long example is from *Gilbert & Bennett Mfg. Co. v. Westinghouse Elec. Corp.*, 445 F. Supp. 537 (D. Mass. 1977). The FTC Used Motor Vehicle Trade Regulation Rule is found at 16 C.F.R. § 455 (1986). A number of states prohibit the disclaimer of implied warranties in the sale of consumer goods. See Millspaugh & Coffinberger, *Sellers' Disclaimers of Implied Warranties: The Legislatures Strike Back*, 13 U.C.C. Law J. 160 (1980).

§ 12.5.3. The "conspicuousness" requirement. FELSENFELD & SIEGEL, WRITING CONTRACTS IN PLAIN ENGLISH, contains excellent suggestions on achieving conspicuousness.

The common law approach is entertainingly discussed in Mellinkoff, *How to Make Contracts Illegible*, 5 Stan. L. Rev. 418 (1953).

The effective disclaimer is from *Southern Carolina Electric & Gas Company v. Combustion Engineering, Inc.*, 283 S.C. 182, 322 S.E.2d 453 (1984). The ineffective disclaimer is from *Tribble Trucking Corp. v. General Motors Corp.*, 14 U.C.C. Rep. Serv. (Callaghan) 63 (N.D. Ga. 1973). *Tribble* and *Southern Carolina* give the drafter a good framework upon which to build. Note that though the drafting was adequate in *Southern Carolina*, the expense of litigation would have been avoided had the disclaimer complied with the "conspicuous" requirement.

§ 12.6. Conflicts among warranties. See WHITE & SUMMERS, UNIFORM COMMERCIAL CODE § 12-7 (5th ed.). The leading case is *Koellmer v. Chrysler Motors Corp.*, 6 Conn. Cir. Ct. 478, 276 A.2d 807 (1970), *cert. denied*, 160 Conn. 590, 274 A.2d 884 (1971).

§ 12.7. Limitation of remedies. See WHITE & SUMMERS, UNIFORM COMMERCIAL CODE §§ 12-8 to 12-12 (5th ed.). The example is adapted from 5A HART & WILLIER § 24.51[5] Form 2-1.

§ 12.8. Magnuson-Moss. The Act is found at 15 U.S.C. § 2301 *et seq.* (1982). The Black Star warranty is found in the Federal Trade Commission Manual for Business, *Writing Readable Warranties*, which is a useful handbook on Magnuson-Moss warranties. It is available at the FTC web site.

The source of the quote is H.R. Rep. No. 93-1107, 93d Cong., 2d Sess. 13, reprinted in [1974] U.S. Code Cong. & Ad. News 7706, quoted in *Skelton v. General Motors Corp.*, 660 F.2d 311, 314 n. 2 (7th Cir. 1981), *cert. denied*, 456 U.S. 974 (1982).

15 U.S.C. § 2301(1) (1982) provides:

> The term "consumer product" means any tangible personal property which is distributed in commerce and which is normally used for personal, family, or household purposes (including any such property intended to be attached to or installed in any real property without regard to whether it is so attached or installed).

The definition of "written warranty" is found in 15 U.S.C. § 2301(6) (1982).

Magnuson-Moss permits consumers damaged by a violation of the act to bring private actions. One advantage of a Magnuson-Moss claim over a U.C.C. claim is that successful consumers can recover costs and attorneys' fees, which are expressly permitted in a Magnuson-Moss action but not in a U.C.C. action. 15 U.S.C. § 2310(d)(2) (1982).

The limitation of duration of an implied warranty may not be meaningful. An implied warranty means that the goods are merchantable at the time of delivery. The "duration" of an implied warranty, such as 30 days, is an alien concept under the U.C.C.. Possible interpretations of the duration requirement are that it refers to the time during which the purchaser must notify the seller of the defect, or that it operates as a presumption that the defect existed at the time of delivery. NATIONAL CONSUMER LAW CENTER, SALES OF GOODS AND SERVICES § 33.3.1 (2d ed. 1989 & Supp. 1991). If it refers to a statute of limitations, then the time would be unreasonably short. Schroeder, *Private Actions under the Magnuson-Moss Warranty Act*, 66 Calif. L. Rev. 1, 20-21 (1978).

A drafting checklist may be found in 5 HART & WILLIER § 22.32. A detailed discussion of the Magnuson-Moss requirements is beyond the scope of this work. 5 HART & WILLIER § 22A.11 App. A, contains this checklist of terms required and prohibited by the Magnuson-Moss Warranty Act:

[1]   Full Warranty Terms

    [a]   Required Terms

        (1)   A caption which reads: Full [statement of duration] Warranty."

        (2)   Time at which warranty commences, if different from the purchase date.

        (3)   Statement of the remedy which the warrantor will afford the consumer.

        (4)   Description of the parts covered.

        (5)   Any conditions to the right of performance.

        (6)   An explanation of the steps that a consumer must take to obtain performance.

        (7)   The name and address of the warrantor.

        (8)   The name and address of any division of the warrantor that will service the products, or a toll-free telephone number from which information can be obtained.

        (9)   Information about any informal dispute mechanism that must be used by the consumer.

        (10)   The identity of the persons to whom the warranty runs if not to every consumer owner during the warranty period.

        (11)   The legend: "This warranty gives you specific legal rights, and you may also have other rights which vary from state to state."

    [b]   Prohibited Provisions

        (1)   Disclaimer of implied warranties.

        (2)   Limitation of implied warranties.

        (3)   Limitation of duration of implied warranties.

    (4)   Requirement that consumer pay labor charges.

    (5)   Provision that consumer's only remedy is that of a refund.

    (6)   Provision that consumer will pay for depreciation if refund is provided.

    (7)   Requirement that warranty be registered with warrantor.

    (8)   Requirement that warranty product be used only with warrantor's goods, unless the warrantor provides those goods free of charge, or the FTC grants a waiver.

    (9)   Any "deceptive" clauses.

[2]   Limited Warranty Terms

[a]   Required Provisions

The requirements are the same as for a full warranty, except the following must appear:

    (1)   The caption "Limited Warranty."

    (2)   Any limitation on the duration of implied warranties with the required legend.

    (3)   Any modification of remedies, e.g. limitation on the right to collect incidental damages, with the required legend.

[b]   Prohibited Provisions

    (1)   Disclaimers of implied warranties.

    (2)   Modification of implied warranties.

    (3)   Any "deceptive" clauses.

§ 12.10. Exercises.

1. Research. For example, Montana has added these provisions to 2-316(3):

(d) in sales of cattle, hogs, sheep, or horses, there are no implied warranties, as defined in this chapter, that the cattle, hogs, sheep, or horses are free from sickness or disease; and

(e) in sales of any seed for planting (including both botanical and vegetative types of seed, whether certified or not), there are no implied warranties, as defined in this chapter, that the seeds are free from disease, virus, or any kind of pathogenic organisms.

The buyer who is aware of these statutes should draft an express warranty in the contract.

Many other states do not permit the disclaimer of implied warranties in consumer transactions. What is the effect of a disclaimer in such a state? I would argue that it is a violation of the Consumer Protection Act. See § 4.6.

2. Creation of Warranties.

a. This was considered an "opinion" rather than an express warranty, especially when coupled with a warning of possible adverse reaction on label. There was an implied warranty of merchantability that the product was fit for use as a hair dye. See *Carpenter v. Alberto Culver Co.*, 28 Mich. App. 399, 184 N.W.2d 547 (1970).

b. There was no warranty, but there was a misrepresentation by dealer to buyer that there was a warranty. See *Hensley v. Colonial Dodge, Inc.*, 69 Mich. App. 597, 245 N.W.2d 142 (1976).

c. There was an express warranty. Courts consistently have held that promises of safety represent affirmations of fact. See *Hauter v. Zogarts*, 14 Cal. 3d 104, 534 P.2d 377, 120 Cal. Rptr. 681 (1975).

d. The representations in a sales brochure are express warranties if the purchaser relies on the statements. See *Drier v. Perfection, Inc.*, 259 N.W.2d 496 (S.D. 1977).

e. The statements are not express warranties but mere sales "puffing" and expression of seller's opinion. *Performance Motors, Inc. v. Allen*, 280 N.C. 385, 186 S.E.2d 161 (1972).

f. The statements are express warranties. There is no warranty of merchantability because the seller is not in the boat business. There is no warranty of fitness for a particular purpose. *Smith v. Stewart*, 233 Kan. 904, 667 P.2d 358 (1983).

3. Disclaimers and Limitations.

a. The specific disclaimers are ineffective because not conspicuous. The limitation of remedies is probably effective in a commercial contract. *Greenspun v. American Adhesives, Inc.*, 320 F. Supp. 442 (E.D. Pa. 1970).

b. This language is not effective as a general disclaimer or implied warranties. "As is" describes the quality of the goods sold, as does "as they stand," "with all faults," and similar terms. These terms alert the buyer that he assumes all risk as to the quality of the goods involved. "In lieu of" does not similarly alert the buyer to the condition of the goods. *Insurance Co. of North America v. Automatic Sprinkler Corp. of America*, 67 Ohio St. 2d 91, 423 N.E.2d 151 (1981).

c. The limitation is not effective because it is inconspicuous. Even though the agreement was commercial and therefore not "prima facie unconscionable," the court found that the parties had not bargained for the limitation of remedies. "If it is contained in a printed clause which was not conspicuous or brought to the buyer's attention, the seller had no reasonable expectation that the buyer understood that his remedies were being limited to repair or replacement." *Id.* at 155 (quoting NORDSTROM, LAW OF SALES 276).

4. Magnuson-Moss. These problems and much of the discussion that follows are adapted from GREENFIELD, CONSUMER TRANSACTIONS (2d ed. 1991). U.C.C. § 2-313 requires an affirmation of fact or a promise that *relates to the goods*. Magnuson-Moss § 101(6) requires an affirmation of fact or a promise that relates to the nature of the material or workmanship *and* affirms that the material or workmanship is defect free or will meet a specified level of performance *over a specified period of time*. The requirement "over a specified period of time" is ambiguous. Does it modify the conjunctive "affirmation of fact or promise" *and* "affirms that the material or workmanship..." or the disjunctive "*or* will meet a specified level of performance." The first interpretation is endorsed by the Regulations. Section 700.3(a) states in part, "Section 101(6) provides that a written affirmation of fact or a written promise of a specified level of performance must relate to a specified period of time in order to be considered a `written warranty.'"

a. This is a U.C.C. warranty but not a Magnuson-Moss warranty. Even if the statement can be said to affirm that the coat may be washed without falling apart, the absence of a specified period of time prevents it from being a Magnuson-Moss warranty.

b. Same result as *a*.

c. This is not a warranty under either statute. See Magnuson-Moss § 103(b), Regulations § 700.5. Section 700.3(b) states that sellers should not characterize language like that in Problems *a* and *c* as "warranties." A seller who does violates the FTC Act. Magnuson-Moss § 110(b), FTC Act § 5. A seller who characterizes the statement as a "full warranty" is obliged to comply with the standards of § 104 (§ 104(e)).

d. This is not a warranty under either statute. Because of the thirty-day limit, this statement is not exempted by § 103(b) and Regulations § 700.5(b). But it does not meet the requirements of § 101(6).

5. Purchase of a used car.

a. Important Facts. The sales contract says in three places that there are no warranties. A statement called "Disclaimer of Warranties" was signed by the customer. A statement that "This car is sold as is and not guaranteed" is initialed by the customer. And the words "This car is sold `as is'--no warranty" is written under "accessories" on the contract. Furthermore, the Buyers Guide states "AS IS-NO WARRANTY." The language on the Guide states: "You will pay all costs for any repairs. The dealer assumes no responsibility for any repairs regardless of any oral statements about the vehicle." The Guide, which is incorporated in the contract, and the contract itself, make clear that Terry Higgins purchased the car "as is." Nevertheless, the salesman told Terry that the car was in "Tip-top condition and it broke down less than 17 miles later.

b. Relevant Statutes. The sale of the car is governed by UCC Article Two. The Buyers Guide is regulated by the FTC Used Motor Vehicle Trade Regulation Rule, 16 CFR § 455. A state Consumer Protection Act may also be applicable.

c. What is the legal effect of the salesman's statements?

Under the facts, Ryman's statement that the car was in "tip-top condition" may constitute an express warranty. On the other hand, a warranty must be a statement of fact and not an opinion. 2-313(1)(a). In *Wat Henry Pontiac v. Bradley*, 202 Okla. 82, 210 P.2d 348 (1949), the court held that representations that a car was in "A-1 shape" and in "perfect condition" were affirmations of fact. But it is hard to construe "tip-top" as an affirmation of fact or promise. It is more likely "sales puffing." Note that the Buyers Guide warns the buyer that "Spoken promises are difficult to enforce."

  d. Is a representation made by a salesperson binding on the seller?

This is almost a non-issue, for the law is clear that the master is responsible when the servant is acting within his or her authority. The master may be charged with liability to a third person when the servant's conduct was of the kind he or she was employed to perform and when the conduct occurred substantially within authorized time and space limits. RESTATEMENT (SECOND) OF AGENCY § 228 (1958). Here, it would be reasonable for Terry to assume that Ryman had authority to sell the cars and to negotiate sales terms, including warranties.

  e. Is the representation admissible in evidence?

The sales contract is a written agreement that purports to represent the entire understanding of the parties. It states, "Purchaser agrees that this Order cancels and supersedes any prior agreement and as of the date hereof comprises the complete and exclusive statement of the terms of the agreement relating to the subject matters covered hereby...." Evidence of an oral statement is probably barred by the parol evidence rule, § 2-202.

An exception to the parol evidence rule is that the oral representation is admissible to prove that a contract was not formed because of fraud. Therefore Terry may try to prove that the statement fraudulently induced him to purchase the car. The elements of fraud are set out in *United States v. Willard E. Fraser Co.*, 308 F. Supp. 557 (D. Mont. 1970), *aff'd per curiam*, 459 F.2d 483 (9th Cir. 1972). One element of fraud is a misrepresentation of fact. As with the express warranty issue, Terry would have a difficult time proving that this statement was a fact rather than opinion or sales puffing.

  f. Was the exclusion effective?

In *Society National Bank v. Pemberton*, 63 Ohio Misc. 26, 17 Ohio Op. 3d 342, 409 N.E.2d 1073 (Akron Mun. Ct. 1979), the seller told the purchaser prior to the purchase that the vehicle was suitable for snow plowing. The written agreement contained a disclaimer of warranties. The court held that while the disclaimer effectively excluded implied warranties, it failed to exclude an express warranty that was part of the basis of the bargain. Similarly, in *Whitaker v. Farmhand, Inc.*, 173 Mont. 345, 567 P.2d 916 (1977), the Montana Supreme Court held that in a conflict between an express warranty given by a salesperson and language of exclusion, the warranty prevails.

Under the reasoning of these cases, if the statement were an express warranty, it may not have been excluded. However, neither of these cases discusses the applicability of the parol evidence rule. Because the purpose of the rule is to give finality to the written contract, Terry's evidence of a term that would vary the contract would probably not be admissible. 2-316(1).

g. Did Big Sky violate the FTC Regulation?

The FTC found that the chief problem in used car sales is that salespersons make oral statements that contradict the final sales terms and are not legally binding. Federal Trade Commission, Trade Regulation Rule Concerning the Sale of Used Motor Vehicles, Statement of Basis and Purpose and Regulatory Analysis, 49 Fed. Reg. 45,692 at 45,698 (1984). This finding led to the adoption of 16 CFR § 455, The Used Motor Vehicle Trade Regulation Rule.

§ 455.1(a) states that "It is a deceptive act or practice for any used vehicle dealer....(1) To misrepresent the terms of any warranty offered in connection with the sale of a used vehicle; and (3) To represent that a used vehicle is sold with a warranty when the vehicle is sold without any warranty. § 455.4 states "You may not make any statements, oral or written, or take other actions which alter or contradict the disclosures required by § 455.2 and 455.3 [the window form]."

Under the facts, Ryman's statement may have indicated that there was a warranty when there was not. His oral statement, if it suggested a warranty, contradicted the window sticker which said that the car was sold "as is." A subtle issue is whether parol evidence should be allowed to prove a violation of the rule. It should be allowed, for the evidence is not offered to vary the contract, but to show that the seller committed a deceptive act or practice.

h. Did Big Sky violate a Consumer Protection Act?

Consumer Protection Acts prohibit "unfair or deceptive acts or practices in the conduct of any trade or commerce." This language mirrors The FTC Act, 15 U.S.C. 45(a) (1982). According to § 455.1 (c) of the Used Car Rule, a violation of § 455.4 is a *per se* violation of the FTC Act but a violation of § 455.1 is not. To prove a violation of § 455.1, Terry would have to prove that the acts or practices were unfair or deceptive. There are numerous authorities articulating this standard. The most relevant may be *Clayton v. McCary*, 426 F. Supp. 248 (N.D. Ohio 1976) and *Attaway v. Tom's Auto Sales, Inc.*, 144 Ga. App. 813, 242 S.E.2d 740 (1978), holding that it is an unfair or deceptive act or practice for a seller to disclaim an oral warranty with a subsequent "as is" contract. See also *State v. Ralph Williams' Northwest Chrysler Plymouth, Inc.*, 87 Wash. 2d 298, 553 P.2d 423 (1976), *appeal dismissed sub nom. Ralph Williams' Northwest Chrysler Plymouth, Inc. v. Washington*, 430 U.S. 952 (1977); Annot., *Practices Forbidden by State Deceptive Trade Practice and Consumer Protection Acts*, 89 A.L.R.3d 449 (1978).

i. Are there other grounds for finding the exclusion ineffective?

A court may set aside an "as is" disclaimer. Section 2-316 states that "unless the circumstances indicate otherwise," warranties may be excluded by the "as is" language. A contract of adhesion in which the buyer has no bargaining rights and the agreement is prepared by the seller may present such circumstances. *E.g., Knipp v. Weinbaum*, 351 So. 2d 1081 (Fla. Dist. Ct. App. 1977), *cert. denied*, 357 So. 2d 188 (Fla. 1978). On the other hand, the clarity of the FTC window form and the contract may indicate that Terry should have known what he was doing. If the disclaimer is effective, there is no remedy under Magnuson-Moss.

j. If the statement was not a warranty (and it probably was not), does Terry have any remedy?

If the statement is not a warranty, the only express warranty is that the goods are an automobile. Is there a breach of that express warranty when a major system of a car with 30,000 miles on it fails after 16.5 miles? Under the facts as stated by the mechanic, the seller would not have known that the part might fail. The contract has allocated all risk to the buyer. Under present law, that allocation of risk is not unconscionable under the circumstances, although a court could imply that a purchaser is entitled to a reasonable level of performance. In *Meyer v. Packard Cleveland Motor Co.*, 106 Ohio St. 328, 140 N.E. 118 (1922), the Ohio Supreme Court held that a "dump truck" sold with no other express warranties, does not mean "a shape of 5-ton size, but a thing fitted for practical, useful, substantial service as a dump truck." Similarly, it could be argued that Terry is entitled to have the car perform as basic transportation.

In *La Vere v. R.M. Burritt Motors, Inc.*, 112 Misc. 2d 225, 446 N.Y.S.2d 851 (Small Claims Ct. Oswego Co. 1982), plaintiff purchased a used truck "as is" that broke down three blocks later. Using its equitable powers, the court held that the circumstances existing at the time of formation, including unequal knowledge, unequal bargaining power, and a contract provided by the seller contributed to a finding of unconscionability.

k. What damages could Terry recover?

Terry is unlikely to succeed on a tort theory. In *Kopischke v. First Continental Corp.*, 187 Mont. 471, 610 P.2d 668 (1980), the Montana Supreme Court held that a used car dealer has a duty to discover and repair any defects which are patent or discoverable in the exercise of ordinary care. Here, the mechanic informed Terry that the problem was latent.

If the disclaimer is set aside and Terry is able to prove that the warranty was given, there is a breach of warranty. The remedy for breach of warranty under § 2-714(2) would be the difference between the value of the car as warranted and as accepted, probably the cost of repair. Terry would not recover attorneys' fees. A statement describing goods as a car is not a Magnuson-Moss warranty.

If Big Sky violated the Used Car Rule, it violated the FTC Act, 15 U.S.C. § 45. But the FTC Act does not permit private actions. To obtain private relief, Terry may pursue a claim under a Consumer Protection Act. Most CPAs permit the recovery of actual loss or minimum damages, punitive damages, and reasonable attorneys' fees.

6. Negotiation Exercise.

What is the default rule? Other than the fact that the car is a 1998 Ford Windstar, there are no express warranties. Are there implied warranties? The facts do not suggest an implied warranty of fitness for a particular purpose.

Is there an implied warranty of merchantability? This warranty is given only by merchants. Is Lynn a merchant for this purpose? UCC § 2-104(1) provides:

"**Merchant**" means a person who deals in goods of the kind or otherwise by his occupation holds himself out as having knowledge or skill peculiar to the practices or goods involved in the transaction or to whom such knowledge or skill may be attributed by his employment of an agent or broker or other intermediary who by his occupation holds himself out as having such knowledge or skill.

Official Comment 2 provides in part:

> On the other hand, in Section 2-314 on the warranty of merchantability, such warranty is implied only "if the seller is a merchant with respect to goods of that kind." Obviously this qualification restricts the implied warranty to a much smaller group than everyone who is engaged in business and requires a professional status as to particular kinds of goods.

The issue comes down to whether a person who sells one or two cars a year is engaged in the business of car sales so as to come within that definition. If yes, then Lynn gives the warranty; if no, Lynn does not. There may be an incentive for both parties to avoid this issue by agreeing to an express warranty.

They should begin by disclaiming the implied warranty under § 2-316. This can be done either the hard way under § 2-316(2) with conspicuous language that uses the word *merchantability* such as:

> ALL WARRANTIES, INCLUDING THE IMPLIED WARRANTY OF MERCHANTABILITY, ARE HEREBY DISCLAIMED.

or the easy way under § 2-316(3) with language such as:

> This car is sold AS IS.

[Note that if Revised Article 2 is enacted, assuming this is a consumer contract, the required language under § 2-316(2) is:

> The seller undertakes no responsibility for the quality of the goods except as otherwise provided in this contract.

Sellers may well use that language as the default language rather than determining whether a transaction is a consumer transaction or not, because the subsection also provides that "Language that satisfies the requirements of this subsection for a consumer contract also satisfies its requirements for any other contract."]

The parties can then negotiate the terms of an express warranty. They should determine what systems are covered, e.g. just the transmission or all systems, and the duration, which could be expressed in terms of time, miles, or both.

They might also determine whether to limit the remedies. For example, they might provide for the seller to only pay for parts, or for labor, or for both but only up to a certain dollar amount.

Chapter 13
Damages

§ 13.1. Introduction.

The quote from Leff is found in, *Injury, Ignorance and Spite -- The Dynamics of Coercive Collection*, 80 Yale L.J. 1, 27 (1970).

The planner can also build forms of protection into the contract that make a lawsuit unnecessary or that make the circumstances more favorable for a client should a lawsuit occur. For example, a creditor may be able to obtain advance payment, take a security interest in goods sold, obtain a lien in connection with the transaction, cut off services, or induce the debtor to pay in order to enhance its position in the community, for example, by improving its credit. Most of these forms of protection are beyond the scope of a traditional contracts class. They are dealt with in courses involving U.C.C. Article 9, Remedies, or Consumer Transactions. It may nevertheless be important to note them in connection with the steps a planner can take in practicing preventive law.

§ 13.2. Specific Performance.

It is interesting to consider what impact the Uniform Player Contract provision would have had on the court in *Philadelphia Ball Club v. Lajoie*, 202 Pa. 210, 51 A. 973 (1902). Perhaps reflecting love of a different game, Farnsworth and Young reproduce the Professional Football Player's Contract in SELECTIONS FOR CONTRACTS. That contract contains a similar provision in ¶ 3.

The U.C.C. language is from 5A HART & WILLIER, FORMS AND PROCEDURES UNDER THE U.C.C. § 24.51[6][d], Clauses 714 and 715.

§ 13.3. Money damages.

The language inserted by B is adapted from the Federal Express Airbill.

This section looks at only one problem that arises under the U.C.C. 5A HART & WILLIER, FORMS AND PROCEDURES UNDER THE U.C.C. § 24 contains many alternative provisions for other rights and remedies of buyer and seller. Other remedies and provisions that may be drafted based on them can be studied with profit. For example, the Code allows the injured party to recover incidental damages. Provisions denying seller incidental damages or awarding specific incidentals, are found at § 24.41[6][b], Clauses 666 and 667. Similar provisions with respect to buyer are found at § 24.51[5], Clauses 708 and 709. Another area in which the drafter may choose among various provisions is buyer's choice between cover damages under 2-712 and market damages under 2-713.

With respect to consequential damages, § 2-715 ties in with §§ 2-711 to 2-714. There is no corresponding provision for seller's consequential damages, presumably because breach of the promise to pay does not give rise to consequential damages. See §§ 2-706(1), 2-708, 2-710; *Nobs Chemical Co., Inc. v. Koppers Co.*, 616 F.2d 212 (5th Cir. 1980)..

§ 13.4. Liquidated Damages.

SWEET, LEGAL ASPECTS OF ARCHITECTURE, ENGINEERING AND THE CONSTRUCTION PROCESS 405 states:

> In [construction] contracts it is almost impossible to estimate the economic loss caused by delay....The amount selected is more likely determined by what the owner believes is necessary to make it more economical for the contractor to perform on time than to delay and pay damages. While courts do not overtly concede they are doing so, their enforcement of liquidated damages clauses for delay in many construction contracts amounts to enforcing reasonable penalties.

The example of a liquidated damages clause is adapted from 7 Am. Jur. Legal Forms 2d Damages § 83:15. See Dunbar, Drafting the Liquidated Damage Clause -- When and How, 20 Ohio St. L.J. 221 (1959).

§ 13.5. Arbitration.

In *Standard Chlorine of Delaware, Inc. v. Leonard*, 384 F.2d 304, 305 (2d Cir. 1967), Judge Kaufman stated:

> Arbitration is often thought of as a quick and efficient method for determining controversies. Unfortunately, cases involving arbitration clauses sometimes are best remembered as monuments to delay because of the litigation and appeals antecedent to the actual arbitration.

Cases illustrating the interpretation of carelessly drafted arbitration clauses include *F.J. Siller and Co. v. City of Hart*, 400 Mich. 578, 255 N.W.2d 347 (1977), and *Recognition Equipment, Inc. v. NCR Corp.*, 532 F. Supp 271 (N.D. Tex. 1981). In *F.J. Siller*, the contract stated:

> Both parties to this Contract agree that as conditions precedent to the filing of an action in any court [specified disputes] shall be referred to arbitration for decision and award.

The court rejected the interpretation that the parties' use of the term "condition precedent" indicated that the arbitrator's decision was not final. In *Recognition Equipment*, the parties specified remedies for certain breaches and added:

In the event of any other default hereunder, either party may seek relief as would be appropriate at law or in equity.

The agreement also contained a standard arbitration clause. The court held that the arbitration clause and not the quoted clause governed the dispute.

The broad and narrow clauses are adapted from AAA forms found in RODMAN, WEST'S COMMERCIAL ARBITRATION §§ 4.25 and 4.26. Among the many cases determining whether a clause is to be read broadly or narrowly is *Refinery Employees Union of Lake Charles Area v. Continental Oil Co.*, 268 F.2d 447, 453 nn. 6-7 (5th Cir. 1959), *cert. denied*, 361 U.S. 896 (1959).

Materials on drafting and avoiding arbitration clauses include RODMAN, WEST'S COMMERCIAL ARBITRATION ch. 5; 44 AM. JUR. TRIALS, TACTICS AND STRATEGY OF PLEADING § 54; Brenner, *Arbitration: Compulsion and Avoidance*, 17 Forum 656 (1982).

§ 13.6. Attorneys' Fees.

Some states require that an attorneys' fees provision be read reciprocally, so that if the contract permits one party may recover fees, the other may also. See, *e.g.*, Cal. Civ. Code § 1717. The second example is from the Citibank plain language consumer loan note, found in FELSENFELD & SIEGEL, WRITING CONTRACTS IN PLAIN ENGLISH 241. There is a great deal of litigation concerning the meaning of the word *prevailing* when the prevailing party is entitled to fees and concerning the computation of fees.

§ 13.7. Punitive Damages.

In *Seaman's Direct Buying Service, Inc. v. Standard Oil Company of California*, 36 Cal. 3d 752, 686 P.2d 1158, 206 Cal. Rptr. 354 (1984), Justice Bird stated in dissent:

> A breach of contract may also constitute a tortious breach of the covenant of good faith and fair dealing in a situation where the possibility that the contract will be breached is not accepted or reasonably expected by the parties.

> This could happen, for example, if at the time of contracting, the parties expressly indicate their understanding that a breach would be impermissible. Or, it could happen if it were clear from the inception of the contract that contract damages would be unavailable or would be inadequate compensation for a breach. Under these circumstances, a breach of the contract could well constitute a tortious breach of the duty of good faith and fair dealing.

Insurance and employment contracts are good examples of the latter situation. Both the insurer and the insured know that, once an injury has occurred, the insured or the insured's beneficiary will suffer great hardship if benefits are not paid promptly. Thus, a breach of contract by the insurer will almost certainly cause a type of harm for which contract damages would be inadequate. Insureds, therefore, are justified in expecting that their insurance contract will *not* be breached. Similarly, breach of an employment contract by the employer can, in some situations, cause severe harm to an employee's reputation and ability to find new employment. The harm caused cannot be undone by an award of back pay. Thus, employees may be entitled to expect that their contracts will not be breached for frivolous or improper reasons.

These are just a few examples. If a plaintiff can show that, under the circumstances or characteristics of his contract, he was justified in expecting that the other party would not breach, then a voluntary breach by that party could well constitute a violation of the duty to deal fairly and in good faith.

Many cases and law review articles refer to this body of law, which now seems to be in decline. On the "special relationship," see the criteria in *Wallis v. Superior Court*, 160 Cal. App. 3d 1109, 207 Cal. Rptr. 123 (1984).

§ 13.8. Exercise.

1. Research. For example, Mont. Code Ann. § 28-3-704 provides:

Contractual right to attorney fees treated as reciprocal. Whenever, by virtue of the provisions of any contract or obligation in the nature of a contract made and entered into at any time after July 1, 1971, one party to such contract or obligation has an express right to recover attorney fees from any other party to the contract or obligation in the event the party having that right shall bring an action upon the contract or obligation, then in any action on such contract or obligation all parties to the contract or obligation shall be deemed to have the same right to recover attorney fees and the prevailing party in any such action, whether by virtue of the express contractual right or by virtue of this section, shall be entitled to recover his reasonable attorney fees from the losing party or parties.

The drafter who is aware of this statute may still provide that only his or client receives attorney fees, but should advise the client of the statute's effect.

Many consumer protection statutes, state and federal, provide for attorneys fees. The drafter should be aware of whether the transaction is governed by such a statute.

2. Creditor's remedies. What happens if you don't pay a bill? It is obviously a breach of contract. But some creditors have protected themselves better than others by thinking about what might happen in the future and planning for it. The subject of damages is intensely practical. Determining after the fact that there is a good legal claim for breach of contract may be less important than planning ahead to obtain a remedy. In the example, some of the creditors have built in devices to protect their client in the event of breach.

In a number of cases, the creditor has probably taken a security interest in the goods. For example, the obligations to pay for the house, the car, and the television set are probably all secured by the goods, which can be taken back by the creditor in the event of nonpayment. The contractor may have filed a statutory mechanic's lien to secure payment for the work done. Similarly, the county probably has a statutory lien against property on which taxes have not been paid.

The Power Company may have the right to terminate service if the bill is unpaid. It may have gained further leverage by requiring an advance payment or by assessing a re-connection fee that deters breach. The credit card company probably assesses a high interest rate on unpaid bills. Ultimately, debtors who does not pay may do damage to their credit reputations. The attorney and the local merchants are probably in the worst position. They are probably unsecured and have no contractual provisions that may induce payment.

3. The lost deal. Clearly you have a claim for breach of contract. However, because the contract price was so close to the market price, your damages are negligible. From the seller's point of view, this was an excellent opportunity for "efficient breach." Knowing your damages would be negligible, the seller was able to breach, earn a higher profit, pay your damages, and still come out ahead. Furthermore, because of the high transaction costs in making the claim and your inability to recover attorneys' fees, the seller knows you will probably not bother to pursue the claim.

You might, however, be able to claim that the seller had committed an "unfair or deceptive act or practice" under the Consumer Protection Act. If that were the case, you might be able to recover punitive damages, minimum damages, and attorneys' fees. As a drafting matter, the seller might have disclosed, "Seller has no obligation under this agreement if Seller receives a better offer for this vehicle." If such a provision is unfair, including it in the contract will probably not aid seller. But if it is deceptive, disclosure could be a defense.

4. The missed game. This problem is adapted from a similar problem in Goetz & Scott, *Liquidated Damages: Penalties and the Just Compensation Principle: Some Notes on an Enforcement Model and a Theory of Efficient Breach*, 77 Colum. L. Rev. 554, 578-79 (1977).

The case obviously makes a strong visceral appeal for liquidated damages. After all, the parties wanted performance and not breach. The inescapable fact, however, is that the liquidated damages provision is a penalty for breach. It is not related to the actual damages the parties would sustain in the event of breach. On the other hand, it was freely negotiated. As with consideration, if the parties thought that it was a fair price to pay for the security of performance, why should a court question their judgment?

Goetz & Scott conclude that although under traditional rules the provision would be unenforceable, economic analysis furthers the conclusion that the traditional rules should be supplanted.

5. Over-lawyering. The second version seems to me to add at least three things to the first version. The most obvious is the grant of attorney's fees. Because it does not provide for attorney's fees, the first draft would be governed by the "American Rule," with each side paying its own fees. The second draft falls under the exception that permits parties by agreement to assume responsibility for the attorney's fees of the other party.

Secondly, the second draft specifically authorizes injunctive relief. Although this authorization will not be binding on a court, it might assist the Licensor when arguing for injunctive relief that the parties in a negotiated agreement recognized the possibility and provided for it. In fact, although this would certainly have upset McCormack, the drafter might have gone even further and added recitals explaining to the court why the parties believed injunctive relief was appropriate. See § 15.4.4.

Finally, and more subtly, the first draft does not set out the consequence of the Company's breach: is it merely breach of promise, entitling the Licensor to damages, or is it material breach (breach of condition), entitling the Licensor to terminate the agreement? The second draft makes the Licensor's performance expressly conditional on the Company's performance. See Chapter 10, *Promise and Condition*.

McCormack's point is that the attorney has changed the *tone* of the agreement from one of cooperation to confrontation. While this is undoubtedly true, the lawyer did so by building in substantive protections for the client. If the client desires the friendlier tone, the attorney must counsel the client that some protection in the event of breach is being forfeited.

Perhaps it is the legalese in the first draft that is responsible for communicating confrontation. Using techniques from Chapter 17, *The Language of Drafting*, the legalese can be eliminated:

If Company uses the Licensor's trademark on products other than athletic shoes, Licensor may immediately terminate this agreement. On termination, Company forfeits its rights under this agreement, including the right to dispose of any inventory bearing Licensor's trademarks. Company agrees that Licensor has the right to enforce this obligation by injunctive relief. In any action against Company for breach of its obligations, Company shall pay Licensor's attorneys' fees.

6. The Shipment Contract. This language is from the Federal Express USA Airbill. It is a great example of the pervasive influence of the *Hadley* rules, and a good opportunity to remind students that such rules are default rules that the parties are free to draft around, as they have done here. You might want to go over the differences between the "direct, incidental, special, or consequential" damages that are excluded in the second provision. Note that "knowledge" is not a factor, so it does not matter whether or not I tell an agent of my potential losses. According to the final paragraph, I get my $15 back, but to get any greater recovery, according to the first paragraph, I must pay a premium.

7. Ethics. It is not unethical to advise breaking a contract. To paraphrase Oliver Wendell Holmes, the decision to breach a contract is an economic decision, not a moral one. If it is in the interests of ABC to do so, the lawyer can assist them. With the help of the *Hadley* rules, the lawyer can advise the client on the costs of breach. The President and the lawyer are privileged to interfere with the contract because they must act for the best interests of ABC, which may include breaking a contract. See Oregon Formal Ethics Opinion No. 1991-92, which concludes:

> From [DR 7-101 and 7-102] it should be clear that Attorney cannot help Client defraud others. As long as Attorney refrains from such wrongful conduct and does not aid or abet Client in such wrongful conduct, Attorney may assist Client with respect to breach of contract matters.

Chapter 14
Third Parties

§ 14.2. Third Party Beneficiaries.

The distinction between intended and incidental beneficiaries is expressed in RESTATEMENT (SECOND) § 302.

The language from a life insurance contract is from KRUEGER & WAGGONER, THE LIFE INSURANCE POLICY CONTRACT Appendix A (Little Brown 1953). Chapter II, entitled "A Few Simple Rules of Contract Law and Their Application to Life Insurance Contracts," is an excellent illustration of the application of contract principles in drafting.

Example *1* is from the American Institute of Architects, Labor and Material Payment Bond, found in SWEET, LEGAL ASPECTS OF ARCHITECTURE, ENGINEERING AND THE CONSTRUCTION PROCESS Appendix C. An excellent discussion of bonds is found in SWEET, ch. 17. Example *2* is from *Hrushka v. State*, 117 N.H. 1022, 381 A.2d 326, 327 (1977).

§ 14.3. Assignment of rights.

The assignment provision is adapted from 5 HART & WILLIER FORMS AND PROCEDURES UNDER THE U.C.C. § 21.08[3] clause 11. The assignment agreement and notice are adapted from 18 AM. JUR. LEGAL FORMS 2D § 253: 260, 268. Note that warranties of an assignor arise by operation of law. RESTATEMENT (SECOND) § 333. The drafter may nevertheless wish to include these warranties in the document. See AM. JUR. form 259.

2B AM. JUR. LEGAL FORMS 2D § 25:30, contains this checklist of matters to be considered in drafting an assignment of contract rights:

☐ Name and address of assignor.

☐ Status of obligor, such as married, a minor, etc.

☐ Name and address of assignee.

☐ Name and address of any obligor on rights assigned.

☐ Statement of consideration

☐ Statement and description of contract rights assigned.

☐ Description of property to which rights assigned relate, if appropriate.

☐   Date rights arose in assignor.

☐   Incorporation of other instruments.

☐   Description of rights reserved, if any.

☐   Warranties of assignor.

☐   Appointment of assignee as assignor's attorney.

☐   Indemnification of assignee, if appropriate.

☐   Consent to assignment by other parties to contract.

☐   Provision for cancellation of assignment.

☐   Date of assignment.

☐   Signature.

☐   Acknowledgment, if required.

§ 14.4. Delegation of duties.

The delegation clause in a contract is adapted from 5 HART & WILLIER FORMS AND PROCEDURES UNDER THE U.C.C. § 21.08[3] clause 12. Mortgage assumption is found at 13A AM. JUR. LEGAL FORMS 2D § 179:551 et seq.

§ 14.5. Is an assignment a transfer?

Note that U.C.C. § 2-210(4) provides the presumption that an assignment of "the contract" is an assignment of rights and a delegation of duties. The provision indicating the contrary is adapted from 5 HART & WILLIER FORMS AND PROCEDURES UNDER THE U.C.C. § 21.08[3] clause 7.

§ 14.6. Contractual prohibitions.

Note that U.C.C. § 9-406 makes ineffective the prohibition of the assignment of a right to payment for goods sold or services rendered.

The provision prohibiting assignment and delegation is adapted from 5 HART & WILLIER FORMS AND PROCEDURES UNDER THE U.C.C. § 21.08[3] clause 6. On the consequences of breach, RESTATEMENT (SECOND) § 322 Comment c states in part:

Where there is a promise not to assign but no provision that an assignment is ineffective, the question whether breach of the promise discharges the obligor's duty depends on all the circumstances. See §§ 237, 241.

§ 14.7. Novation.

The example of a novation is adapted from 13B AM. JUR. LEGAL FORMS 2D § 187:16. Section 187:4 contains the following checklist of matters to be considered when drafting a novation:

☐   Names and addresses of relevant parties.

        --Parties to original contract.
        --New party to be substituted for one of the original parties.

☐   Existence of valid original contract.

        --Description of obligations under original contract, if appropriate.

☐   Designation of instrument as a novation.

        --Statement that original contract extinguished and superseded by present agreement.

☐   Type of novation.

        --Substitution of new obligor or debtor.

        --Substitution of new obligee or creditor.

        --Substitution of new obligation.

☐   Terms of novation.

☐   Consideration.

☐   Consent of all parties.

☐   Date and place of execution.

☐   Signature of parties.

§ 14.8. Exercises.

1. Language of assignment and delegation. This form is adapted from 18 AM. JUR. LEGAL FORMS 2D § 253:271 (Agreement to delegate performance under sales contract).

This form typifies the failure of drafters to distinguish between assignment and delegation. The parties' intention to delegate duties should be clarified by the use of the language of delegation. Also, the obligation of the delegate to perform should be spelled out. A revision might look like this:

> I, *ABC Co.*, delegating party, hereby delegate to *DEF Co.*, delegate, the duty to perform all undertakings specified in Sections 5 and 6 of an agreement dated October 1, 1988 between myself and *XYZ Co.* for the sale of *1000 widgets* for *$5000*.

> In consideration of delegate's promise to perform the undertakings, I shall pay delegate the amount of *$4800*, payable 30 days after delivery.

> Dated *September 1, 1988*.

2. Sale of a business. In the contract with B, A has the right to obtain parts and the duty to pay money. In the contract with C, A has the duty to furnish goods and the right to receive money. The drafter must examine the existing contracts to determine whether assignment or delegation is prohibited by express language or by the circumstances.

In the contract between A and D, A will assign his rights and delegate his duties under the existing contracts to D. The parties must also determine whether to draft a prohibition of assignment or delegation in the contract between them.

Note that the agreement between A and D does not discharge A's obligations under the existing contracts with B and with C. If A is to be discharged from these agreements, the parties should enter into a novation.

3. Re-sale of a business. This problem is best solved through a novation. The parties to the original contract, A and D, will substitute a new contract between A and E with the intention of extinguishing the original contract. The agreement might look like this:

> Agreement made [date], between A [original party], D [discharged party], and E [substituted party].

> Recitals:

> A. A and D entered into a contract, herein referred to as the original contract, on [date], that provided D would [describe obligation of D].

B. D desires to be discharged from the performance of the obligations enumerated in the original contract.

C. A desires to release D from his obligations as described in the original contract on condition that E agrees to perform the obligations and to be bound by the terms of the original contract.

For the reasons recited above, and in consideration of the mutual covenants contained herein, the parties agree as follows:

1. E shall perform the obligations of D that are enumerated under the original contract, and E agrees to be bound by all the terms of the original contract in every way as if he were an original party thereto.

2. A hereby releases D from all claims for any liability that has arisen or may have arisen in respect to the original contract. A accepts the liability of E in lieu of the liability of D. A shall be bound by the terms of the original contract in every way as if E was named in the original contract in place of D as a party thereto.

3. This agreement supersedes the original contract entered into by A and D, and all the rights and obligations under the original contract are completely extinguished. A copy of the original contract is attached hereto and incorporated herein by reference to define the extent of the liability of E under the agreement.

4. This agreement has been executed in triplicate, and all the parties to this agreement have received a signed copy of it.

5. A, D, and E consent to all the provisions of this agreement.

In witness whereof, the parties have executed this agreement the day and year first above written.

This form is adapted from 13B AM. JUR. LEGAL FORMS 2D § 187:11 (Novation by substitution of new party for discharged party). The recitals are useful to provide the background that led up to this agreement and to clarify the transaction for the reader. Note that the recitals do not contain language of obligation.

4. Additional Exercise. Consider this assignment from 2B AM. JUR. LEGAL FORMS 2D § 25:31:

For value received, I, assignor herein, ___1___, of ___2___ [address], City of __ 3____, State of ___4___, assign, transfer, and set over to ___5___, assignee herein, of __

  6   [address], City of ____7____, State of ____8____, all my right, title, and interest in and to the within and foregoing agreement, subject to all the terms and conditions thereof.

I remise, release, and quitclaim to assignee, all my right, title, and interest in and to the property within described and agreed to be conveyed.

Dated ____9____, 20 10 .

In witness whereof, I have executed this assignment at ____11____, [place of execution] the day and year above written.

[Signature of assignor]

ACCEPTANCE OF ASSIGNMENT

_____ [Assignee] hereby accepts the foregoing instrument, subject to all the terms and conditions thereof.

Dated _____, 20 __.

[Signature of assignee]

Is this document an assignment of rights or a transfer? Suppose the assignor had the duty to pay B $5000 for 1000 widgets to be delivered by B. What are the assignor's rights and duties after the document has been executed? How would you redraft it for clarity? Consider these points:

Why "assign, transfer, and set over"? Do the surplus words add anything to "assign" other than confusion?

Why "all my right, title and interest"? This sounds like more than rights.

Why "the within and foregoing agreement"? Does this refer to two agreements, the agreement between assignor and B, and the agreement between assignor and assignee?

Why "subject to all the terms and conditions thereof"? If there is an assignment of rights, then the assignee receives no greater rights than the assignor is entitled to.

Why the second paragraph?

An acceptance is necessary to make a contract, but which is the "foregoing instrument"? Again, isn't any acceptance "subject to all the terms and conditions" in a contract?

Would the agreement be any less compelling if it read as follows:

Dated ____9____, 20_10_.

      For value received, I, assignor, ____1____, of ____2____ [address], City of ___3___, State of ____4____, assign to ____5____, assignee, of ____6____ [address], City of ____7____, State of ____8____, all my rights under an agreement with B attached hereto.

      Executed at ____11____, [place of execution] the day and year above written.

                                     [Signature of assignor]

                        Accepted: [Signature of assignee]

PART II

How the Principles of Drafting Are Exemplified in Contracts

Chapter 15
The Framework of a Contract

§ 15.1. Introduction.

Most agreements require substantive knowledge of specialized transactions. This book considers the substance only of first-year Contracts. I believe that the process of drafting is the same however complex the agreement. Through this book students should become accustomed to expressing the agreement after understanding the substance.

§ 15.2. The use of forms.

In considering whether an agreement serves the client's purposes, JOHN E. TRACY, HINTS ON ENTERING THE PRACTICE OF LAW (1933), states:

> Nothing is so embarrassing as to have a client ask what certain language in a contract means and, on looking at it, discover that this was certain language copied from a form which was in no way applicable to your client's particular matter.

MELLINKOFF, THE LANGUAGE OF THE LAW, contains a fascinating history of formbooks. He notes at 199 that many of the early formbooks were intended not for lawyers but for laymen:

> Such books preserved in detail a continuity of archaic English, bad grammar, and deficient punctuation, in form available to every scrivener and dabbler in the law, without the slightest knowledge of what he was writing.

Macneil, *A Primer of Contract Planning*, 48 S. Cal. L. Rev. 627 (1975), offers this advice on the use of forms:

> The lawyer is justified in using an unaltered form only when he knows from prior experience or otherwise that the proposed relationship will be identical to the one for which the form was designed, and that the form is still well designed for its purpose.
> ...
> Advantages of forms in legal framework planning itself are obvious: they are convenient and efficient. There is, however, vast variation in the quality of forms. Moreover, using any form can be dangerous. First, the legal framework contained in the form simply may not fit the relationship being planned. In addition, however good the form may be as far as it goes, it may not constitute complete legal framework planning. Finally, a form may have become outdated because of changes in the law. Macneil, 655 (footnotes omitted).

This book includes a number of examples from commonly available formbooks, such as AM. JUR. LEGAL FORMS and WEST'S LEGAL FORMS. In conjunction with those formbooks, the reader should study the substantive text referred to in the formbook, such as AM. JUR. itself. I have found most useful those formbooks that discuss substantive law and present alternative forms that reflect alternative substantive provisions. For example, 5 HART & WILLIER, FORMS AND PROCEDURES UNDER THE U.C.C. (Matthew Bender 1986) and FELSENFELD & SIEGEL, SIMPLIFIED CONSUMER CREDIT FORMS (Warren, Gorham & Lamont 1978). These days, forms are also available in software packages or can be downloaded from internet sites.

DICKERSON, FUNDAMENTALS OF LEGAL DRAFTING § 4.11 (2d ed.) (footnotes omitted) contains this helpful advice on the use of form books:

> Before turning to the specific matters of form and style set forth in the following chapters, let us consider briefly the use of forms or form books, which is so often deplored. The time-pressed draftsman naturally turns to any resource that will hasten his progress and perhaps even improve the result. But the problem is really broader: When are specific legal problems sufficiently similar that their treatment can be standardized in legal boilerplate? Besides form books, lawyers normally keep copies of their earlier efforts for possible use in dealing with later problems. Some of these develop into office forms. In the same way, legislative draftsmen look to existing statutes. Lawyers steeped in case precedent and heavily pressed for time readily see the value of instrumental precedent.

> But just as the values are generally the same, so also are the pitfalls. Just as blind adherence to judicial precedent is hazardous, so also is the blind use of forms, even when they have been developed by the lawyer for his own use or enacted in statutory form by a legislature. Despite the similarities that make feasible the use of forms, new situations often present significantly different elements. And so the draftsman should carefully weigh the appropriateness of a form to the case at hand each time he is prompted to use it. Indeed, the danger that the form will lull him into a false sense of accomplishment is so great that in other than the most routine situations he is wise to use it mainly as a cross check. He must not forget that he has been engaged to exercise his professional judgment, not to serve as a mere retrieval system.

> There is still another consideration. In their natural preoccupation with substantive results, some published form books have treated matters of structure, form, and style so cautiously that they have tended to perpetuate the drafting ineptitudes of the past. In drawing heavily on adjudicated documents, they have included an unfortunate percentage of inadequately drafted provisions.

Sources on the architecture of agreements include DICKERSON, FUNDAMENTALS OF LEGAL DRAFTING ch. 5 (2d ed.); DICK, LEGAL DRAFTING ch. 4 (2d ed.); FELSENFELD & SIEGEL, WRITING CONTRACTS IN PLAIN ENGLISH ch. 8 (1981). A most aesthetically pleasing book, actually using architectural examples, is JILL J. RAMSFIELD, THE LAW AS ARCHITECTURE: BUILDING LEGAL DOCUMENTS (West 2000).

§ 15.3. Zero-base drafting.

Siegel & Glascoff, *Case History: Simplifying an Apartment Lease*, in DRAFTING DOCUMENTS IN PLAIN LANGUAGE 169-205 (PLI 1981) is an excellent unit, involving drafting an apartment lease using the "zero base" technique. At 191 the authors suggest these four steps for "zero base" drafting:

Step 1:   Outline the document based on the contents of the original.

Step 2:   Evaluate the rights and responsibilities of both parties as stated in case law and legislation.

Step 3:   Assess the issues involving business risk, based on provisions from the original document and an evaluation of business records. This assessment may show the need for new provisions or even whole new categories of information.

Step 4:   Draft the simplified document using [plain language techniques].

§ 15.4. The structure of a contract.

§ 15.4.1. Description of the instrument. Materials on beginning a contract include Kirk, *Legal Drafting: How Should a Document Begin?*, 3 Tex. Tech L. Rev. 233 (1972); PARHAM, THE FUNDAMENTALS OF LEGAL WRITING ch. 3 (1967); DICK, LEGAL DRAFTING ch. 8 (2d ed. 1985).

§ 15.4.2. Caption. See § 17.12, Exercise 2, for another example. The Connecticut Plain Language Law provides that a consumer contract is written in plain language if:

> It uses personal pronouns, the actual or shortened names of the parties to the contract, or both, when referring to those parties; ...

Conn. Gen. Stat. § 42-152(b)(3), (c)(6) (1985).

MELLINKOFF, LEGAL WRITING SENSE AND NONSENSE 140-44 goes through the steps of editing a caption. He begins with this:

> THIS AGREEMENT, made and entered into this 10th day of January, 1981, in the City of Los Angeles, State of California, by and between John Doak, hereinafter sometimes referred to as and called the Party of the First Part, and the Plotz Corporation, a corporation duly organized and existing under and by virtue of the laws of the State of Delaware, hereinafter sometimes referred to as and called the Party of the Second Part.

> WITNESSETH:

He ends with this:

AGREEMENT

January 10, 1981

Los Angeles, California

JOHN DOAK and PLOTZ CORPORATION of Delaware AGREE:

§ 15.4.3. Transition. The rental agreement that fails to contain words of agreement is adapted from Kirk, *Legal Drafting: How Should A Document Begin?*, 3 Tex. Tech L. Rev. 233, 261-62 (1972).

§ 15.4.4. Recitals. See Chapter 7, *Interpretation*, and § 17.12, Exercise 2, for additional information. The source of the quote regarding ambiguity is *Ex Parte Dawes*, 17 Q.B.D. 275 (1886).

COOPER, WRITING IN LAW PRACTICE 275-76, contains sound advice on the use of recitals:

> Recitals. These are the "Whereases" in which some draftsmen delight, and which some invariably eschew.
>
> Those who favor their use assert that when you are relying on representations which have induced the making of the contract, the recitals in the "whereas" clauses constitute admissions against interest which may be employed to create an estoppel. Further, they assert, such recitals serve to illuminate the intention and purpose of the parties, and thus aid in the construction of the agreement.
>
> Draftsmen of the opposite persuasion urge that the employment of a string of "Whereases" is both clumsy and obsolete. In those rare cases in which it is necessary to explain the facts or representations or assurances on the basis of which the parties are contracting, they assert, the purpose can be accomplished much more economically by stating the facts in narrative form in a single paragraph. If the purpose is to create a condition or warranty, they say, it is much safer to create the condition or warranty by specific provisions in the main portion of the agreement.
>
> Would you accept the following middle-of-the-road view as a fair suggestion? Do not interject "Whereases" merely because you like their sound, as some Psalmists scattered "Selahs" throughout their psalms. Use them only where you discover a need, and then guardedly.

§ 15.4.5. Definitions. See §§ 7.5.1 and 17.12, Exercise 3, for additional information. See also CHILD, DRAFTING LEGAL DOCUMENTS ch. 10 (2d ed.).

The Humpty Dumpty example is from ROBINSON, DEFINITION 80-81 (1965).

On the meaning of *best efforts*, see 2 FARNSWORTH, CONTRACTS § 7.17(c) (2d ed. 1998).

§ 15.5. Exercises.

1. Revising a form. The original agreement:

MEMORANDUM OF AGREEMENT

This memorandum of agreement, made this _____ day of _____, 20__, by and between _____, of the city of _____, county of _____, state of _____, hereinafter sometimes referred to as the party of the first part and _____ _____, of the city of _____, county of _____, state of _____, hereinafter sometimes referred to as the party of the second part, witnesseth the agreement of the aforesaid parties hereto, as follows, to wit:

1. The party of the first part agrees to purchase and the party of the second part agrees to sell _____ for a total price of _____ dollars ($).

2. The party of the second part agrees to deliver the goods as described in paragraph 1 hereinabove to the party of the first part at _____on the _____ day of _____ ____.

3. The party of the first part agrees to pay the party of the second part the total price set forth in paragraph 1 hereinabove at the time of delivery as set forth in paragraph 2 hereinabove.

4. In witness whereof, the parties have set their hands and seals to this Agreement as of the date first above written.

_____(s)   _____(s)
Party of the first part   Party of the second part

Address _____   Address _____

The drafter might begin by giving the parties names. Because the client may use this form in the future, you would not want to call them Zilch and Smith. You could call them Buyer and Seller, Owner and Artist, or I and You. For example:

MEMORANDUM OF AGREEMENT

This memorandum of agreement, made this _____ day of _____, __, by and between _
John Zilch , of the city of _____, county of _____, state of
_____ ("Buyer") and Sheila Smith , of the city of _____, county of
_____, state of _____ ("Seller"), witnesseth the agreement of the aforesaid parties
hereto, as follows, to wit:

1. Buyer agrees to purchase and Seller agrees to sell _____ for a total price of __
_____ dollars ($).

2. Seller agrees to deliver the goods as described in paragraph 1 hereinabove to Buyer at _
_____, on the _____ day of _____, __.

3. Buyer agrees to pay Seller the total price set forth in paragraph 1 hereinabove at the
time of delivery as set forth in paragraph 2 hereinabove.

4. In witness whereof, the parties have set their hands and seals to this Agreement as of
the date first above written.

_____(s)   _____(s)
Buyer   Seller

Address _____   Address _____

You have already removed a substantial amount of clutter. You might now modernize
the date and eliminate the residences in the caption, for they appear in the closing:

MEMORANDUM OF AGREEMENT

This memorandum of agreement, made and entered _____, 20__, by and between _
John Zilch ("Buyer") and Sheila Smith ("Seller"), witnesseth the agreement of the
aforesaid parties hereto, as follows, to wit:

Now you can eliminate the phrases that employ two words to do the work of one
("twofers") and the archaic expressions:

AGREEMENT

This agreement, made _____, 20__, between John Zilch ("Buyer") and Sheila
Smith ("Seller").

1. Buyer agrees to purchase and Seller agrees to sell _____ for a total price of _____ dollars ($).

2. Seller agrees to deliver the goods as described in paragraph 1 to Buyer at _____ on _____, 20__.

3. Buyer agrees to pay Seller the total price set forth in paragraph 1 at the time of delivery as set forth in paragraph 2.

_____(s)   _____(s)
Buyer   Seller

Address _____   Address _____

These changes have been made:

Before	After
Memorandum of Agreement made and entered witnesseth aforesaid hereto to wit hereinabove	Agreement made

A closing such as Paragraph 4 adds a certain formality to the agreement, but adds nothing of substance. Note, however, that if the caption did not contain a date, you might want to include a date in a closing paragraph.

Finally, you might make the heading more specific, add language of agreement, make the caption a complete sentence, and add language of obligation in the body of the agreement.

SALES AGREEMENT

   John Zilch ("Buyer") and Sheila Smith ("Seller") agree as follows:

1. Buyer shall purchase and Seller shall sell _____ for a total price of _____ dollars ($).

2. Seller shall deliver the goods as described in paragraph 1 to Buyer at _____ on _____, 20__.

3. Buyer shall pay Seller the total price set forth in paragraph 1 at the time of delivery as set forth in paragraph 2.

4. Signed _____, 20_.

_____   _____
Buyer   Seller

Address _____   Address _____

2. Zero-base drafting.

Let us compare the standard revision of a draft with zero-base drafting. Here is the provision regarding security deposits as found in a lease used in Tennessee:

SECURITY DEPOSIT   LESSEE agrees to pay LESSOR the sum of $_____ as a security deposit upon the execution of this lease, the receipt of which is hereby acknowledged. If LESSEE shall promptly pay the rent as provided herein, and if he shall comply with each and all of the terms and conditions of this written lease which are to be performed be LESSEE during LESSEE'S entire tenancy, then upon the termination of this tenancy, and after the surrender of the possession of the leased premises according to the terms of this lease, in good and clean condition, reasonable wear and tear excepted, LESSOR will refund to LESSEE the said sum within two (2) weeks following 30 day written notice. It is understood and agreed that this Security Deposit is forfeited if for any reason the Applicant does not occupy these quarters also. If this lease is signed by more than one person as LESSEE, the LESSOR may make return of the Security Deposit or any part thereof to any one or more of the persons constituting the LESSEE without further liability therefore to any other person or LESSEE who may have contributed all or part of said deposit. LESSEE understands and agrees that only that portion of the Security Deposit above the fair and reasonable cost necessary to repair the walls, floors, cabinets, carpet, drapes, windows, plumbing fixtures, range, refrigerator and furniture or premises, will be refunded.

ESCROW   All monies paid as deposits shall be held in _____ in escrow account number _____

To revise this provision, we first break the existing language down into component parts:

SECURITY DEPOSIT

1. LESSEE agrees to pay LESSOR the sum of $_____ as a security deposit upon the execution of this lease, the receipt of which is hereby acknowledged.

2. If

        LESSEE shall promptly pay the rent as provided herein, and

        if he shall comply with each and all of the terms and conditions of this written lease which are to be performed be LESSEE during LESSEE'S entire tenancy,

then

        upon the termination of this tenancy, and

        after the surrender of the possession of the leased premises according to the terms of this lease, in good and clean condition, reasonable wear and tear excepted,

LESSOR will refund to LESSEE the said sum within two (2) weeks following 30 day written notice.

3. It is understood and agreed that this Security Deposit is forfeited if for any reason the Applicant does not occupy these quarters also.

4. If this lease is signed by more than one person as LESSEE, the LESSOR may make return of the Security Deposit or any part thereof to any one or more of the persons constituting the LESSEE without further liability therefore to any other person or LESSEE who may have contributed all or part of said deposit.

5. LESSEE understands and agrees that only that portion of the Security Deposit above the fair and reasonable cost necessary to repair the walls, floors, cabinets, carpet, drapes, windows, plumbing fixtures, range, refrigerator and furniture or premises, will be refunded.

ESCROW   All monies paid as deposits shall be held in _____ in escrow account number _____

      We can now better comprehend each part and the relationship of each part to the whole. In Part (1), does it make sense to say LESSEE "agrees to pay" an amount "which is hereby acknowledged"? If it is acknowledged, it has been paid. We can combine this provision with the ESCROW provision, changing that provision to the active voice, making clear that it is an obligation of the LESSOR. Let's also make it easier to keep the parties straight by calling LESSOR "Landlord" and LESSEE "Tenant":

Tenant has paid Landlord $_____ as a security deposit. Landlord shall place the security deposit in _____ in escrow account number _____

Part (2) states a legal rule as a logical "If...then" proposition. See § 7.5.4. We might better communicate the proposition to the reader (the tenant) if we start with the result (return of the security deposit) and then enumerate the events that must occur to reach that result. Because Part (3) is also an event which must occur to bring about the result, we can add it to the enumeration:

Landlord shall refund the full amount of the security deposit within 14 days after the termination of this lease if Tenant:

1. gives LANDLORD written notice of at least 30 days before termination of the lease;
2. always pays rent when due;
3. does not violate the terms of this lease;
4. occupies the PREMISES;
5. vacates the PREMISES no later than the date this lease terminates; AND
6. leaves the PREMISES clean and undamaged, except for reasonable wear and tear.

It is not clear what the drafter means by "within two (2) weeks following 30 day written notice." It could mean that the tenant must give 30 days notice of termination and the landlord must return the deposit within 14 days after the termination. Or it could mean that the tenant must give written notice demanding return of the security deposit and landlord must return it within 14 days after the notice date. We should examine the document for internal consistency, to see if anything is said elsewhere about notice of termination. We should also discuss this question with our client, the landlord.

Part (5) should now logically follow, as it describes what happens if one of the enumerated events does not occur. The enumeration of particular areas of the premises seems unnecessary in that provision. I have decided to use the general term "premises" instead of risking an argument about whether something not enumerated needed cleaning or repair (see § 7.3.):

If the premises are not clean and undamaged upon termination of this lease, Landlord may refund only that part of the security deposit above the cost of reasonable cleaning and repair.

Finally, we can add a simplified version of Part (4):

If this lease is signed by more than one Tenant, Landlord may return the security deposit to any Tenant regardless of which Tenant paid the security deposit.

Let's put all the revisions together to see what the provision looks like in plain language:

SECURITY DEPOSIT

Tenant has paid Landlord $_____ as a security deposit. Landlord shall place the security deposit in _____ in escrow account number _____

Landlord shall refund the full amount of the security deposit within 14 days after the termination of this lease if Tenant:

    1. gives LANDLORD written notice of at least 30 days before termination of the lease;

    2. always pays rent when due;

    3. does not violate the terms of this lease;

    4. occupies the PREMISES;

    5. vacates the PREMISES no later than the date this lease terminates; AND

    6. leaves the PREMISES clean and undamaged, except for reasonable wear and tear.

If the premises are not clean and undamaged upon termination of this lease, Landlord may refund only that part of the security deposit above the cost of reasonable cleaning and repair.

If this lease is signed by more than one Tenant, Landlord may return the security deposit to any Tenant regardless of which Tenant paid the security deposit.

We now have a clear provision, but do we have a legal one? Over the years, boilerplate tends to accrete language that results because of experiences of the client, court decisions, or additional risks the client contemplates. The language loses one of its original purposes, to conform to the statutory requirements. This provision is from a Tennessee lease, so we must examine the Tennessee statute, which is based on the Uniform Residential Landlord and Tenant Act. The relevant section provides:

§ 66-28-301. Security deposits

(a) All landlords of residential property requiring security deposits prior to occupancy shall be required to deposit all tenants' security deposits in an account used only for that purpose, in any bank or other lending institution subject to regulation by the state of Tennessee or any agency of the United States government. Prospective tenants shall be informed of the location of the separate account and the account number.

(b) At the termination of occupancy, the landlord shall inspect the premises and compile a comprehensive listing of any damage to the unit which is the basis for any charge against the security deposit and the estimated dollar cost of repairing such damage. The tenant shall then have the right to inspect the premises to ascertain the accuracy of such listing. The landlord and the tenant shall sign such listing, which signatures shall be conclusive evidence of the accuracy of such listing. If the tenant shall refuse to sign such listing, he shall state specifically in writing the items on the list to which he dissents, and shall sign such statement of dissent. If the tenant has moved or is otherwise inaccessible to the landlord, the landlord shall mail a copy of the listing of damages and estimated cost of repairs to the tenant at his last known mailing address.

(c) No landlord shall be entitled to retain any portion of a security deposit if the security deposit was not deposited in a separate account as required by subsection (a) and if the final damage listing required by subsection (b) is not provided.

(d) A tenant who disputes the accuracy of the final damage listing given pursuant to subsection (b) may bring an action in a circuit or general sessions court of competent jurisdiction of this state. Tenant's claim shall be limited to those items from which the tenant specifically dissented in accordance with the listing or specifically dissented in accordance with subsection (b) of this section; otherwise the tenant shall not be entitled to recover any damages under this section.

(e) Should a tenant vacate the premises with unpaid rent due and owing, and without making a demand for return of deposit, the landlord may, after thirty (30) days, remove the deposit from the account and apply the moneys to the unpaid debt.

(f) In the event the tenant leaves not owing rent and having any refund due, the landlord shall send notification to the last known or reasonable determinable address, of the amount of any refund due the tenant. In the event the landlord shall not have received a response from the tenant within sixty (60) days from the sending of such notification, the landlord may remove the deposit from the account and retain it free from any claim of the tenant or any person claiming in his behalf.

(g) This section does not preclude the landlord or tenant from recovering other damages to which they may be entitled under this chapter.

We can now draft a zero-base provision, starting not from the boilerplate but from the language of the statute:

Security Deposit

Tenant has paid Landlord $_____ as a security deposit. Landlord shall place the security deposit in _____ in escrow account number _____

Upon termination of this lease, Landlord must inspect the premises and make a comprehensive listing of any damage. Landlord shall:

      1. state in the listing any damage which is to be deducted from the security
deposit; and
      2. state the estimated cost of repairing the damage; and
      3. sign the listing;
      4. give the listing to Tenant or, if Tenant is unavailable, mail it to Tenant's last
known mailing address.

If Landlord does not give the listing to Tenant, Landlord may not retain any portion of
the security deposit.
Tenant may inspect the premises to determine the accuracy of the Landlord's listing. If
Tenant signs the listing, the signatures are conclusive evidence of the accuracy of the
listing. If Tenant does not sign the listing, Tenant shall:
      1. state specifically in writing the items in the listing to which Tenant disagrees;
and
      2. sign this statement.

If Tenant vacates the premises owing rent and does not demand the return of the security
deposit, Landlord may, after 30 days, apply the security deposit to the unpaid debt.

If Tenant vacates the premises not owing rent, Landlord shall, within 30 days, mail notice
to Tenant's last known mailing address informing Tenant that Tenant has a refund of the
security deposit due. Landlord may keep the security deposit if Tenant does not claim
the refund within 60 days from the date notice was sent.

    The zero-base version tracks the language of the statute more closely. The enumeration
of landlord's duties is preceded by *must*, indicating that these events are conditions precedent.
See § 17.6.3. The consequence of failure to bring about those events is specified. See § 10.6.2.
We have improved upon the statute by using gender-neutral language. See § 17.4.

    One significant difference is that the original lease provided for loss of the security
deposit in a number of circumstances, including violation of any lease term. Section 66-28-104
(12) of the Act defines a security deposit as security against financial loss by the landlord due to
damage to the premises. A landlord who retains the security deposit for reasons other than
damage to the premises may be in violation of the statute.

    On the other hand, § 66-28-301(d), detailing the action a tenant who disputes the
accuracy of the listing may bring, was omitted from the zero-base draft. While the drafter should
describe the rights and obligations of each party, it does not seem necessary to explain how each
party may secure relief. While we should specify the consequences of the tenant's breach, we
need not inform the tenant how to secure a remedy if landlord does not meet its obligations.

    Legitimate business concerns of the landlord, not prohibited by the statute, could be
added to the zero-base draft. The drafter should, as with all agreements, maintain an annotated

version of the lease in order to keep track of the source of the language. This technique will keep boilerplate fresh and meaningful. See § 19.4.

3. Organization of an Agreement. The Agreement is, of course, in alphabetical order, which makes no sense. I make a transparency of the agreement and ask students where they would put the various provisions. It seems easy to start with the Recitals and Definitions and the beginning, followed by the Operative Terms relating to sales, delivery, and billing. There is a cluster of terms having to do with dates, which might logically succeed those terms; they also might arguably precede them, as there seems to be a prior agreement in the picture. We then have two classes of Boilerplate: those that are specific to this transaction and those that are found in contracts generally. Finally, we put the Signatures at the end. It might look something like this:

13	Recitals
6	Definitions
16	Sale Quantities
14	Sale Charges
17	Sale Scheduling Provisions
15	Sale of Other Products or Services
7	Delivery
3	Billing and Payment
4	Commencement Date
19	Termination of Prior Agreement on Commencement Date
8	Effective Date and Term
12	Obligations Upon Expiration or Termination
1	Appropriations Refinancing Act Incorporated by Reference
11	Notices and Information Exchange
5	Contract Revisions and Waivers
9	Entire Agreement
10	Governing Law and Dispute Resolution
2	Assignment
20	Uncontrollable Forces
18	Signatures

4. Organization of a term. The drafter probably thought it was very clear to state the duties of each party. The problem is, as we have seen in Chapter 10, *Promise and Condition*, often duties are not immediately performable; some event must occur before they are due. Here, we can't tell when each party has to perform a duty without reference to the performance by the other party. It would therefore have been better to put them in chronological order, showing the relationship between the performances. When I tried to put them in chronological order, I'm not sure I succeeded. It does not help that the drafter violated the Golden Rule (see § 9.3), calling the document variously Energy Efficiency Task Order, Task Order, and Customer Task Order. I assume these all refer to the same thing. I would have to go back to my client to ask exactly what they expected to have happen when. My best guess for the chronological order is this:

(2)(a) Customer shall request BPA services under this Agreement.

(1)(a) BPA shall provide an Energy Efficiency Task Order in response to Customer's request for service.

(2)(b) Customer shall provide BPA with a signed Energy Efficiency Task Order within 45 days indicating its acceptance or rejection of BPA's offer to provide the services requested.

(1)(d) BPA may elect to accept, counter propose, or reject a Customer Task Order.

(1)(b) BPA shall commence implementation of the Task Order when it receives and accepts the Task Order from Customer. BPA may accomplish the work, at the discretion of BPA, by using BPA employees or through the use of partners.

(1)(c) BPA or its partners shall perform agreed-upon services as specified in the Energy Efficiency Task Order approved by Customer.

(2)(c) Customer shall provide BPA with access to necessary information and facilities as agreed to by the Parties necessary to provide the energy efficiency products and services.

(2)(d) Securing necessary environmental permits or waivers are the responsibility of Customer, unless other arrangements are made by the Parties.

5. The Personal Management Contract. The terms of this contract looks as though they were shuffled and dealt randomly. The caption gets off to a good start and is logically followed by a recital. The first term, Appointment, however, also begins with a recital. Is this really background information, or is it a substantive term? Note that the "Manager" in the caption has now become the "Personal Manager."

The recital is then followed by a definition. The definition does not entirely make sense. It is unlikely that "here now known or hereafter invented" were intended to modify "Artist's name and likeness." Definitions don't have to be in a separate section, especially if they define only terms used in the provision, but here the defined term may be used in the rest of the agreement.

Following the third term there are words of transition. But even if the first term was a recital, aren't the second and third substantive terms? The language of transition should have preceded these terms.

6. The Golden Rule of Drafting.

a. Can Seller delay service until Buyer removes hazardous material? The phrase "removal of any hazardous material (e.g., asbestos) or correction of any hazardous condition" in the first sentence has become "corrects the hazardous condition" in the second sentence. What has become of "removal of any hazardous material"?

b. The "Telecommunications Service Provider Purchase and License Agreement" becomes the "Telecommunications Service Provider and License Agreement" and finally the "Telco and Service Provider Agreement." Are these all the same thing?

c. "Confidential Information or any technical data" becomes just "Confidential Information." What has become of "technical data?"

Chapter 16
Operative Language and Boilerplate Terms

§ 16.1. **Introduction**. The quote is from 3A CORBIN, CONTRACTS 13.

§ 16.2. **Stating obligations.**

On the extent to which the drafter should provide for contingencies, see the contract for the sale of an orange in Teacher's Manual § 3.1. Note that language that may not be appropriate for the sale of a single orange may be appropriate for the sale of a truckload.

§ 16.3. **Representations and warranties.**

In THE LANGUAGE OF THE LAW 78, Mellinkoff is critical of the "twofers" in this passage:

> If Borrower shall have made any representation or warranty herein or in any report, financial or other statement or instrument furnished pursuant thereto which shall be in any material respect false and/or erroneous and/or incorrect...

He does not criticize the phrase "representation or warranty," however, indicating that the two words have different meanings. While the meaning may differ on some occasions, in this particular passage it seems that "representation" would do. Because it concerns a "representation or warranty" that is false, erroneous, or incorrect, it cannot refer to a promise.

The examples of representations with remedies specified are from 16 AM. JUR. LEGAL FORMS 2D 226.

MANDEL, THE PREPARATION OF COMMERCIAL INSTRUMENTS 23-26, makes the point in this way:

Representations, Warranties and Conditions

All material representations relied upon by your client should be set forth in the contract as express warranties. This will protect your client against innocent as well as fraudulent misrepresentations and will give him an action for breach of warranty. You do this by simply stating in your contract, in a separate paragraph, that the named party "represents and warrants" the particular set of facts upon which your client is relying. Bear in mind that representations of law as distinguished from fact are generally not actionable and should not be relied on. To avoid any question as to whether the representations are to survive the closing or other consummation of the transaction, a statement to that effect should be added, if that is the intent.

Where the transaction is conditioned upon a particular representation, the representation should be expressed as a condition, as well as a warranty. No particular wording is necessary to create a condition, but language which clearly evinces such an intent on the part of the parties is necessary. Words commonly used to denote a condition are "on condition," "provided," "if," "only if," "unless and until," "when, as and if," and words of similar import.

To illustrate the foregoing, let us assume that your client is buying a business by acquiring all the outstanding shares of stock of a corporation, and that the purchase price is being fixed with relation to certain stated assets and liabilities, and a consequent net worth. It is also fixed with relation to the earnings record of the corporation for a specified number of past years. The sellers should be required to "represent and warrant" the precise state of affairs for which the purchaser has bargained, including (1) that the corporation is validly organized and in good standing under the laws of X state; (2) that the sellers are the owners of all the issued and outstanding shares of the capital stock of the corporation, and that such shares have been validly issued and are fully paid and non-assessable; (3) that the sellers are the sole owners thereof and own such shares free and clear of all liens and encumbrances; (4) that the assets and liabilities of the corporation, including contingent obligations, are fully and correctly reflected on an identified balance sheet (or that the net worth of the corporation is not less than x dollars); (5) that the operations and income of the corporation are accurately reflected on identified income statements; (6) that such statements have been prepared in accordance with generally accepted accounting principles consistently applied; (7) that all income, franchise and other taxes assessed against or payable by the corporation have been fully paid or provided for; (8) that there is no pending or threatened litigation involving the corporation (except as expressly set forth), and so on. Identification of the statements can be made by stating that they have been initialed by the parties or by annexing them to the contract.

You should also consider making these warranties conditions, as is generally done. Thus, you may wish to provide that if an independent audit by an accountant selected by your client discloses a net worth lower than a stated figure or lower than as represented and warranted by the sellers, or if there is a material adverse change in the affairs of the corporation prior to the closing date, or if certain other representations or warranties are not true as of the closing date, your client will not be obligated to go through with the transaction, and that in such event he shall be entitled to the return of any consideration paid by him under the contract plus reasonable expenses, including counsel fees, incurred by him, and that thereupon the parties shall be released of all further obligations.

You may also wish to provide for indemnification from the seller if subsequent events show that the stock had a lower value than was believed to be the case at the time of the closing. It is common practice to provide, for example, that the sellers will indemnify the buyers against undisclosed liabilities, including taxes, not reflected or reserved against in the financial statements relied upon.

You should provide that until the closing the seller will not enter into any new contracts or commitments (beyond a stated amount) or incur any liabilities other than in the usual and ordinary course of business. Also, it will not pay dividends or make any other distributions to stockholders, will not issue or redeem stock, and so on, so that on the closing your client will get the business intact and without being saddled with unexpected burdens.

The foregoing discussion assumes that you represent a buyer. Suppose you represent a seller who is selling certain property "as is," without any representations as to quality, value, etc. In such a case, you will wish to exclude any implied representations. Your contract should reflect that fact by an appropriate provision stating in substance that the seller has made no representations, or that all oral representations shall be deemed merged in the writing, or that the buyer has inspected the subject matter of the transaction and is not relying on any representations of the seller. In some situations it may be appropriate to provide that certain representations shall not survive the closing.

§ 16.5. Boilerplate.

There are many other examples of declarations. 5 HART & WILLIER, FORMS AND PROCEDURES UNDER THE U.C.C. § 21.00 contains an excellent "Basic Guide and Checklist for Drafting Contracts" that explains the substance of each declaration.

§ 16.5.1 Headings.

Regarding the substantive effect of headings, recall the example in § 7.7, Exercise 4. A separation agreement provided:

> *Cost of living increase.* "Base alimony" is defined as $100 per week. In the first calendar year, Husband shall pay Wife the base alimony. In each subsequent calendar year, Husband shall pay Wife the base alimony plus a cost of living increase. The cost of living increase is the base alimony multiplied by the inflation rate for the prior year as determined by the Department of Labor.

The Husband argued an interpretation that would give the wife no increase after the second year. The caption "Cost of living increase," however, weighs against that interpretation. Perhaps the declaration would have aided the husband.

The warranty case is *Colgan v. Agway, Inc.*, 150 Vt. 373, 553 A.2d 143 (1988).

§ 16.5.2. Choice of Law. Assume that the Company Master Terms agreement in Part III of this book is between a Company that is incorporated in Delaware and has its only office in New York. Yet section 9.4 provides:

> This Agreement shall for all purposes be governed by and interpreted in accordance with the laws of the Commonwealth of Virginia without reference to its conflicts of laws provisions.

Why did the drafter choose Virginia law? Hint: This is a software licensing agreement. I don't know for sure, but I bet the answer is that Virginia is, as of this date, one of only two states that has enacted UCITA (Maryland is the other one).

§ 16.5.4. Jury Trial. The court found that a jury trail was not effectively waived in *Kloss v. Edward D. Jones & Co.*, 2002 MT 129.

§ 16.5.5. Notice. The common law rules, such as they are, can be found in MERRILL ON NOTICE (1952).

Occasionally regulations will require a particular form of notice or provide a "safe harbor." Revised Article 9 §§ 9-613 and 9-614 contain safe harbor forms for the notice of the disposition of collateral.

The form that needs updating is discussed in detail in HOWARD DARMSTADTER, HEREOF, THEREOF, AND EVERYWHEREOF 109-113.

On whether to use paper or electronic notices, see ABIGAIL J. SELLER & RICHARD H.R. HARPER, THE MYTH OF THE PAPERLESS OFFICE. Paper has certain affordances not shared by electronic messages. A piece of paper sent to a large organization is likely to get routed to the correct person or department. But if the staff changes, will an email addressed to a particular person be effective? Even if it reaches that person, will the person send the notice to the right place for administration?

§ 16.7. Exercises.

1. The coal contract. This provision is very hard to read. Note that it is all one sentence. As with much poor writing, the primary problem seems to be poor thinking. If the drafter had thought more clearly about what was being said, he or she could have stated it more clearly. "Easy reading is the result of hard writing" is the predicate to "Easy writing is the result of hard thinking." It might be best to approach revision of this paragraph by thinking about what the drafter was trying to say and framing that content in the proper operative language.

This paragraph can be attacked on a word processor, on which we can pull it apart, reorganize it, and put it back together in a clearer structure. We can pull it apart as follows:

5.   **Failure of Seller to Deliver Coal of Prescribed Quality.**

I. It being essential that the coal covered by this contract shall meet the requirements of the Gas Company in the production of coke and gas of substantially the same structure and strength as that heretofore produced from coal furnished by the Coal Company to the Gas Company and that said coal shall contain on an average of thirty per cent (30%) of volatile matter,

II. it is understood that if the coal delivered hereunder, as sampled and analyzed dry basis, after being crushed ready to go to the ovens of the Gas Company, fails for thirty (30) consecutive days to maintain an average for said thirty (30) days sufficient to produce coke of such structure as that heretofore produced from coal furnished by said Coal Company, and

III. it is practicable for the Gas Company to remedy such deficiency in quality by the mixture of not exceeding thirty per cent (30%) of other coal with the coal furnished by the Coal Company, the Gas Company may to the extent necessary for the purpose of such mixture purchase other coal; and to the extent that other coal may be thus purchased, the amount which it shall be required to take of the Coal Company shall be reduced; but

IV. in the event it is impossible to remedy such deficiency by such mixture of not exceeding thirty per cent (30%) of other coal, the Gas Company shall be entitled to cancel this contract;

V. but the Coal Company shall not be responsible for any damages which the Gas Company may suffer from any such deficiency or from the cancellation of such contract; except as provided in Sections 8 and 9.

Working through the content, we see the following analytical and drafting issues:

I. This provision stresses the importance of the structure and strength of the coal. But what is the legal significance of the provision? It could be a *recital*, used to give weight to a provision treating breach of this particular provision as material. It could be a *warranty*, promising a certain level of performance in the future. It probably makes more sense to regard it as a warranty. Note carefully what is warranted: that the coal will produce

> coke and gas of substantially the same structure and strength as that heretofore produced from coal furnished by the Coal Company to the Gas Company and that said coal shall contain on an average of thirty per cent (30%) of volatile matter.

II. This provision states what constitutes a breach of the warranty. Note that there is a breach if the coal fails:

> to produce coke of such structure as that heretofore produced from coal furnished by said Coal Company

This language differs from the language of the warranty in (I) in at least three ways: gas is not mentioned, there is a remedy only for different *structure* but not different *strength*, and there is no mention of volatile matter. Recall the Golden Rule of Drafting:

Never change your language unless you wish to change your meaning, and always change your language if you wish to change your meaning.

In this case, because the drafter changed the language, it can be assumed that the stated remedy applies only to the stated violation and not to the other warranted terms. This problem could be resolved either by repeating the same words of by using *definition*, defining the term and then repeating the definition rather than the term.

III. This provision provides for a way for the Gas Company to remedy the breach. Is it discretionary or mandatory that it do this? The language used, *may*, suggests that it is discretionary.

This provision, as well as (IV) and (V) refer to "such deficiency." The drafter should always avoid *such* as archaic, but here it is also inexact. The phrase "such deficiency" assumes that the deficiency has been defined. Here we have another problem of definition: assuming the reader knows what a term refers to when it has not been defined. This problem can be easily corrected by defining *deficiency*.

IV. This provision states when the breach is material, allowing the Gas Company the remedy of canceling the contract. This remedy is permitted only when the remedy in III is "impossible," while III provides for when it is "practicable." It can be argued that these possibilities are not exhaustive; something can be impracticable, but not impossible, as attested by U.C.C. § 2-615. Again, the Golden Rule was violated. When creating a decision tree, make sure all possible branches are covered. Here, "practicable" and "impracticable" will cover the territory. Of course, the law is often indeterminate as to when performance is impracticable. The drafter may wish to leave this term vague or clarify it to prevent a future dispute.

V. This provision addresses whether in addition to termination as a remedy, the Gas Company can also recover damages.

Cleaned up according to this analysis, the paragraph might look like this:

> ### 5.   Failure of Seller to Deliver Coal of Prescribed Quality.
>
> The Coal Company shall deliver coal that meets the requirements of the Gas Company in the production of coke and gas of substantially the same structure and strength as that heretofore produced from coal furnished by the Coal Company to the Gas Company and that contains an average of thirty per cent (30%) of volatile matter ("the standard").
>
> If the coal delivered hereunder, as sampled and analyzed dry basis, after being crushed ready to go to the ovens of the Gas Company, fails to maintain the standard for thirty (30) consecutive days on an average for those thirty (30) days ("the deficiency"), then:
>
> if it is practicable for the Gas Company to remedy the deficiency by the mixture of not exceeding thirty per cent (30%) of other coal with the coal furnished by the Coal Company, the Gas Company may to the extent necessary for that purpose purchase other coal and accordingly reduce the amount which it is required to take from the Coal Company.
>
> if it is impracticable for the Gas Company to remedy the deficiency by the mixture of not exceeding thirty per cent (30%) of other coal, the Gas Company may cancel this contract.
>
> The Coal Company shall not be responsible for any damages the Gas Company may suffer from the deficiency or from the cancellation of the contract except as provided in Sections 8 and 9.

The passage was easily improved once we determined what the drafter meant to say, used concepts of legal analysis and drafting to state that meaning, and stated it with clarity.

2. Redrafting a form provision. This provision would be much more readable -- and therefore usable by the parties -- if it were written in an enumerated style. Without changing any substance, we can reform the text as follows:

Notices. All notices required or permitted under this Agreement will be in writing and will be deemed given:

(a) when delivered personally;

(b) when sent by confirmed telex or facsimile (followed by the actual document in air mail/air courier);

(c) three (3) days after having been sent by registered or certified mail, return receipt requested, postage prepaid (or six (6) days for international mail); or

(d) one (1) day after deposit with a commercial express courier specifying next day delivery (or two (2) days for international courier packages specifying 2-day delivery), with written verification of receipt.

All communications will be sent to the addresses set forth on the cover sheet of this Agreement or such other address as may be designated by a party by giving written notice to the other party pursuant to this paragraph.

The four methods by which a party can give notice now stand out and can be more readily used. It is also clear that the last sentence modifies all four methods and not just the one that preceded it. Now that we can more easily read it, we can examine the substance of this provision. This notice provision seems more modern, but it still does not contemplate electronic substitutes for writing, such as the "record" now found in UCC § 9-102(69). Perhaps this is intentional. Working with the client, the drafter can decide whether the office can accommodate an electronic notice or relies on paper.

Chapter 17
The Language of Drafting

§ 17.1. Introduction.

There are many sources for the language of drafting, including Kirk, *Legal Drafting: Curing Unexpressive Language*, 3 Tex. Tech L. Rev. 23 (1971); Kirk, *Legal Drafting: Some Elements of Technique*, 4 Tex. Tech L. Rev. 297 (1973); Lindey, *Let's Write Better Contracts*, 3 Prac. Law. 32 (Jan. 1957); Maxey, *Fundamentals of Draftsmanship--A Guide for the Apprentice in Preparing Agreements*, 51 Pa. B.A.Q. 47 (Jan. 1980).

More information about the rules stated in this chapter, including sources, may be found in the discussion of the Exercises in § 17.12.

§ 17.3. Use the active voice. Dickerson refers to the use of *shall* as a false imperative in FUNDAMENTALS OF LEGAL DRAFTING § 6.7 (2d ed.).

§ 17.4. Draft in gender-neutral language. Excellent advise on eliminating sexist language is found in Charrow & Erhardt, CLEAR AND EFFECTIVE LEGAL WRITING 44-45.

§ 17.6. Language of obligation, authorization, and condition. Dickerson's rules are found in FUNDAMENTALS OF LEGAL DRAFTING § 9.4.

The problem of the interpretation of *must* was nicely illustrated in *State v. Beanblossom*, 2002 MT 351. Defendant was convicted of violating MCA § 61-8-401. He alleged that the arresting officer failed to administer a breathalyzer test as required by MCA § 61-8-402(2). The statute provides in pertinent part:

61-8-402. Blood or breath tests for alcohol, drugs, or both.

(1) A person who operates or is in actual physical control of a vehicle upon ways of this state open to the public is considered to have given consent to a test or tests of the person's blood or breath for the purpose of determining any measured amount or detected presence of alcohol or drugs in the person's body.

(2) (a) The test or tests must be administered at the direction of a peace officer when:
    (i) the officer has reasonable grounds to believe that the person has been driving or has been in actual physical control of a vehicle upon ways of this state open to the public while under the influence of alcohol, drugs, or a combination of the two and the person has been placed under arrest for a violation of 61-8-401;

The majority found that the language, "The test or tests must be administered at the direction of a peace officer when ... the officer has reasonable grounds to believe that the person has been driving ... while under the influence of alcohol," merely mandates who may administer a breath test and does not require the administration of breath tests. This interpretation is buttressed by MCA § 61-8-401, which provide that evidence other than the breathalyzer test can be used to prove that the person was driving under the influence.

A dissenting judge disagreed:

> When construing a statute, this Court's role is to simply ascertain and declare what is in terms or in substance contained therein, not to put its own result-oriented spin on otherwise clear language. Every child understands the meaning of "must," however, if there's any question, Webster's Ninth New Collegiate Dictionary defines it in part as "b: be required by law, custom, or moral conscience . . . to be obliged to . . . ."

While that may be dictionary definition of *must*, the court should have cited THE STATE OF MONTANA BILL DRAFTING MANUAL, which provides at § 2-5:

> Use "shall" when imposing a duty on a person or entity (Active)

> Use "must" when the subject is a thing rather than a person or entity. (Passive)

§ 17.12. Exercises.

1. Editing.

a. A contract should speak in the present tense:

> Acceptance *occurs* when the Multiservice System performs without Major Failure over a period of thirty (30) days after delivery ("Acceptance Period"). Major Failure(s) *is* defined as follows:

b. This sentence should be in the active voice:

> Buyer shall pay all shipping, rigging, and other destination charges.

c. This sentence may prove the exception to the rule. The passive voice is acceptable where the emphasis is on the *result*, not on who has responsibility for doing it. Compare:

> Seller shall pay Broker a commission of 6% if a buyer is procured.

> Seller shall pay Broker a commission of 6% if the Broker procures a buyer.

The passive form is correct if the Broker receives the commission upon the result occurring even if the Broker does not bring about that result. See § 10.8, Exercise 5.

d. This looks right to me. Not everything has to be edited!

e. Use *shall* for obligations. Service Provider *shall* not distribute the Products to third parties, including resellers, other than for use in conjunction with Network Services.

f. Use *may* for discretion. Service Provider *may* determine its resale prices unilaterally.

g. This might be best in the present tense, as it is a representation of a present condition:

> Company represents that all Hardware delivered to Service Provider *is* free of liens and encumbrances.

However, it is most important for Service Provider to consider what the remedy is if the representation is not true.

h. *During the term of this Agreement* -- This strikes me as surplusage that can be deleted -- when else are we talking about?
and/or -- this one can be *or*
if it chooses -- this is also surplusage, since the operative verb was *may*
In the event that -- make it *if*
will -- make it *shall*
such delivery -- make it *the delivery*
orders ... will be shipped -- make it active -- *Company shall ship orders*
Company shall have the right -- Company *may*
such alternate order and delivery process is implemented by Company -- make it active --
> *Company implements*
Let's put this all together:
> Company may make the Products which are to be supplied outside the United States available for order in and delivery from an alternate central location or a Company affiliate. If Company does so, Service Provider shall order the Products according to the procedures set forth at the time the delivery becomes available. At that time, Company shall ship orders in conformance with Company's policies according to the availability and expedited leadtimes described in the procedures. Company may change delivery terms and include additional charges, if any, at the time Company implements the alternate order and delivery process.

i. An initial draft might look like this:

Purchaser shall:

(1)   submit to UM Productions signed copies of all Artist contracts negotiated by Purchaser in connection with the engagement not later than 21 days prior to performance.

(2)   submit to UM Productions Artist contract riders associated with this performance immediately upon return of this signed contract. Requirements contained in the Artist contract riders are subject to approval by UM Productions.

Once that parallel construction is clear, we could compact it further:

Purchaser shall submit to UM Productions:

(1)   signed copies of all Artist contracts negotiated by Purchaser in connection with the engagement not later than 21 days prior to performance.

(2)   Artist contract riders associated with this performance immediately upon return of this signed contract. Requirements contained in the Artist contract riders are subject to approval by UM Productions.

It seems odd that the contracts under (1) don't need to be submitted until 21 days prior to performance while the contract riders under (2) need to be returned immediately. This is a substantive question to put to the client, not to change in drafting.

2. The coal contract. The greatest weakness in this provision is the drafter's failure to state clearly the obligations of the parties. Use *shall* to mean "has a duty to" and *may* to mean "is authorized to." The first paragraph states an obligation. The obligation, however, is stated in the passive voice: "the coal to be delivered *shall* ...." Obviously it is not coal that is under an obligation, it is the Coal Company. This should be rewritten in the active voice: "The Coal Company shall deliver coal that ..."

What is the obligation? Note that it is written in three different ways: 1) the coal must closely approximate previous deliveries, 2) it must approximate the specified breakdown, and 3) it must meet certain absolutes. It would seem that these three standards are redundant and that any one would suffice, perhaps the third as presenting the clearest standard. The standard is written in the future ("will not"). This obligation can be rewritten in the present, for the contract should be seen as continually speaking.

To revise the next part of the provision, it will be helpful first to highlight all language of obligation, authorization, or condition precedent. This task can easily be accomplished with a search and replace feature on your word processor.

> 1 The Gas Company *may* test each carload of coal upon receipt at its plant, and if it *shall* not
> 2 meet the requirements specified herein, the Gas Company *shall* at once notify the Coal
> 3 Company of the fact and set said car aside as subject to the order of the Coal Company. If
> 4 the Coal Company *shall* question the correctness of such test, it *shall* have the right to have
> 5 such carload of coal tested by a competent chemist of its own selection. If the chemists of
> 6 the parties disagree in the results of their respective tests, then the parties *shall* select a third
> 7 chemist competent and disinterested in every way, who *shall* test said car of coal and
> 8 whose determination *shall* be final and binding on both parties.

Then, analyze each use of the relevant terms. The use of *may* in line 1 is correct, for the Gas Company does not have an obligation to test the coal. The *shall* in line 1 makes no sense, as the coal is under no obligation to meet requirements; make it *does*. The *shall* in line 2 does not express an obligation, it expresses a condition precedent; make it *must*. In line 4, the *shall* expresses the future; make it the present *questions*. In line 4, "shall have the right" is language of discretion; make it *may*. The *shall* in line 6 correctly expresses an obligation. The chemists are third parties who cannot be obligated by this agreement. The use of *shall* in lines 7 and 8 probably represents the future; make it *will*. The rewritten passage looks like this:

> The Gas Company *may* test each carload of coal upon receipt at its plant, and if it *does* not meet the requirements specified herein, the Gas Company *must* at once notify the Coal Company of the fact and set said car aside as subject to the order of the Coal Company. If the Coal Company *questions* the correctness of such test, it *may* have such carload of coal tested by a competent chemist of its own selection. If the chemists of the parties disagree in the results of their respective tests, then the parties shall select a third chemist competent and disinterested in every way, who *will* test said car of coal and whose determination *will* be final and binding on both parties.

Other problems with the provision include use of *herein*, which should be avoided as legalese. Is there any question which requirements are in issue? If there is, then use definition to make them clearer. The word *said* should also be avoided. Here, it is not even used properly, for the provision refers to the *said car* even though *car* was not previously used. The provision also violates the Golden Rule of drafting:

> Never change your language unless you wish to change your meaning, and always change your language if you wish to change your meaning.

In line 1, the provision refers to *each carload of coal*. In line 3, the language has become *said car*. In line 5 it is back to *such carload of coal* but in line 7 has reverted to *said car of coal*. It is bad enough that the drafter has used *said* and *such*. Merely archaic expression, however, has become imprecise expression when there is no referent for *said*, and potentially ambiguous expression when the language is changed. Consistent use of *the carload of coal* would have avoided any problem.

The last sentence is an anti-waiver provision. The Gas Company wants to make clear that its failure to act should not keep it from acting in the future. *Provided* is a weak term in drafting. Sometimes it refers to an exception, sometimes to a condition. Here, it seems to be neither. It is simply a declaration that can be stated as such.

The revised provision might look like this:

---

2.   **Quality.** The Coal Company shall deliver coal that upon fair tests, dry basis, in carload lots, shows not less than twenty-eight and one-half per cent (28 1/2%) volatile matter, not more than eight per cent (8%) ash, and not more than eight-tenths of one percent (.8 of 1%) sulphur in ash ("the requirements").

The Gas Company may test each carload of coal upon receipt at its plant, and if the carload does not meet the requirements, it shall at once notify the Coal Company of the fact and set the carload aside as subject to the order of the Coal Company.

If the Coal Company questions the correctness of the test, it may have the carload of coal tested by a competent chemist of its own selection. If the chemists of the parties disagree in the results of their respective tests, then the parties shall select a third chemist competent and disinterested in every way, who will test the carload of coal and whose determination will be final and binding on both parties.

The failure of the Gas Company at any time to make the tests and to make complaint does not estop it from thereafter making the tests and complaint of the quality of the coal, although there may be no apparent change in quality.

---

3. Shareholders' Agreement.

This is a generally well-drafted agreement. It presents an opportunity to improve a form through application of the principles discussed in this chapter as well as principles found in other chapters. Perhaps the process also illustrates H.G. Wells' dictum that "No passion in the world, no love or hate, is equal to the passion to alter someone else's draft."

1. The caption. See § 15.4.2. There can be no quarrel with the straightforward description of the instrument: it is a Shareholders' Agreement. The caption serves to identify the parties and their legal relationship (Corporation and Shareholder). The shorthand identifications are appropriate, for they are accurate and easy for the reader to follow.

2. The recitals (premises). See § 15.4.4. These recitals contain appropriate background information. The definition of *shares*, however, seems out of place in the recitals, for it is part of the substance of the agreement. The first recital appears to be also a representation. It recites the truism that the shareholders own all the shares of the corporation, but it may also represent

that all those who own shares signed the agreement. One wonders what would happen if a shareholder were overlooked or refused to sign. Could another shareholder argue that the agreement was not binding on him or her on the grounds that it did not bind all the shareholders? Perhaps a substantive provision is desirable stating: "This Agreement is effective only if signed by all Shareholders."

The recitals could be rewritten in a modern style as:

BACKGROUND

1. The Shareholders own all shares of the common stock of the Corporation.

2. The Shareholders and the Corporation desire to restrict the transferability of shares in order that the Corporation remain closely held and in order to avoid incompatible owners.

3. The Shareholders desire to create a market for the shares owned by deceased Shareholders.

The parties agree as follows:

---

3. Definitions. See §§ 7.5.1 and 15.4.5. See also DICKERSON, FUNDAMENTALS OF LEGAL DRAFTING ch. 7 (2d ed.); DICK, LEGAL DRAFTING 73-82 (2d ed.); CHILD, DRAFTING LEGAL DOCUMENTS ch. 10 (2d ed.). The agreement defines two terms: "shares" and "Subject Shares." It uses another, "Transferring Shareholder," without stating the term as a definition. After "shares" is defined, the term "shares of the Corporation is used. Since these are the only shares referred to in the agreement, the definition could have been expanded so that "shares" would always mean shares of the Corporation. "Subject Shares" is defined in Section 1.3; it could have been defined and used earlier. Similarly, "Transferring Shareholder" is referred to in Section 1.4; it could have been stated as a definition and referred to and used earlier. Defining "Transferring Shareholder" has the added benefit of making readily apparent the distinction between a Shareholder who desires to transfer and other Shareholders.

The agreement refers in Section 1.1 to a Shareholder who desires to "sell, transfer, assign, pledge, encumber, or otherwise dispose of or convey (by operation of law or otherwise)." This phrase is frequently, but not consistently, used. For example, the phrase "(by operation of law or otherwise)" is later dropped. And Section 1.5 refers only to "transfer." Changes in the use of a phrase are condemned in the drafting texts as "elegant variation." Recall the Golden Rule of drafting:

> Never change your language unless you wish to change your meaning, and always change your language if you wish to change your meaning.

It might be noted that some of the clause headings use *transfer* as shorthand. In order to clearly indicate that no change in meaning is intended, some drafters include a declaration providing: "The headings and subheadings of clauses contained in this Agreement are used for convenience and ease of reference and do not limit the scope or intent of the clause."

Definitions are appropriate for this agreement, for they are used to achieve clarity and consistency without repetition. The awkward insertion of the definitions could be eliminated by creating a new section of the agreement for definitions. While this section could be placed anywhere in the agreement, it would seem most logical at the beginning. For example:

DEFINITIONS

As used in the agreement:

1. *Shares* means common stock of the Corporation.

2. *Transfer* means to sell, transfer, assign, pledge, encumber or otherwise dispose of or convey (by operation of law or otherwise).

3. *Transferring Shareholder* means a Shareholder who desires to transfer shares.

4. *Subject Shares* means the shares the Transferring Shareholder desires to transfer.

After the defined words are inserted in the text, the agreement looks like this (the defined words are underlined for emphasis only):

AGREEMENT

1.   Restrictions on Transfer.

1.1   Offer of Sale. Except to the extent expressly permitted by this Agreement, Shareholders may not *transfer* any or all of the *shares* unless such shares are first offered to the Corporation and remaining Shareholders in accordance with Section 1 of this Agreement.

1.2   Time and Form of Offer. At least 90 days prior to the date the *Transferring Shareholder* desires to *transfer* any of the *shares*, the *Transferring Shareholder* must offer to sell such shares to the Corporation and remaining Shareholders in accordance with the terms of this Agreement. The offer to the Corporation and remaining Shareholders must (i) be written; (ii) be executed by the *Transferring Shareholder*; (iii) be subject to the terms of this Agreement; and (iv) be transmitted to the Secretary of the Corporation. At the same time such offer is transmitted the *Transferring Shareholder* shall transmit a written statement concerning the proposed *transfer*, which states (i) how the *Transferring Shareholder* proposes to *transfer* any or all of his shares; (ii) the number of shares to be transferred; (iii) the proposed transfer date; (iv) the name, business and residence address of the proposed transferee; (v) the price for which the shares are to be transferred, including the value of any property to be received for the shares (or the amount of the proposed pledge or encumbrance); and (vi) the terms of the proposed transfer (including time of payment of purchase price, interest rate on deferred payments, type of collateral offered to secure purchase price and value of collateral offered to secure purchase price). The Secretary of the Corporation shall, upon receipt of any such offer and statement, transmit a copy of the offer and statement to the remaining Shareholders.

1.3 Corporation's Option to Purchase. The Corporation shall have the option to purchase all of the *Subject Shares* for the purchase price per share set forth in Section 3.2 and upon the other terms provided in this Agreement. The Corporation must send a notice of its election to exercise such option to the *Transferring Shareholder* within 60 days of the Corporation's receipt of the offer described in Section 1.2. If the Corporation does not send such notice of its election within such 60 day period, the Corporation's option to purchase the *Subject Shares* will be considered to have expired. At the end of such 60 day period, the Secretary of the Corporation shall notify all Shareholders whether or not the Corporation elected to exercise the option described herein.

1.4 Shareholder's Option to Purchase. If the Corporation does not elect to exercise its option described in Section 1.3, any or all of the remaining Shareholders may elect to purchase all of the *Subject Shares* for the purchase price per share set forth in Section 3.2 and upon the other terms provided in this Agreement. All Shareholders wishing to purchase all of the *Subject Shares* must send written notice to the Corporation within 75 days of the date they received the offer described in Section 1.2. If more than one Shareholder proposes to purchase all the *Subject Shares*, then those Shareholders will be entitled to purchase the shares of the *Transferring Shareholder* on the basis of their pro rata ownership of the shares. The Secretary of the Corporation shall forthwith send to all Shareholders a notice of which Shareholders, if any, elect to purchase the *Subject Shares*, together with a statement as to the number of *Subject Shares* which each of the Shareholders shall purchase.

1.5 Intervening Death. If a *Transferring Shareholder* dies prior to the closing of the sale and purchase contemplated by this Section 1, the *Subject Shares* shall be the subject of sale and purchase under Section 2.

1.6 Effect of Non-Exercise of Options. If the Corporation and Shareholders do not exercise their purchase options, then the *Subject Shares* may be transferred at any time within 90 days after the expiration of the Shareholders' option to the transferee named in the offer required by Section 1.1, and upon the terms therein stated. In such case the *Subject Shares* shall be free forever of the terms of this Agreement.

1.7   Exceptions. Nothing herein shall prevent the inter vivos transfer by gift, sale or any other means of the stock of this Corporation to those person(s) or trust(s) listed on Exhibit A hereto or any descendants of these individuals listed on Exhibit A, but only if such individual(s) or trust(s), prior to transfer of the stock, agree to be bound by the terms of this Agreement with respect to such stock.

The drafter must use the defined term consistently, without elegant variation. For example, Section 1.7 uses the word *stock* instead of the previously defined *shares*. The drafter must also use the defined term precisely, inserting it only where the substance calls for it. For example, the following sentence appears in Section 1.4:

> If more than one Shareholder proposes to purchase all the *Subject Shares*, then those Shareholders will be entitled to purchase the shares of the *Transferring Shareholder* on the basis of their pro rata ownership of the shares.

The drafter must carefully distinguish between a *Shareholder* and a *Transferring Shareholder*, and between *shares* and *Subject Shares*, using the term intended in the substantive context. Because "Subject Shares" has been defined to mean the shares of the Transferring Shareholder, the provision can be simplified:

> If more than one Shareholder proposes to purchase all the *Subject Shares*, then those Shareholders will be entitled to purchase the *Subject Shares* on the basis of their pro rata ownership of the shares.

4. The active voice. The passive voice is occasionally used in this agreement.

Section 1.1 states:

> unless such shares are first offered to the Corporation and remaining Shareholders in accordance with Section One of this Agreement.

This can be rewritten in the active voice:

> unless the Shareholders first offer the shares to the Corporation and remaining Shareholders in accordance with Section One of this Agreement.

Section 1.6 states:

> then the Subject Shares may be transferred ....

This can be rewritten in the active voice:

> then the Transferring Shareholder may transfer the Subject Shares ....

Section 1.7 states:

> Nothing herein shall prevent the inter vivos transfer by gift, sale or any other means of the stock of this Corporation to those person(s) or trust(s) listed on Exhibit A hereto or any descendants of these individuals listed on Exhibit A, but only if such individual(s) or trust(s), prior to transfer of the stock, agree to be bound by the terms of this Agreement with respect to such stock.

First, let's use the definition of *shares*:

> Nothing herein shall prevent the inter vivos transfer by gift, sale or any other means of *shares* to those person(s) or trust(s) listed on Exhibit A hereto or any descendants of these individuals listed on Exhibit A, but only if such individual(s) or trust(s), prior to transfer of the *shares*, agree to be bound by the terms of this Agreement with respect to such *shares*.

There is also a variation here. The provision begins with "person(s) or trust(s)" but ends with "individual(s) or trust(s)." Either phrase is appropriate, but should be used consistently. The designation of plurals is awkward. Here, *any person or trust* would work, for *any* may be singular or plural.

The provision lacks an actor. It begins with *nothing* as a subject and ends with *such individual(s) or trust(s)* as a subject. Exhibit A pops up in the middle with no sense of who lists someone on Exhibit A. The subject of the sentence should be *shareholders*, for they are the ones whose behavior is governed by the agreement. The provision also uses *shall* for the future tense. Here the action of the Shareholder is authorized, so *may* would be appropriate. The provision might be rewritten as:

> A Shareholder may make an inter vivos transfer of shares by gift, sale or any other means to any person or trust the Shareholder has listed on Exhibit A hereto, or to descendants of any person listed on Exhibit A. The transfer is effective only if the person or trust, prior to transfer of the shares, agrees to be bound by the terms of this Agreement with respect to the shares.

An alternative would be:

> 1.7   Exceptions. An inter vivos transfer of shares by gift, sale or any other means to any person or trust, or to the descendants of any person, is not effective unless:
>
> > 1.7.1 The Shareholder has listed on Exhibit A hereto the name of the person or trust; and
> >
> > 1.7.2 The person or trust, prior to transfer of the shares, agrees to be bound by the terms of this Agreement with respect to the shares.

5. The present tense. The future is occasionally used in this agreement. This usage is confusing when *shall* also conveys an obligation. For example, Section 1.5 states:

> If a Transferring Shareholder dies prior to the closing of the sale and purchase contemplated by this Section 1, the Subject Shares *shall be* the subject of sale and purchase under Section 2.

Obviously, Subject Shares are not obligated to do anything. Here, the future is intended:

> If a Transferring Shareholder dies prior to the closing of the sale and purchase contemplated by this Section 1, the Subject Shares *will be* the subject of sale and purchase under Section 2.

Section 1.3 states:

> The Corporation shall have the option to purchase all of the Subject Shares ....

If the agreement is seen is continuously speaking, then the Corporation does not have this option at some future time; it has the option when the agreement speaks to that issue. This provision can be rewritten in the present tense:

> The Corporation has the option to purchase all of the Subject Shares ....

Section 1.3 also states:

> If the Corporation does not send such notice of its election within such 60 day period, the Corporation's option to purchase the Subject Shares will be considered to have expired.

This provision can be written in the present tense:

> If the Corporation does not send such notice of its election within such 60 day period, the Corporation's option to purchase the Subject Shares expires.

Section 1.6 states:

> In such case the Subject Shares shall be free forever of the terms of this Agreement.

This provision can be rewritten in the present tense:

> In such case the Subject Shares are free forever of the terms of this Agreement.

Section 1.4 states:

> If more than one Shareholder proposes to purchase all the Subject Shares, then those Shareholders *will be entitled* to purchase the Subject Shares on the basis of their pro rata ownership of the shares.

At the time the Shareholders propose to purchase, they are entitled. Therefore, this can be expressed in the present using language of authorization:

> If more than one Shareholder proposes to purchase all the Subject Shares, then those Shareholders *may* purchase the Subject Shares on the basis of their pro rata ownership of the shares.

Exceptions to the general rule that the agreement should be written in the present tense arise when the agreement refers to actions that have occurred prior to the time it speaks or that will occur after the time it speaks.

For example, there is an alternative way to state the sentence in Section 1.4 previously discussed. The event that triggers the result, *proposes to purchase*, is in the present tense. The triggering event can be stated as occurring prior to the resulting event by putting the triggering event in the past tense and the resulting event in the present:

> If more than one Shareholder *has proposed* to purchase all the Subject Shares, then those Shareholders *are entitled* to purchase the shares of the Transferring Shareholder on the basis of their pro rata ownership of the shares.

This solution is consistent with the principle that the agreement is continuously speaking, for in this sentence the agreement deals with an event which is in the past at the time it is addressed. See Kirk, *Legal Drafting: Some Elements of Technique*, 4 Tex. Tech L. Rev 297, 312-13 (1973).

Another example occurs in the next sentence:

> The Secretary of the Corporation *shall* forthwith *send* to all Shareholders a notice of which Shareholders, if any, elect to purchase the Subject Shares, together with a statement as to the number of Subject Shares which each of the Shareholders *shall purchase*.

"Shall send" is language of obligation, but "shall purchase" is a future action. In the latter case, "will purchase" is appropriate.

6. Language of obligation, authorization, and condition.

Section 1.1 states "Shareholders may not transfer any or all of the shares ...." This provision is particularly troublesome. It is the heart of the agreement and deserves attention. What is the intent of this provision? It seems to create a duty not to act. To determine whether there is a prohibition, it is helpful to ask whether there is any sanction for breach. If a shareholder did not comply with this provision, would the shareholder be liable for damages? This is a possibility. Therefore, the provision should tell shareholders more than that they are not authorized to do it, but that they have a duty not to do it. See Kirk, *supra*, 301-03. Using language of negative obligation, the provision might be drafted:

> Shareholders shall not transfer any or all of the shares ....

A simpler example occurs in Section 1.3:

> The Corporation has the option to purchase all of the Subject Shares ....

Because the Corporation has discretionary authority, the provision can be rewritten as:

> The Corporation *may* purchase all of the Subject Shares ....

7. Number.

As a general rule, the drafter should use the singular. DICKERSON, FUNDAMENTALS OF LEGAL DRAFTING § 6.5 (2d ed.). Consider this provision:

> Shareholders shall not transfer any or all of the shares.

In this provision there are two plurals: *Shareholders* and *shares*. The first may easily be rewritten in the singular as "a Shareholder shall not transfer ...." The second is more difficult. The difficulty is compounded by the use of the phrase "any or all." In this expression, three words do the work of one, for *any* can be used in its place. In fact, the phrase can often be dropped entirely. Without any change in meaning, the provision can be rewritten as:

> A Shareholder shall not transfer shares.

However, the technicality can be raised that a shareholder has not been prohibited from transferring a single share. This problem cannot be resolved by rewriting in the singular, for a provision stating "a Shareholder shall not transfer a share" does not prohibit the shareholder from transferring multiple shares. Some drafters resolve this problem through the awkward and imprecise devise of adding a saving clause such as that found in U.C.C. § 1-102(5):

> In this [agreement] unless the context otherwise requires
> (a) words in the singular number include the plural, and in the plural include the singular;
> (b) words of the masculine gender include the feminine and the neuter, and when the sense so indicates words of the neuter gender may refer to any gender.

In the Shareholders' Agreement there is an easier solution. *Shares* is a defined term in this agreement. The definition could clarify that the term incorporates both the singular and the plural. It has been defined to mean "common stock of the corporation." This definition seems to cover all bases. If we substitute "a Shareholder shall not transfer *common stock of the Corporation*," it seems that the Shareholder has been prohibited from transferring one or more than on shares. Therefore we can leave this second plural intact. See Kirk, *supra*, 313-15.

The drafter must be careful to use *any* only where *any or all* was used and not where *all* was intended. For example, Section 1.4 states:

> If the Corporation does not elect to exercise its option described in Section 1.3, *any or all* of the remaining Shareholders may elect to purchase *all* of the Subject Shares for the purchase price per share set forth in Section 3.2 and upon the other terms provided in this Agreement.

When *any or all* refers to the remaining Shareholders, the phrase may be replaced by *any*, but when *all* refers to the Subject Shares, *all* is intended.

8. Gender neutral language. Section 1.2 refers to:

> How the Transferring Shareholder proposes to transfer any or all of *his* shares ....

Because Transferring Shareholders may be of any gender, this can be rewritten in gender neutral language as:

> How the *Transferring Shareholder* proposes to *transfer* the shares ....

9. Words to avoid. A comprehensive list is found in the Appendix to BURNHAM, THE CONTRACT DRAFTING GUIDEBOOK (Michie, 1992). This agreement is thankfully free of most archaic terms. Here are a few that remain:

Such. Drafters frequently use *such* as a demonstrative adjective to refer to the last of a series. The problem is, of course, that *such* means no such thing. Usually, another adjective or an indefinite article can be used instead without any loss in clarity. Not only does *such* not mean "the last one," drafters sometimes carelessly use it to refer to one which is not the last. For clarity, the provision should be rewritten to make clear which previous reference is intended.

Section 1.3 states (as previously rewritten):

> If the Corporation does not send *such* notice of its election within *such* 60 day period, the Corporation's option to purchase the Subject Shares expires.

This agreement refers to only one notice and one 60 day period. The provision can be rewritten as:

> If the Corporation does not send *the* notice of its election within *the* 60 day period, the Corporation's option to purchase the Subject Shares expires.

If there were other notices or periods, the provision should be rewritten to refer to the specific notice or period.

Herein, therein, etc. Opinion differs on the use of these archaic words. They sound "legal" and to replace them may require using more words, as in "in this agreement" or "in that Section." One authority generally advises junking them while another approves of *hereinafter* ("A decent enough little word doing the job of six and deserving of promotion for its hard work") but not *aforesaid* ("A revolting word that has little to recommend it"). MELLINKOFF, LEGAL WRITING: SENSE AND NONSENSE (1982); WINCOR, CONTRACTS IN PLAIN ENGLISH 30 (1976). Perhaps this is a matter of taste, with my own taste favoring infrequent use.

Section 1.6 states:

> If the Corporation and Shareholders do not exercise their purchase options, then the Transferring Shareholder may transfer the Subject Shares at any time within 90 days after the expiration of the Shareholders' option to the transferee named in the *offer* required by Section 1.1, and upon the terms *therein* stated.

Therein is ambiguous: does it refer to the terms in the *offer* or in the *Section*? In fact, the transferee is named in the *statement*, not in the *offer*; the statement is probably intended.

    10. Architecture. A well-crafted agreement looks good. To construct an attractive agreement, as well as to avoid ambiguity, it may be helpful to tabulate large blocks of text that contain lists or conditions. See § 7.5.2. For example, Section 1.2 contains two lists that can be tabulated and renumbered consistently with the numbering of the sections. The Section states:

> The offer to the Corporation and remaining Shareholders must (i) be written; (ii) be executed by the Transferring Shareholder; (iii) be subject to the terms of this Agreement; and (iv) be transmitted to the Secretary of the Corporation. At the same time such offer is transmitted the Transferring Shareholder shall transmit a written statement concerning the proposed transfer, which states (i) how the Transferring Shareholder proposes to transfer any or all of his shares; (ii) the number of shares to be transferred; (iii) the proposed transfer date; (iv) the name, business and residence address of the proposed transferee; (v) the price for which the shares are to be transferred, including the value of any property to be received for the shares (or the amount of the proposed pledge or encumbrance); and (vi) the terms of the proposed transfer (including time of payment of purchase price, interest rate on deferred payments, type of collateral offered to secure purchase price and value of collateral offered to secure purchase price).

This provision can be broken down into lists as follows:

> The offer to the Corporation and remaining Shareholders must:
>
>   1.2.1 be written;
>   1.2.2 be executed by the Transferring Shareholder;
>   1.2.3 be subject to the terms of this Agreement; and
>   1.2.4 be transmitted to the Secretary of the Corporation.

> At the same time the Transferring Shareholder transmits the offer, the Transferring Shareholder shall transmit a written statement concerning the proposed transfer, which states:
>
> 1.2.5 how the Transferring Shareholder proposes to transfer any or all of his shares;
> 1.2.6 the number of shares to be transferred;
> 1.2.7 the proposed transfer date;
> 1.2.8 the name, business and residence address of the proposed transferee;
> 1.2.9 the price for which the shares are to be transferred, including the value of any property to be received for the shares (or the amount of the proposed pledge or encumbrance); and
> 1.2.10 the terms of the proposed transfer (including time of payment of purchase price, interest rate on deferred payments, type of collateral offered to secure purchase price and value of collateral offered to secure purchase price).

After the lists are broken down this way, it is readily apparent that they lack parallel structure. The first list is passive and refers to what the *offer* must do. The fact that it must be transmitted to the Secretary seems out of place, for this item does not describe the offer. The second list is active and refers to what the Transferring Shareholder must do. But the second list does not tell the actor where to send the list. The section does not say what happens if the offer or statement does not comply with the requirements of the lists. The lists can be rewritten as follows:

> To make an effective offer to the Corporation and remaining Shareholders, the Transferring Shareholder must transmit to the Secretary of the Corporation, in writing, the offer and a statement. The offer must:
>
> 1.2.1 be executed by the Transferring Shareholder; and
> 1.2.2 be subject to the terms of this Agreement.

This list is not clear. What does it mean that the offer must "be subject to the terms of this Agreement?" A shareholder looking to the agreement for guidance should be able to understand what is required. Perhaps this is meant: "The offer must state that it is subject to the terms of this Agreement." At this point, a list may not be necessary at all, for the requirements have been reduced to two. The provision can state:

> The offer must state that it is subject to the terms of this Agreement and must be executed by the Transferring Shareholder.

The items enumerated in the statement can be rewritten as follows:

> The statement must state:
>
> 1.2.1 how the Transferring Shareholder proposes to transfer the shares;
> 1.2.2 the number of shares to be transferred;
> 1.2.3 the proposed transfer date;
> 1.2.4 the name, business and residence address of the proposed transferee;
> 1.2.5 the price for which the shares are to be transferred, including the value of any property to be received for the shares (or the amount of the proposed pledge or encumbrance); and
> 1.2.6 the terms of the proposed transfer (including time of payment of purchase price, interest rate on deferred payments, type of collateral offered to secure purchase price and value of collateral offered to secure purchase price).

The sentence that follows can answer the alternative -- what happens if the offer or statement does not comply? -- if we replace the unclear "such offer and statement" with "an offer and statement that complies with this Section," leaving the implication that offers and statements that do not comply with the lists will not be forwarded. This implication has been strengthened by prefacing the list with the requirements for an *effective* offer. That sentence presently reads:

> The Secretary of the Corporation shall, upon receipt of any such offer and statement, transmit a copy of the offer and statement to the remaining Shareholders.

It can be rewritten as:

> The Secretary of the Corporation shall, upon receipt of an offer and statement that complies with this Section, transmit a copy of the offer and statement to the remaining Shareholders.

If we put the entire revised agreement together, it reads as follows:

SHAREHOLDERS' AGREEMENT [Excerpts]

This is an Agreement entered into on   , 20 , between ("Corporation"), and
(collectively referred to as the "Shareholders" and individually as the "Shareholder").

BACKGROUND

1. The Shareholders own all shares of the common stock of the Corporation.

2. The Shareholders and the Corporation desire to restrict the transferability of shares in order that the Corporation remain closely held and in order to avoid incompatible owners.

3. The Shareholders desire to create a market for the shares owned by deceased Shareholders.

DEFINITIONS

As used in the agreement:

1. *Shares* means common stock of the Corporation.

2. *Transfer* means to sell, transfer, assign, pledge, encumber or otherwise dispose of or convey (by operation of law or otherwise).

3. *Transferring Shareholder* means a Shareholder who desires to transfer shares.

4. *Subject Shares* means the shares the Transferring Shareholder desires to transfer.

The parties agree as follows:

AGREEMENT

1.   Restrictions on Transfer.

1.1   Offer of Sale. Except to the extent expressly permitted by this Agreement, a Shareholder shall not transfer shares unless the Shareholder first offers the shares to the Corporation and remaining Shareholders in accordance with Section 1 of this Agreement.

1.2   Time and Form of Offer. At least 90 days prior to the date the Transferring Shareholder desires to transfer any shares, the Transferring Shareholder must offer to sell the shares to the Corporation and remaining Shareholders in accordance with the terms of this Agreement. To make an effective offer to the Corporation and remaining Shareholders, the Transferring Shareholder must transmit to the Secretary of the Corporation, in writing, the offer and a statement. The offer must state that it is subject to the terms of this Agreement and must be executed by the Transferring Shareholder. The statement must state:

1.2.1 how the Transferring Shareholder proposes to transfer the shares;
1.2.2 the number of shares to be transferred;
1.2.3 the proposed transfer date;
1.2.4 the name, business and residence address of the proposed transferee;

1.2.5 the price for which the shares are to be transferred, including the value of any property to be received for the shares (or the amount of the proposed pledge or encumbrance); and

1.2.6 the terms of the proposed transfer (including time of payment of purchase price, interest rate on deferred payments, type of collateral offered to secure purchase price and value of collateral offered to secure purchase price).

The Secretary of the Corporation shall, upon receipt of an offer and statement that complies with this Section, transmit a copy of the offer and statement to the remaining Shareholders.

1.3 Corporation's Option to Purchase. The Corporation may purchase all of the Subject Shares for the purchase price per share set forth in Section 3.2 and upon the other terms provided in this Agreement. The Corporation must send a notice of its election to exercise the option to the Transferring Shareholder within 60 days of the Corporation's receipt of the offer described in Section 1.2. If the Corporation does not send notice of its election within the 60 day period, the Corporation's option to purchase the Subject Shares expires. At the end of the 60 day period, the Secretary of the Corporation shall notify all Shareholders whether or not the Corporation elected to exercise the option described in this Section.

1.4 Shareholder's Option to Purchase. If the Corporation does not elect to exercise its option described in Section 1.3, any of the remaining Shareholders may elect to purchase all of the Subject Shares for the purchase price per share set forth in Section 3.2 and upon the other terms provided in this Agreement. Shareholders wishing to purchase all of the Subject Shares must send written notice to the Corporation within 75 days of the date they received the offer described in Section 1.2. If more than one Shareholder proposes to purchase all the Subject Shares, then those Shareholders may purchase the Subject Shares on the basis of their pro rata ownership of shares. The Secretary of the Corporation shall forthwith send to all Shareholders a notice of which Shareholders, if any, elect to purchase the Subject Shares, together with a statement as to the number of Subject Shares which each of the Shareholders will purchase.

1.5 Intervening Death. If a Transferring Shareholder dies prior to the closing of the sale and purchase contemplated by this Section 1, the Subject Shares will be the subject of sale and purchase under Section 2.

1.6 Effect of Non-Exercise of Options. If the Corporation and Shareholders do not exercise their purchase options, then the Transferring Shareholder may transfer the Subject Shares at any time within 90 days after the expiration of the Shareholders' option to the transferee named in the statement required by Section 1.1, and upon the terms stated in the statement. In this case the Subject Shares are free forever of the terms of this Agreement.

1.7 Exceptions. A Shareholder may make an inter vivos transfer of shares by gift, sale or any other means to any person or trust the Shareholder has listed on Exhibit A of this Agreement, or to descendants of any person listed on Exhibit A. The transfer is effective only if the person or trust, prior to transfer of the shares, agrees to be bound by the terms of this Agreement with respect to the shares.

4. Additional exercise. If you did not revise it earlier, this would be an appropriate time to revise the Fair Clause in § 9.6, Exercise 3.

Chapter 18
Plain Language

§ 18.1. Introduction.

There are a number of fine sources on plain language, including:

FEDERAL TRADE COMMISSION, WRITING READABLE WARRANTIES. This pamphlet is available at the FTC web site, http://www.ftc.gov/bcp/conline/pubs/buspubs/writwarr.htm

FELSENFELD & SIEGEL, WRITING CONTRACTS IN PLAIN ENGLISH (West 1981). The authors were retained by Citibank to revise its consumer loan agreements.

MELLINKOFF, LEGAL WRITING: SENSE & NONSENSE (West 1982).

PRACTISING LAW INSTITUTE, DRAFTING DOCUMENTS IN PLAIN LANGUAGE (1981).

Symposium: Plain English in the Law, 62 Mich. B.J. 941-93 (Nov. 1983).

A number of states have enacted plain language laws, using either the New York model (Gen. Oblig. Law § 5-702), which contains subjective standards, or the Connecticut model (Conn. Gen. Stat. Ann. § 42-151), which provides detailed objective requirements based on the Flesch test. The National Association of Insurance Commissioners' Model Life and Health Insurance Policy Simplification Act and other developments in the insurance area are discussed in PLI, DRAFTING DOCUMENTS IN PLAIN LANGUAGE 131-68.

On plain language in government, see O'HAYRE, GOBBLEDYGOOK HAS GOTTA GO! (reprint 1980). Dickerson's frustrating attempts to persuade the federal government to improve its drafting process are chronicled in MATERIALS ON LEGAL DRAFTING ch. 14 (1981). The attack on gobbledygook has been continued by, among others, the League for Literate Laws. Its publication, the *Dispatch*, may be obtained through the web site at http://users.overland.net/~litlaw/

Carter's executive order is Exec. Order No. 12,044, 43 Fed. Reg. 12661 (1978). One of President Reagan's first acts was to revoke this order. Exec. Order No. 12,291, 46 Fed. Reg. 13193 (1981).

SECURITIES AND EXCHANGE COMMISSION, A PLAIN ENGLISH HANDBOOK: HOW TO CREATE CLEAR SEC DISCLOSURE DOCUMENTS, is available at http://www.sec.gov/pdf/handbook.pdf. Pages 75-83 have great examples of documents Before and After translation into plain language. The process of drafting a disclosure in plain language is discussed in HOWARD DARMSTADTER, HEREOF, THEREOF, AND EVERYWHEREOF 133-49.

An explanation of how forms came to be this way, with some modest suggestions for improvement, is found in Claire A. Hill, *Why Contracts Are Written in "Legalese,"* 77 Chicago-Kent L.R. 59 (2001).

§ 18.2. and § 18.3. Subjective and objective standards of plain language. Mellinkoff, Appendix I, compares and contrasts the different plain language statutes. The Flesch test is criticized (one might say demolished) in Gertrude Block, *Plain Language Laws: Promise v Performance*, 62 Mich. B.J. 950 (Nov. 1983). The New York plain language law is found at N.Y. Gen. Oblig. Law § 5-702 (McKinney 1989). The Model Health Insurance Policy Language Simplification Act is promulgated by the National Association of Insurance Commissioners.

§ 18.4. Plain language and substance. One commentator who analyzed consumer loan agreements found that many clauses are "misinformational:" they are legally unenforceable, but give the impression that the creditor has more rights or the debtor less rights than the law gives them. In comparing New York forms used prior to and subsequent to passage of the plain language law, he found that the types of clauses most often deleted were the misinformational ones. Examples of deleted clauses included those stating that the debtor waived the statute of limitations, that the creditor's opinion as to default was conclusive, and that the creditor had the right to modify the terms of any contract assigned as collateral. Davis, *Revamping Consumer-Credit Contract Law*, 68 Va. L. Rev. 1333, 1369-70 (1982).

On the Citibank agreement, see FELSENFELD & SIEGEL, DRAFTING IN PLAIN LANGUAGE (1981). The quote from FELSENFELD & SIEGEL is at 57.

§ 18.5. The process of plain language drafting.

On Step 1, Read for Style, lawyers sometimes fear that clients will not think they are getting their money's worth unless the agreement contains a sprinkling of legalese. DICK, LEGAL DRAFTING 6 (2d ed.) states:

> Modern clients reject this approach and are no longer impressed with the hocus-pocus. The general level of education is a good deal higher than it has been in the past and people feel that they are entitled to understand the contents of a document. They should be able to read a contract or a will and to have a reasonably good idea of whether their intentions are being carried out. It seems now that there is a certain resentment among clients if too much outdated drafting is used. Many lawyers are unaware how little impressed the average person is by abstract or obsolete words.

On Step 7, Make it look good, see FELKER ET AL., GUIDELINES FOR DOCUMENT DESIGNERS (1981); CHARROW & ERHARDT, CLEAR & EFFECTIVE LEGAL WRITING (1986); FELSENFELD & SIEGEL, WRITING CONTRACTS IN PLAIN ENGLISH (1981).

§ 18.7. Is plain language drafting worth the trouble? On the criticism of Plain English, see David Crump, *Against Plain English: The Case for a Functional Approach to Legal Document Preparation*, 33 Rutgers L.J. 713 (2002).

Charles M. Fox's eminently sensible book, WORKING WITH CONTRACTS, generally approves of forms that capture knowledge, but advises revision for the sake of clarity. For example, in § 4:2:3, he suggests that the provision:

> It is hereby agreed among the parties hereto that upon the occurrence of each and every failure by Borrower to comply and perform in all respects with the covenants, restrictions and limitations set forth in Article 6, Lender shall have and be entitled to exercise, and shall be deemed to have, and be entitled to exercise, the right and privilege to cause the termination and extinguishment of the Loan Commitments, provided, however, that delivery of prior notice of said termination and extinguishment be made to Borrower.

be rewritten as follows:

> If Borrower shall breach any covenant in Article 6, Lender may terminate the Loan Commitments upon notice to Borrower.

James C. Freund, in ANATOMY OF A MERGER (1975) has great advice in Chapter 5 on using forms and a marvelous spoof at 500-01 (footnotes omitted) on the situation where an associate failed to adapt the form to the client's needs:

Scene 3

"WHAT DO THEY TEACH THESE KIDS IN LAW SCHOOL NOWADAYS?"

[Prudent's office, one week later, Friday, December 27. PRUDENT is at his desk; PREPPIE enters.]

PRUDENT: Merry Christmas, Pete. Now look, fella, you'll just have to forgive my candor but time's short and this draft of the Proliferating-Suggestive agreement is an *inferior* job. The problem is that you *just didn't think!* You walked out of here, you went into the library, you grabbed that Screwloose binder off the shelf, you had a photocopy made of the final contract, and you marked it up for purposes of this draft. Don't you realize that the *final* Screwloose agreement represented the culmination of three weeks of intensive negotiation on the part of a pretty smart seller's attorney? You've got to start with the *first draft* of the Screwloose contract!

All that stuff in there about their right to defend lawsuits, and all those materiality and knowledge caveats–they have no place in the *first draft* of an agreement to buy Software;

plus which you forgot about the omission of the tax representation in Screwloose because of that special problem of theirs. And then you left in all that valuation language–average closing price, etc.–which was fine in the Screwloose deal where the pricing was based on the market price over a two-week period right before the closing, but is completely inapplicable here since we're using a fixed number of shares. You have to *think*, boy.

And then, in the one place you *did* a little thinking, Pete, it seems to me you went too far. I know it's *possible* that they'll repeal the Copyright Act some day, but it doesn't really rise to a level of probability sufficient to warrant three pages of provisions conditional upon that event.

Get this thing fixed up, and let me see it first thing Monday. We still have to clear it with the Proliferating people before we can send it out to Suggestive.

PREPPIE: Yes, *sir*.

PRUDENT: And by the way, the Suggestive people asked to see a copy of the agreement from one of our other deals. Send them the Softie contract; it was negotiated by a seller's lawyer who was poised to leave on a non-cancellable charter flight to St. Moritz and who managed to convince his client that I was a superbly evenhanded draftsman . . .

§ 18.8. Computer assistance. It is not so easy to find the readability scores in some word processing programs. Here is where it can be found in the following programs:

In Word Perfect 8.0:

> Tools/Grammatik/Options/Analysis/Readability
> You can then get the Flesch-Kincaid Grade Level.
> By clicking on "Basic Counts," you can get the information on Syllables per Word and Words per Sentence that you can use to compute the Flesch Reading Ease Score. See § 18.3 of DRAFTING CONTRACTS for the formula:
> 1. Multiply Words per Sentence by 1.015.
> 2. Multiply Syllables per Word by 84.6
> 3. Add (1) and (2) together and subtract that figure from 206.835
> The higher the score the better, with a score over 40 qualifying as plain language.

In Word Office 10 (2002):

> Tools/Spelling and Grammar/Options
> Make sure "Show Readability Statistics" is checked.
> You can then get the Flesch-Kincaid Grade Level and the Flesch Reading Ease Score
> when you have completed the grammar checking.

I have also found that each program may give a different score. In particular, check that the program is following the rule that "a unit of words ending with a period, semicolon, or colon ... shall be counted as a sentence." If it does not, you may have to manually enter periods instead of semicolons or colons for the purpose of obtaining a Flesch Reading Ease Score.

§ 18.10. Exercises.

1. Contract for deed.

a. Introduction. This language was the subject of litigation in *Glacier Campground v. Wild Rivers, Inc.*, 184 Mont. 543, 597 P.2d 689 (1978). The court wryly commented on the dangers of putting form language in contracts without reflection:

> Over fifty years ago, in *Wandell v. Johnson* (1924), 71 Mont. 73, 227 P. 58, this Court had occasion to interpret language of a contract for the sale and purchase of real estate, much of which language is substantially similar to that found in the default clause of the contract before us.
>
> ....
>
> The *Wandell* Court expressed its dissatisfaction with the language in the contract before it in these terms:
>
> "No one would have the temerity to suggest that the language of this agreement is either clear or explicit. Indeed, it would be difficult to conceive of a contract expressed more clumsily; hence we are required to resort to the usual rules of construction to ascertain, if possible, what the parties meant by the language they employed." 71 Mont. at 76, 227 P. at 60.
>
> We have essentially the same language before us now, more than fifty years later. It has not been made clear or explicit by the passage of time; it is still clumsy. Thus, we, too, must resort to the usual rules of construction to ascertain, if possible, what the parties meant by the language they employed.

b. Reading for style and precision.

This language is so muddled, that it would probably be best to revise for style before looking at the substance.

Junk antiques:	change to:
said	the
such	the
hereinafter	delete after clarifying

aforesaid   <u>delete</u> after clarifying
hereunto   <u>delete</u>

Note that the habitual use of these junk words can cause substantive problems. For example, "any of the payments" (line 2) must refer to the monthly installment payments. In line 4, however, "said payments" must refer not to the monthly payments in line two but to the entire principal balance.

Twofers: <u>change to</u>

due and payable (line 5)   due
reasonable and sufficient (lines 20-21)   reasonable
right, title, and interest (lines 25, 27)   <u>do not change</u>
by and between (line 19)   <u>see below</u>

One reason plain language has gained slow acceptance is that many lawyers think particular expressions are "terms of art" that cannot be tampered with. While there are a few terms of art, as Mellinkoff points out, most legal language is peculiar rather than precise. "Right, title, and interest" is one of those time-worn expressions that is readily identified by attorneys and judges. I would not change it.

Lack of parallel construction:

Recall the "golden rule" of drafting: Never change your language unless you wish to change your meaning. This passage is full of changes. For example:

"failure of Purchasers to make ... or to perform" (lines 1-2) becomes "failed to perform and make" (lines 10-11) and "failure to perform" (line 22).

"election" (line 5) becomes "option" (line 7).

"forfeited and determined" (line 7) becomes "cancel and determine" (line 9) and "acceleration" (lines 14, 17).

"Seller" sometimes becomes "Sellers."

Undefined terms:

"such default" (lines 12-13, 16) -- what is the default?
"said acceleration" (lines 14, 16-17) -- what is the acceleration?
"premises aforesaid" (line 32) -- in documents, *premises* means "that which precedes;" in property, "land and buildings." Which is intended here? Clarify.

Wordiness:

"covenants on their part hereby made and entered into" (lines 3 and 22-23) -- who else made promises the other party can enforce? Strike "on their part hereby made and entered into."

"It is mutually understood and agreed by and between the parties to this contract" (lines 19-20) -- that is what a contract is! Strike it.

"should the said" (line 12) -- make it *if*.

"In case of the failure of the said Purchasers" (line 1) -- this is passive. This provision concerns what happens if the Purchasers don't do something. Make them the subject: "If Purchasers fail".

With the garbage cleaned up, and the terms we want to clarify noted in italics, we get this:

DEFAULT. If Purchasers *fail to make* any payment of principal or interest, *or to perform* any covenant, then the whole of payments and interest shall, at the *election* of Sellers, become immediately due, except as *hereinafter* provided, and this Contract shall, at the *option* of Sellers, be *forfeited and determined* by giving Purchasers 60 days' notice, in writing, of the intention of Sellers to *cancel and determine* this Contract and any covenants and payments which Purchasers have *failed to perform and make*; and the time when and the place where payment can be made; if Purchasers make good the *default* within the 60-day period, then their rights under this Contract shall be fully reinstated, and *acceleration* of payments shall fail; however, should Purchasers fail to make good any *default* within the 60-day period, the *acceleration* shall be good and this Contract may be terminated by Sellers as *aforesaid*.

60 days is a reasonable notice to be given Purchasers in case of their *failure to perform* any covenant and shall be sufficient to cancel all obligations on the part of Sellers and fully invest them with all *right, title and interest* agreed to be conveyed, and Purchasers shall forfeit all payments made on this Contract, and all *right, title and interest* in all buildings, or other improvements shall be retained by Sellers, in full satisfaction and as a reasonable rental for the property and in liquidation of all their damages, and they shall have the right to take possession of the land and *premises*.

c. Identifying the problem.

Now we can take the contents apart in order to discover the substance of this provision:

DEFAULT. If Purchasers *fail to make* any payment of principal or interest, *or to perform* any covenant,

This is a triggering event. If Purchasers fail to do something, a certain result will occur.

> then the whole of payments and interest shall, at the *election* of Sellers, become immediately *due,*

This is the result. But note Sellers have the election to bring this result about or not.

> except as *hereinafter* provided,

This language creates an exception to the result. Because the exception is stated "hereinafter," we will have to stay tuned to see what the exception is.

> and this Contract shall, at the *option* of Sellers, be *forfeited and determined* by giving Purchasers 60 days' notice, in writing, of
> > the intention of Sellers to *cancel and determine* this Contract and
> > any covenants and payments which Purchasers have *failed to perform and make*;
> > > and
> > the time when and the place where payment can be made;

This is a notice provision. Apparently if Sellers elect to bring about the result, Sellers must give this notice. The provision should have been stated earlier, when the agreement explained how the result could be brought about.

> if Purchasers make good the *default* within the 60-day period, then their rights under this Contract shall be fully reinstated, and *acceleration* of payments shall fail;

This is apparently the exception, indicating when the result will not occur. It explains how Purchaser may cure the problem.

> however, should Purchasers fail to make good any *default* within the 60-day period, the *acceleration* shall be good and this Contract may be terminated by Sellers as *aforesaid.*

This indicates what happens if Purchaser does not cure the problem.

> 60 days is a reasonable and sufficient notice to be given Purchasers in case of their *failure to perform* any covenant and shall be sufficient to cancel all obligations on the part of Sellers and fully invest them with all *right, title and interest* agreed to be conveyed,

This provision appears to be inserted to indicate that Purchaser agrees 60 days is not an unconscionable period of time to cure the breach. It is probably meaningless, for a court would probably ignore agreement to an unconscionable provision. The provision also seems to be doing substantive work, however, for it states that "60 days" cancels Sellers' obligations and invests them with title. The provision must be stated more clearly, for "60 days" cannot do that.

> *and* Purchasers shall forfeit all payments made on this Contract,
> and all *right, title and interest* in all buildings, *or* other improvements shall be retained by Sellers, in full satisfaction and as a reasonable rental for the property and in liquidation of all their damages,

> and they shall have the right to take possession of the land and *premises*.

These are apparently all events that will occur if Purchasers do not cure the default. Note the problems here with *and* and *or*. The first *and* in this passage should be *or*. Sellers may recover the accelerated balance or take the property back; clearly Sellers may not do both. The first *or* should be an *and*; if Sellers takes back the buildings, Sellers would want to take back the improvements as well.

d. Outlining a solution.

We can now outline the provision:

Trigger:	If Purchasers defaults
Result:	Sellers may accelerate

> Sellers must give notice containing:
>> how Purchasers failed
>>
>> how Purchasers may perform
>>
>> 60 days notice

Result A:	If Purchasers cure, acceleration is voided
Result B:	If Purchasers do not cure, everything is due

> The 60 days is reasonable
>
> The contract is terminated
>
> Sellers forfeit all payments
>
> Sellers keep all buildings
>
> Sellers get possession

e. The section in plain language.

DEFAULT. If Purchasers fail to make any payment of principal or interest, or fail to perform any covenant, Sellers may elect to accelerate the entire principal balance.

To exercise this election, Sellers shall give Purchasers 60 days' notice, in writing, specifying:

1. the intention of Sellers to accelerate payments under the contract; and

2. the covenants or payments which Purchasers have failed to perform or make; and

3. the time when and the place where payment can be made.

If Purchasers cure the failure within the 60-day period, the acceleration of payments shall fail and their rights under the contract shall be fully reinstated.

If Purchasers do not cure the failure within the 60-day period, the acceleration shall be good and Sellers may:

1. bring an action to collect the amount due; or:

2. cancel the contract and

a. retain all the right, title and interest agreed to be conveyed; and

b. retain all payments made on the contract and all right, title and interest in all buildings and other improvements, as a reasonable rental for the property and in liquidation of all damages; and

c. have the right to take possession of the land and property.

f. Subjective and objective standards of plain language.

Under the objective test for plain language, the original draft had 5 sentences, 329 words, and 509 syllables.

$$
\begin{array}{lr}
\text{words/sentences x 1.015} & = 66.79 \\
\text{syllables/words x 84.6} & = \underline{130.89} \\
\text{total} & = 197.68 \\
206.835 - 196.50 & = 9.15
\end{array}
$$

In the revision, there are 10 sentences, 185 words, and 290 syllables.

words/sentences x 1.015   = 18.77
syllables/words x 84.6   = 132.62
total   = 151.39
206.835 - 151.39   = 55.45

Note that the score for syllables per word is no better in the revision than in the original. The score was improved by increasing the number of sentences and by decreasing the sentence length.

2. Lease.

The provision as originally drafted:

DAMAGE TO PREMISES. The LESSEE further covenants and agrees to take good care of the premises hereby leased, and the fixtures of same, and commit and suffer no waste of any kind therein; that LESSEE shall pay for all repairs required to be made to the floors, walls, ceilings, paint, plastering, plumbing work, pipes, fixtures or any other part of leased premises, whenever damage or injury to same shall have resulted from any misuse or neglect on the part of Lessee or members of family, guests, or employees of LESSEE; that Leased premises shall be used only as a family dwelling. LESSEE shall not perform any maintenance, adjustment, or repair on heating or air conditioning, and plumbing, stoves, refrigerators or other appliances or equipment of LESSOR but said maintenance, adjustment or repair shall be done only by LESSOR'S employees, contractors or agents, and LESSEE agrees to notify LESSOR accurately and promptly of any problem arising from such equipment, its location and cause, if possible; Lessee agrees to allow repairmen to enter leased premises to remedy said problems; and LESSOR shall not be liable for damages due to the temporary breakdown or discontinuance of same. Locks may not be changed, nor any additional locks put on any doors without written permission of the LESSOR. LESSOR is not responsible to provide access to the premises in the event LESSEE accidently or otherwise locks himself/herself out of the premises. LESSEE is responsible for the cost of lost keys or the replacement of locks. Nails, tacks, brads, screws, stick-on picture hangers or tape shall not be used on the woodwork, walls, floors or ceilings of said premises. It is permissible to use small nails that are specifically designed for hanging pictures on the walls. The use of gasoline and/or similar combustibles for cleaning or for other purposes is strictly prohibited. LESSEE shall so use the premises so as not to cause any increase in the insurance rates. LESSOR shall not be responsible or liable to the LESSEE, or any other person claiming by or through LESSEE, for any injury or damage resulting from bursting, stoppage or leaking of plumbing, gas, water, sewer, or other pipes; nor for any damage or injury arising from the acts or neglect of co-tenants, their families or guests or any owners or occupants of adjacent or contiguous property; nor for any damage or injury caused by fire, water damage, snow, ice, wind or any other natural calamity. No outside or attic aerials or antennas will be permitted on the building or premises. LESSOR and/or his representatives may enter the leased premises at any reasonable time to make such repairs and alterations as may be deemed necessary by LESSOR for the safety and preservation of the premises, or exhibiting the leased premises for sale, lease or mortgage financing.

The provision unchanged but broken down into blocks of text which are numbered for convenience:

DAMAGE TO PREMISES

The LESSEE further covenants and agrees to

1. take good care of the premises hereby leased, and the fixtures of same, and commit and suffer no waste of any kind therein;

2. that LESSEE shall pay for all repairs required to be made to the floors, walls, ceilings, paint, plastering, plumbing work, pipes, fixtures or any other part of leased premises, whenever damage or injury to same shall have resulted from any misuse or neglect on the part of Lessee or members of family, guests, or employees of LESSEE;

3. that Leased premises shall be used only as a family dwelling.

4. LESSEE shall not perform any maintenance, adjustment, or repair on heating or air conditioning, and plumbing, stoves, refrigerators or other appliances or equipment of LESSOR but said maintenance, adjustment or repair shall be done only by LESSOR'S employees, contractors or agents, and LESSEE agrees to notify LESSOR accurately and promptly of any problem arising from such equipment, its location and cause, if possible; Lessee agrees to allow repairmen to enter leased premises to remedy said problems; and LESSOR shall not be liable for damages due to the temporary breakdown or discontinuance of same.

5. Locks may not be changed, nor any additional locks put on any doors without written permission of the LESSOR. LESSOR is not responsible to provide access to the premises in the event LESSEE accidently or otherwise locks himself/herself out of the premises. LESSEE is responsible for the cost of lost keys or the replacement of locks.

6. Nails, tacks, brads, screws, stick-on picture hangers or tape shall not be used on the woodwork, walls, floors or ceilings of said premises. It is permissible to use small nails that are specifically designed for hanging pictures on the walls.

7. The use of gasoline and/or similar combustibles for cleaning or for other purposes is strictly prohibited.

8. LESSEE shall so use the premises so as not to cause any increase in the insurance rates.

9. LESSOR shall not be responsible or liable to the LESSEE, or any other person claiming by or through LESSEE, for any injury or damage resulting from bursting, stoppage or leaking of plumbing, gas, water, sewer, or other pipes; nor for any damage or injury arising from the acts or neglect of co-tenants, their families or guests or any owners or occupants of adjacent or contiguous property; nor for any damage or injury caused by fire, water damage, snow, ice, wind or any other natural calamity.

10. No outside or attic aerials or antennas will be permitted on the building or premises.

11. LESSOR and/or his representatives may enter the leased premises at any reasonable time to make such repairs and alterations as may be deemed necessary by LESSOR for the safety and preservation of the premises, or exhibiting the leased premises for sale, lease or mortgage financing.

Let us now redraft some of the blocks of text using the techniques discussed in Chapter 17, *The Language of Drafting*, and Chapter 18, *Plain Language*:

1. take good care of the premises hereby leased, and the fixtures of same, and commit and suffer no waste of any kind therein;

Division into sections and language of obligation. We will break down the one long provision beginning "The Lessee further covenants and agrees to" into individual provisions, each beginning with language of obligation: *Lessee shall*.

Archaic language. *Hereby*, *same*, and *therein* can all be deleted. Is there really any question about which premises we are referring to?

Twofers. We might wonder whether there is any distinction between the *premises* and the *fixtures*. If there is a distinction, we could probably eliminate it by definition, defining the premises to include the fixtures. What about "commit and suffer?" Perhaps there is a distinction in that waste could be committed by others on the premises. Perhaps we could embrace both terms with a word such as *allow*.

Redundancy. What does "of any kind" add to "no waste?" Perhaps we can delete it.

We might end up with something like this:

1. LESSEE shall take good care of the premises and allow no waste.

Let us examine the second provision:

2. that LESSEE shall pay for all repairs required to be made to the floors, walls, ceilings, paint, plastering, plumbing work, pipes, fixtures or any other part of leased premises, whenever damage or injury to same shall have resulted from any misuse or neglect on the part of Lessee or members of family, guests, or employees of LESSEE;

General and particular. What does the listing of particulars add to the general "any part of leased premises?"

Twofers. What is the difference between *damage* and *injury* in the context of physical damage to the premises?

Redundancy. Why *leased premises* and not just *premises*?

Legalese. Why *to same*? Is there any doubt what damage we are talking about?

Present tense. *Shall have resulted*? Give me a break. Make it the present, *results*.

We might end up with something like this:

2. LESSEE shall pay for all repairs required to be made to any part of the premises, whenever the damage results from any misuse or neglect on the part of LESSEE or members of family, guests, or employees of LESSEE.

Let us examine one more:

3. that Leased premises shall be used only as a family dwelling.

Active voice. Who has the obligation? Certainly not the *premises*. Make *Lessee* the subject:

3. LESSEE shall use the premises only as a family dwelling.

After working through each of these provisions, we should reorganize them to conform to the architecture of the agreement. Those that have nothing to do with "Damage to Premises" should be moved to other locations in the agreement.

Here is one example of the redrafted text:

1. LESSEE shall take good care of the premises and the fixtures, and commit and suffer no waste of any kind.

2. LESSEE shall pay for all repairs required to be made to any part of the premises, whenever the damage results from any misuse or neglect on the part of LESSEE or members of family, guests, or employees of LESSEE.

3. LESSEE shall use the premises only as a family dwelling.

4. LESSEE shall not perform any maintenance, adjustment, or repair to LESSOR's appliances or equipment. If possible, LESSEE shall notify LESSOR accurately and promptly of any problem with appliances or equipment. LESSOR shall perform the maintenance, adjustment or repair. LESSEE shall allow repairmen to enter the premises to remedy the problems. LESSOR is not liable for damages due to the temporary breakdown or discontinuance of appliances or equipment.

5. LESSEE shall not change locks nor install additional locks on any doors. LESSOR is not responsible to provide access to the premises if LESSEE locks himself/herself out of the premises. LESSEE shall pay for the cost of lost keys and the replacement of locks.

6. LESSEE shall not use nails, tacks, brads, screws, stick-on picture hangers or tape on the woodwork, walls, floors or ceilings of the premises. LESSEE may use small nails that are specifically designed for hanging pictures on the walls.

7. LESSEE shall not use gasoline or similar combustibles for cleaning or for other purposes.

8. LESSEE shall not use the premises so as to cause any increase in the insurance rates.

9. LESSOR is not liable to LESSEE, or any other person claiming by or through LESSEE, for any injury or damage resulting from:

> bursting, stoppage or leaking of plumbing, gas, water, sewer, or other pipes;

> the acts or neglect of co-tenants, their families or guests or any owners or occupants of adjacent or contiguous property; or

> fire, water damage, snow, ice, wind or any other natural calamity.

10. LESSEE shall not attach an outside or attic aerial or antenna on the building or premises.

11. LESSOR or LESSOR's representatives may enter the premises at any reasonable time to make such repairs or alterations as LESSOR considers necessary for the safety or preservation of the premises, or to exhibit the premises for sale, lease or mortgage financing.

We might also want to consider whether to replace LESSOR and LESSEE with names that are easier to tell apart, such as LANDLORD and TENANT.

3. The Owner Operator Lease Agreement. Here is my next to final draft:

OWNER OPERATOR LEASE AGREEMENT

AGREEMENT between _____ Trucking, a corporation, ("CARRIER") and

_____

(Name)   (Address)   (City)   (State)   (Zip)
("CONTRACTOR").

1. DEFINITIONS

1.1. "Equipment" means the motor carrier equipment described in Appendix A, which is attached to and made a part of this Agreement.

1.2. "Rules and regulations" means the applicable requirements of the Interstate Commerce Commission, the U.S. Department of Transportation, or the various states in the United States and provinces in Canada.

2. BACKGROUND

2.1. CARRIER is a for-hire motor carrier that transports goods in the United States and Canada. CARRIER holds operating authority from the Interstate Commerce Commission and from one or more state and Canadian provincial agencies responsible for the regulation of motor carrier operations.

2.2. CONTRACTOR is the owner of the equipment. As an independent contractor, CONTRACTOR operates the equipment or employs drivers to operate it.

2.3. The parties desire that CONTRACTOR lease to CARRIER the equipment, furnished with driver, under the terms of this Agreement.

IT IS AGREED:

3. TERM AND EQUIPMENT

3.1. <u>Term.</u> CONTRACTOR leases the equipment to CARRIER for the period from _____ to _____.

3.2. <u>Contractor's Legal Title.</u> CONTRACTOR represents that it holds full legal title to the equipment or that it has the legal right to exercise full control over the equipment. CONTRACTOR shall furnish CARRIER with all the information and documents of title or registration that will enable CARRIER to identify the equipment.

3.3. <u>Possession and Use of Equipment.</u> For the term of this Agreement, possession and use of the equipment is entirely vested in CARRIER. CARRIER's possession and use is good against all the world, including CONTRACTOR.

3.4. <u>Condition of Equipment.</u> CONTRACTOR warrants that the equipment is complete with all required accessories, and is in good, safe, and efficient operating condition and appearance. CONTRACTOR shall maintain the equipment in good, safe, and efficient operating condition and appearance at no expense to CARRIER. CONTRACTOR may choose where any necessary repair or maintenance is done and who does it.

3.5. <u>Inspection.</u> CONTRACTOR shall submit the equipment for CARRIER's inspection at the time CARRIER takes possession and at other times as required by rules and regulations. Before taking possession of the equipment, CARRIER shall inspect it to make certain that it complies in every respect with all rules and regulations. If the original inspection reveals that the equipment does not comply with any rule or regulation, CONTRACTOR must make it comply. If CONTRACTOR does not do so, this Agreement immediately terminates.

4. PAYMENT AND RESERVE FUND

4.1. <u>Payment.</u> CARRIER shall pay CONTRACTOR for each trip CONTRACTOR makes under this Agreement according to the Schedule of Compensation in Appendix B, which is attached to and made a part of this Agreement. To modify Appendix B, the parties must either (a) note the modification on Appendix B and initial it, or (b) substitute a new Appendix B and sign and date it.

CARRIER shall pay CONTRACTOR for completed use of the equipment within fifteen (15) business days (or sooner if CARRIER desires) after CONTRACTOR turns in to CARRIER the properly prepared and executed paperwork. The paperwork includes signed delivery tickets, bills of lading, driver's logs, and other trip documents CARRIER needs to secure payment from shippers. CARRIER may require CONTRACTOR to furnish additional trip documents, but this is not necessary for payment.

At the time of payment, CONTRACTOR may inspect a copy of the rated freight bill. Exception: CARRIER may delete the names of shippers and consignees in cases where payments are based on a percentage of gross freight revenue for a shipment. CONTRACTOR may always examine copies of CARRIER's applicable tariff.

4.2. <u>Payments to CONTRACTOR.</u> If CARRIER's consignors or consignees pay CONTRACTOR any amount for transportation or other charges under CARRIER's shipping or billing documents, CONTRACTOR shall collect and promptly remit that amount to CARRIER. CONTRACTOR is liable for any amount that it fails to collect when the amount is specified on the shipping or billing documents.

4.3. <u>Reserve.</u> On signing this Agreement, CONTRACTOR shall deposit with CARRIER _____ Dollars ($_____) to establish a reserve fund. CARRIER may withhold _____ Dollars ($_____) from each payment until the reserve amount equals _____ Dollars ($_____). CARRIER may continue to withhold money from time to time to maintain the reserve fund at that level. CARRIER may apply the reserve funds at CARRIER's discretion to cover CONTRACTOR's obligations arising out of this Agreement. CARRIER may also use the reserve funds to cover license fees and to reimburse CARRIER for losses and expenses caused by CONTRACTOR's failure to comply with Paragraph 9.2.

CARRIER shall account to CONTRACTOR for any transaction involving the reserve fund, either by (a) clearly showing each transaction on individual settlement sheets or by (b) providing a monthly accounting of any transactions involving the fund. CONTRACTOR may demand an accounting of transactions involving the fund at any time.

CARRIER shall pay interest on the reserve fund on at least a quarterly basis. To calculate the balance of the fund on which interest is paid, CARRIER may deduct a sum equal to the average advance made to CONTRACTOR during the period of time for which interest is paid. The interest rate will be established on the date the interest period begins and will equal the average yield or equivalent coupon issue yield on 91-day, 13-week Treasury bills as established in the weekly auction by the Department of the Treasury.

When this Agreement terminates, if and only if CONTRACTOR has complied with the terms of paragraphs 6.2 and 9.2, CARRIER shall refund to CONTRACTOR the remaining balance of the reserve fund and any accrued interest. CARRIER shall also furnish CONTRACTOR with a final accounting specifying all deductions made. CARRIER shall refund the remaining balance no later than forty-five (45) days from the date this Agreement terminates.

5. COSTS AND EXPENSES

5.1. <u>Equipment Loss or Damage.</u> CARRIER is not liable to CONTRACTOR for loss of the equipment or damage to it. Exception: CARRIER is liable if the loss or damage is caused by the intentional or negligent act of CARRIER's employees while acting within the scope of their employment. However, CARRIER is liable only to the extent CONTRACTOR is not compensated for the loss or damage by insurance or otherwise.

5.2. <u>Cargo Claims.</u> CONTRACTOR shall deliver cargo that is dispatched and loaded on the vehicles to the consignees(s) with reasonable diligence, speed and care. CONTRACTOR shall be responsible for the first $ _____ of any cargo claim, as well as any expense incurred by CARRIER in the settlement and investigation of a claim. CONTRACTOR shall also be liable for any cargo claim recovery in excess of CARRIER's cargo insurance policy limits.

CARRIER may deduct from CONTRACTOR's payment any claims for damage or shortage of cargo or any property damage to CARRIER's equipment. CARRIER shall provide CONTRACTOR with a written explanation and itemization for any deduction 15 days before it makes the deduction.

5.3. <u>Personal Injury or Death.</u> CONTRACTOR assumes the risk of any personal injury or death that results from performance of this Agreement. CONTRACTOR assumes the risk whether the personal injury or death is caused by CONTRACTOR's own equipment, by equipment furnished by CARRIER, or by the employees of CONTRACTOR or CARRIER. Exception: CONTRACTOR does not assume the risk if the personal injury or death is caused by the intentional or negligent acts of CARRIER's employees while acting within the scope of their employment.

5.4. <u>Expenses Caused by CONTRACTOR.</u> If CARRIER incurs any liability, expense, cost or attorneys' fees because of what CONTRACTOR does or does not do under this Agreement, CONTRACTOR shall indemnify and save harmless CARRIER from the liability, expense, cost, or attorneys' fees.

5.5. <u>Trailer and Accessorial Equipment.</u> If CARRIER supplies the trailer equipment and the accessorial equipment ("the trailer" and "the accessories" in this provision) to CONTRACTOR, CARRIER shall maintain the trailer and pay the cost of fuel for the accessories. CONTRACTOR is liable for loss of or damage to the trailer or accessories while they are in CONTRACTOR'S possession or custody. Exception: CONTRACTOR is not liable for loss or damage for which CARRIER is compensated by insurance or otherwise. However, CONTRACTOR shall indemnify CARRIER for any loss CARRIER suffers even though it is covered by insurance.

If CONTRACTOR supplies the trailer and the accessories, then CONTRACTOR shall maintain the trailer and pay the cost of fuel for the accessories. CONTRACTOR shall also be responsible for insurance on the trailer and the accessories according to Paragraph 5.7.

[signature lines omitted]

This draft accomplished most plain language goals, but to improve readability even more, I did one more draft using "we" and "you" instead of "carrier" and "contractor." That draft looks like this:

OWNER OPERATOR LEASE AGREEMENT

AGREEMENT between _____ Trucking, a corporation, ("CARRIER") and

_____
(Name)   (Address)   (City)   (State)   (Zip)
("CONTRACTOR").

1. DEFINITIONS

1.1. "Equipment" means the motor carrier equipment described in Appendix A, which is attached to and made a part of this Agreement.

1.2. "Rules and regulations" means the applicable requirements of the Interstate Commerce Commission, the U.S. Department of Transportation, or the various states in the United States and provinces in Canada.

1.3. "We," "us," and "our" means the CARRIER, _____ Trucking.

1.4. "You" and "your" means the CONTRACTOR.

2. BACKGROUND

2.1. We are a for-hire motor carrier that transports goods in the United States and Canada. We hold operating authority from the Interstate Commerce Commission and from one or more state and Canadian provincial agencies responsible for the regulation of motor carrier operations.

2.2. You are the owner of the equipment. As an independent contractor, you operate the equipment or employ drivers to operate it.

2.3. The parties desire that you lease to us the equipment, furnished with driver, under the terms of this Agreement.

IT IS AGREED:

3. TERM AND EQUIPMENT

3.1. <u>Term.</u> You lease the equipment to us for the period from _____ to _____.

3.2. <u>Contractor's Legal Title.</u> You represent that you hold full legal title to the equipment or that you have the legal right to exercise full control over the equipment. You shall furnish us with all the information and documents of title or registration that will enable us to identify the equipment.

3.3. <u>Possession and Use of Equipment.</u> For the term of this Agreement, possession and use of the equipment is entirely vested in us. Our possession and use is good against all the world, including you.

3.4. <u>Condition of Equipment.</u> You warrant that the equipment is complete with all required accessories, and is in good, safe, and efficient operating condition and appearance. You shall maintain the equipment in good, safe, and efficient operating condition and appearance at no expense to us. You may choose where any necessary repair or maintenance is done and who does it.

3.5. <u>Inspection.</u> You shall submit the equipment for our inspection at the time we take possession and at other times as required by rules and regulations. Before taking possession of the equipment, we shall inspect it to make certain that it complies in every respect with all rules and regulations. If the original inspection reveals that the equipment does not comply with any rule or regulation, you must make it comply. If you do not do so, this Agreement immediately terminates.

4. PAYMENT AND RESERVE FUND

4.1. <u>Payment.</u> We shall pay you for each trip you make under this Agreement according to the Schedule of Compensation in Appendix B, which is attached to and made a part of this Agreement. To modify Appendix B, the parties must either (a) note the modification on Appendix B and initial it, or (b) substitute a new Appendix B and sign and date it.

We shall pay you for completed use of the equipment within fifteen (15) business days (or sooner if we desire) after you turn in to us the properly prepared and executed paperwork. The paperwork includes signed delivery tickets, bills of lading, driver's logs, and other trip documents we need to secure payment from shippers. We may require you to furnish additional trip documents, but this is not necessary for payment.

At the time of payment, you may inspect a copy of the rated freight bill. Exception: we may delete the names of shippers and consignees in cases where payments are based on a percentage of gross freight revenue for a shipment. You may always examine copies of our applicable tariff.

4.2. <u>Payments to CONTRACTOR.</u> If our consignors or consignees pay you any amount for transportation or other charges under our shipping or billing documents, you shall collect and promptly remit that amount to us. You are liable for any amount that you fail to collect when the amount is specified on the shipping or billing documents.

4.3. <u>Reserve.</u> On signing this Agreement, you shall deposit with us

_____

Dollars ($_____) to establish a reserve fund. We may withhold _____
Dollars ($_____) from each payment until the reserve amount equals
_____ Dollars ($_____). We may continue to withhold money from time to time to maintain the reserve fund at that level. We may apply the reserve funds at our discretion to cover your obligations arising out of this Agreement. We may also use the reserve funds to cover license fees and to reimburse us for losses and expenses caused by your failure to comply with Paragraph 9.2.

We shall account to you for any transaction involving the reserve fund, either by (a) clearly showing each transaction on individual settlement sheets or by (b) providing a monthly accounting of any transactions involving the fund. You may demand an accounting of transactions involving the fund at any time.

We shall pay interest on the reserve fund on at least a quarterly basis. To calculate the balance of the fund on which interest is paid, we may deduct a sum equal to the average advance made to you during the period of time for which interest is paid. The interest rate will be established on the date the interest period begins and will equal the average yield or equivalent coupon issue yield on 91-day, 13-week Treasury bills as established in the weekly auction by the Department of the Treasury.

When this Agreement terminates, if and only if you have complied with the terms of paragraphs 6.2 and 9.2, we shall refund to you the remaining balance of the reserve fund and any accrued interest. We shall also furnish you with a final accounting specifying all deductions made. We shall refund the remaining balance no later than forty-five (45) days from the date this Agreement terminates.

5. COSTS AND EXPENSES

5.1. <u>Equipment Loss or Damage.</u> We are not liable to you for loss of the equipment or damage to it. Exception: we are liable if the loss or damage is caused by the intentional or negligent act of our employees while acting within the scope of their employment. However, we are liable only to the extent you are not compensated for the loss or damage by insurance or otherwise.

5.2. Cargo Claims. You shall deliver cargo that is dispatched and loaded on the vehicles to the consignees(s) with reasonable diligence, speed and care. You shall be responsible for the first $ _____ of any cargo claim, as well as any expense incurred by us in the settlement and investigation of a claim. You shall also be liable for any cargo claim recovery in excess of our cargo insurance policy limits.

We may deduct from your payment any claims for damage or shortage of cargo or any property damage to our equipment. We shall provide you with a written explanation and itemization for any deduction 15 days before we make the deduction.

5.3. Personal Injury or Death. You assume the risk of any personal injury or death that results from performance of this Agreement. You assume the risk whether the personal injury or death is caused by your own equipment, by equipment furnished by us, or by the employees of you or us. Exception: you do not assume the risk if the personal injury or death is caused by the intentional or negligent acts of our employees while acting within the scope of their employment.

5.4. Expenses Caused by CONTRACTOR. If we incur any liability, expense, cost or attorneys' fees because of what you do or do not do under this Agreement, you shall indemnify and save us harmless from the liability, expense, cost, or attorneys' fees.

5.5. Trailer and Accessorial Equipment. If we supply the trailer equipment and the accessorial equipment ("the trailer" and "the accessories" in this provision) to you, we shall maintain the trailer and pay the cost of fuel for the accessories. You are liable for loss of or damage to the trailer or accessories while they are in your possession or custody. Exception: you are not liable for loss or damage for which we are compensated by insurance or otherwise. However, you shall indemnify us for any loss we suffer even though we are covered by insurance.

If you supply the trailer and the accessories, then you shall maintain the trailer and pay the cost of fuel for the accessories. You shall also be responsible for insurance on the trailer and accessories according to Paragraph 5.7.

[signature lines omitted]

4. Notice to Guests.

It is interesting to use this exercise as a diagnostic to see how many students jump in to edit the individual words and how many step back to take in the big picture, perhaps rewriting the provision from scratch.

I think it is helpful to understand what the "drafter" of this notice did -- he simply posted the text of the statute. Does that effectively carry out the statutory mandate? I think not. The statute seems to say that if you provide a safe and tell the guests that, then you are not liable. This notice does not say that the proprietor has a safe.

The big picture drafters might come up with a redraft like "We have a safe. Use it or lose it." The editors will note that the notice consists of one long sentence that contains string phrases. Each approach has value and we have to learn to see through both ends of the telescope.

5. Computer Exercise: Plain Language.

Here are the comments that Grammatik IV made on the original draft of the lease in Exercise 2:

DAMAGE TO PREMISES.
[#Long sentences can be difficult to read and understand. Consider revising so that no more than one complete thought is expressed in each sentence.]
The LESSEE further covenants and agrees to take good care of the premises
[#Omit, or revise.]
hereby leased, and the fixtures of same, and commit and suffer no waste of any kind therein; that LESSEE shall pay for all repairs required to be made to the floors, walls, ceilings, paint, plastering, plumbing work, pipes, fixtures or any other part of leased premises, whenever damage or injury to
[#An adjective (`same`) is usually not followed by a verb (`shall`). You may need to use an adverbial form of `same` (e.g., `quickly` instead of `quick`), or you may need a comma before `shall`.]
same shall have resulted from any misuse or neglect
[#Simplify.]
on the part of Lessee or members of family, guests, or employees of LESSEE; that Leased premises shall be used only as a family dwelling.
[#Long sentences can be difficult to read and understand. Consider revising so that no more than one complete thought is expressed in each sentence.]
LESSEE shall not
[#Use form of `do` (except for film and stage performers).]
perform any maintenance, adjustment, or repair on heating or air conditioning, and plumbing, stoves, refrigerators or other appliances or equipment of LESSOR but said

maintenance, adjustment or repair shall be done only by LESSOR'S employees, contractors or agents, and LESSEE agrees to notify LESSOR accurately and promptly of any problem arising from such equipment, its location and cause, if possible; Lessee agrees to allow repairmen to enter leased premises to remedy said problems; and LESSOR shall not be liable for damages due to the temporary breakdown or discontinuance of same. Locks may not

[#**Passive voice: `be changed`. Consider revising using active voice. See Help for more information.**]

be changed, nor any additional locks put on any doors without written permission of the LESSOR. LESSOR is not responsible to provide access to the premises in the event LESSEE accidently or otherwise locks himself/herself out of the premises. LESSEE is responsible for the cost of lost keys or the replacement of locks. Nails, tacks, brads, screws, stick-on picture hangers or tape shall not

[#**Passive voice: `be used`. Consider revising using active voice. See Help for more information.**]

be used on the woodwork, walls, floors or ceilings of said premises. It is permissible to use small nails that

[#**Passive voice: `are designed`. Consider revising using active voice. See Help for more information.**]

are specifically designed for hanging pictures on the walls. The use of gasoline

[#**Simplify.**]

and/or similar combustibles for cleaning or for other purposes

[#**Passive voice: `is prohibited`. Consider revising using active voice. See Help for more information.**]

is strictly prohibited. LESSEE shall so use the premises so as not to cause any increase in the insurance rates.

[#**Long sentences can be difficult to read and understand. Consider revising so that no more than one complete thought is expressed in each sentence.**]

LESSOR shall not be responsible or liable to the LESSEE, or any other person claiming by or through LESSEE, for any injury or damage resulting from bursting, stoppage or leaking of plumbing, gas, water, sewer, or other pipes; nor for any damage or injury arising from the acts or neglect of co-tenants, their families or guests or any owners or occupants of adjacent or contiguous property; nor for any damage or injury caused by fire, water damage, snow, ice, wind or any other natural calamity. No outside or attic aerials or antennas will be permitted on the building or premises.

[#**Long sentences can be difficult to read and understand. Consider revising so that no more than one complete thought is expressed in each sentence.**]

LESSOR

[#**Simplify.**]

and/or his representatives may enter the leased premises at any reasonable time to make such repairs and alterations as may be deemed necessary by LESSOR for the safety and preservation of the premises, or exhibiting the leased premises for sale, lease or mortgage financing.

Here is the statistical summary from that same draft:

```
=================== Grammatik IV ===================
```

Summary for A:\lease1

Problems marked/detected: 0/14

Readability Statistics

   Flesch Reading Ease: 33
   Gunning's Fog Index: 22
   Flesch-Kincaid Grade Level: 18

Paragraph Statistics

   Number of paragraphs: 1
   Average length: 13.0 sentences

Sentence Statistics

   Number of sentences: 13
   Average length: 36.2 words
   End with `?`:   0
   End with `!`:   0
   Passive voice: 4
   Short (< 14 words): 2
   Long (> 30 words): 4

Word Statistics

   Number of words: 471
   Prepositions: 61
   Average length: 4.88 letters
   Syllables per word: 1.62

Note particularly that the Flesch Reading Ease score is 33, below the passing score of 40, and the Flesch-Kincaid Grade Level is 18, indicating that high school graduates and even law school graduates would have difficulty with the passage!

Here is the statistical summary from the revised draft:

```
=================== Grammatik IV ===================
```

Summary for A:\lease2

Problems marked/detected: 0/15

Readability Statistics

   Flesch Reading Ease: 54
   Gunning's Fog Index: 15
   Flesch-Kincaid Grade Level: 11

Paragraph Statistics

   Number of paragraphs: 14
   Average length: 1.3 sentences

Sentence Statistics

   Number of sentences: 19
   Average length: 19.1 words
   End with `?`:   0
   End with `!`:   0
   Passive voice: 1
   Short (< 14 words): 9
   Long (> 30 words): 2

Word Statistics

   Number of words: 363
   Prepositions: 49
   Average length: 4.91 letters
   Syllables per word: 1.58

Note that the Flesch Reading Ease score is now an above-passing 54 and the Flesch-Kincaid Grade Level of 11 indicates that the text can be read by high school graduates. Readability was improved mostly by shorter sentences and to some extent by shorter words.

    6. Additional exercise. Siegel & Glascoff have an excellent section called "Case History: Simplifying an Apartment Lease" in PLI, DRAFTING DOCUMENTS IN PLAIN LANGUAGE 169-205 that contrasts the two methods of simplifying an existing form: "translating" and "zero-base" drafting. Consider, for example, the Standard Listing Agreement in § 10.8, Exercise 4, as a zero-base draft of the broker's agreement in § 18.6.

Chapter 19
Drafting with a Computer

§ 19.1. Introduction.

Helpful guides to technological issues include PERRITT, HOW TO PRACTICE LAW WITH COMPUTERS (1988, supplemented periodically) and BRAEMAN & SHELLENBERGER, FROM YELLOW PADS TO COMPUTERS (2d ed. 1991). Because technological changes occur so rapidly, attorneys should consult such periodicals as Law Practice Management and The Lawyers' PC. Attorneys interested in Document Assembly/Expert Systems may wish to join the Section of Law Practice Management of the ABA and obtain the Document Assembly and Practice Systems Report.

§ 19.2.2. Word processing improves your written expression.

b. Readability. In a terrific sendup of grammar checking programs, Mike Royko ran The Gettysburg Address through a grammar checker, which found 13 problems. Chicago Tribune, March 8, 1990, at 3:

Lincoln's speech doesn't compute

Mike Royko

The ad caught my eye and intrigued me. It was for a computer program and it said: "Write better in 30 days or your money back!"

I'm not a computer nut, but I'm familiar with computer programs that correct spelling and have built-in dictionaries.

But the ad for this program said that it would correct "stylistic errors." Style. That's a big part of what writing is about.

So I decided to check it out. I stopped by the computer store to give it a test run. I wanted to see what the program would say about the style of a short piece of writing that has always been one of my favorites.

I typed it into the computer just as the author is said to have written and delivered it.

Then the computer printed out its critique. Here's the final product, with the computer's comments in parentheses:

Fourscore and seven years ago our fathers brought forth on this continent, a new nation, conceived in Liberty, and dedicated to the proposition that all men are created equal. (No. 1. Long sentences can be difficult to read and understand. Consider revising so that no more than one complete thought is expressed in each sentence. No. 2. Passive voice: "are created." Consider revising, using active voice. See Help for more information. No. 3. Usually a paragraph should have more than one sentence.)

Now we are engaged (No. 4. Passive voice: "are engaged." Consider revising using active voice. See Help for more information.) in a great civil war, testing whether that nation or any nation so conceived and so dedicated can long endure. We are met (No. 5. Passive voice: "are met." Consider revising using active voice. See Help for more information.) on a great battlefield of that war. We have come to dedicate a portion of that field, as a final resting place for those who here gave their lives that that (No. 6. Delete doubled word or punctuation mark.) nation might live. It is altogether fitting and proper that we should do this.

But, (No. 7. Use "But" sparingly to start a sentence.) in a larger sense, we cannot dedicate - we cannot consecrate - we cannot hallow - this ground. The brave men, living and dead, who struggled here, have consecrated it far above our poor power to add or detract. The world will little note nor long remember (No. 8. An adjective "long" is usually not followed by a verb "remember." You may need to use an adverbial form of "long" (e.g. "quickly" instead of "quick"), or you may need a comma before "remember.") what we say here, but it can never forget what they did here. It is for us, the living, rather (No. 9. This word usually adds little and should be omitted.) to be dedicated here to the unfinished work which (No. 10. "That" is almost always preferred to "which" in this situation. If you really mean "which," then it usually needs to be preceded by a comma. See Help key for more information.) they who fought here have thus far so nobly advanced. (No. 11. Long sentences can be difficult to read and understand. Consider revising so that no more than one complete thought is expressed in each sentence.) It is rather (No. 12. This word usually adds little and should be omitted.) for us to be here dedicated to the great task remaining before us - that from these honored dead we take increased devotion to that cause for which they gave the last full measure of devotion; that we here highly resolve that these dead (No. 13. Usually "these" should be followed by a plural noun.) shall not have died in vain; that this nation, under God, shall have a new birth of freedom; and that government of the people, by the people, for the people, shall not perish from the earth.

(Problems marked/detected: 13/13)

That's something. As often as I've read this speech, getting a lump in my throat every time, I didn't detect even one stylistic problem, much less 13. Shows how little I know.

But I suppose we really shouldn't expect anything better from someone who grew up in a log cabin, hoofed to a one-room schoolhouse, and never made it to college.

We might remember, though, that Abe Lincoln was at a stylistic disadvantage when he wrote what has become known as his Gettysburg Address. The poor guy didn't have a "Help Key" to push.

And even with his 13 stylistic flaws, we can say one thing in Abe's behalf: he sure as hell wasn't a computer nerd. So run that through your program and spit it out.

c. Aesthetics. The disclaimer was found ineffective in *Dorman v. Int'l Harvester Co.*, 46 Cal. App. 3d 11, 120 Cal. Rptr. 516 (1975).

§ 19.6. Comparison by computer. Burnham, *The Hazards of Using Plain English*, 8 The Compleat Lawyer 46 (Summer 1991), discusses the legal consequences that arise when one attorney alters another's draft on a computer without informing the other.

§ 19.7. Exercises.

1. Document assembly.

Steps 1 and 2. Identify and bracket the variables:

EMPLOYMENT AGREEMENT

AGREEMENT made **[February 1, 1993]**, between Washington Corporation, a corporation duly organized and existing under the laws of the State of Montana ("Company"), and **[Trevor Burnham]** ("Employee").

Company and Employee agree as follows:

ARTICLE I

Term

The term of this Agreement shall commence as of the date set forth above and shall continue for **[three years]**.

ARTICLE II

Duties

Company shall employ Employee as **[Corporate Counsel]** of Company with the following responsibilities:

[all legal matters relating to intellectual property, including patents, trademarks, and copyrights.]

Employee shall report to **[Company's President]** and shall be under the supervision and control of **[Company's President]**. Employee shall be available to perform such duties on a **[full-time]** basis.

ARTICLE III

Compensation

3.1   *Base Salary*. Company shall pay Employee a salary of **[$50,000]** per annum ("Base Salary") payable in equal monthly installments. The Base Salary is subject to periodic review (with the first review being on **[August 1, 1993]**) and may be adjusted from time to time by mutual agreement of Employee and Company's Board of Directors ("the Board").

3.2   *Other Benefits*. In addition to the Base Salary, Company shall provide Employee, in the discretion of the Board, such other benefits as management employees in similar positions in Company receive, except that Employee will be subject to any qualification requirements contained in Company's insurance or benefit plans.

[3.3   *Auto*. Company shall, at its discretion, provide Employee with either a Company Automobile or a $200 per month auto allowance.]

Step 3. Create the secondary document:

date of agreement:
name of employee:
term of agreement (how many months or years):
employee's job title:
employee's responsibilities:
who does employee report to:
who supervises employee:
full-time or part-time:
base salary:
first salary review: [as a default provision, make it 6 months from <u>date of agreement</u>
        above]
company auto provision: [if not expressly indicated, leave it out]

Step 4. Test it with some actual facts.

2. Redlining.

a. While this agreement may not have been difficult to compare by hand, imagine reading through a 20-page document.

b. In WordPerfect, the comparison revealed the following:

2.   <u>Assumption of Indebtedness</u>. Buyer hereby covenants, promises and agrees (a) to assume the payment for $400, ~~promises and agrees (a) to assume the payment for $450,~~000.00 of the Note and to pay at the times, in the manner and in all respects as therein provided, (b) to perform each and all of the covenants, agreements, and obligations in the Mortgage and in the other security instruments securing the Note to be performed by Mortgagor therein, at the time, in the manner and in all respects as therein provided, and (c) to be bound by each and all of the terms and provisions of the Note and the Mortgage as though such documents had originally been made, executed and delivered by Smith and Buyer. ~~executed and delivered by Buyer.~~

c. In CiteRite, the comparison looked like this:

2.   <u>Assumption of Indebtedness</u>. Buyer hereby covenants, promises and agrees (a) to assume the payment for $400,000.00 **[$450,000.00]** of the Note and to pay at the times, in the manner and in all respects as therein provided, (b) to perform each and all of the covenants, agreements, and obligations in the Mortgage and in the other security instruments securing the Note to be performed by Mortgagor therein, at the time, in the manner and in all respects as therein provided, and (c) to be bound by each and all of the terms and provisions of the Note and the Mortgage as though such documents had originally been made, executed and delivered by **[Smith and]** Buyer.

PART III

How to Read a Contract

Part III
How to Read and Analyze a Contract

Exercise 1. Agreement for the Sale of Goods.

1.   First Pass: Orientation

Ascertain the general theme of the contract. The description of the instrument makes clear what this is: an agreement for the sale of goods. Other than the names of the parties, there is little to learn from the caption and there are no recitals. The primary exchange of promises is found in ¶ 1: Seller promises to sell the goods and buyer to pay for them.

This looks like a fairly thorough agreement, but its structure is simple. The language of transition is part of the caption and there are no recitals or definitions. The closing is also exceptionally simple. The terms are all either operative terms or boilerplate.

The goals of the parties are to foresee and possibly shift any risks associated with their performance as buyer and seller of goods. Because this contract involves the sale of goods, it is governed by U.C.C. Article 2. Any gaps in it will be filled in first by that statute and then by the common law.

2.   Second Pass: Explication

The boilerplate terms begin with ¶ 16.

¶ 16 begins as a standard merger clause to bar extrinsic evidence. The next provisions are more unusual. The default rule under the Code is that trade usage, course of dealing, and course of performance are read into the contract for purposes of interpretation. This provision changes the default rule. Similarly, it provides that a word has the meaning given it by the Code and not by the business the parties are in. See Chapter 6.

¶ 17 is a variation on the merger clause, specifically providing that Seller has made not representations or warranties except those found in the writing.

¶ 18 is language tracking § 2-209(2) to provide a private statute of frauds for modifications. See Chapter 11.

¶ 19 is language that makes it harder for a party to waive rights arising when the other party is in breach.

¶ 20 changes the default rule by prohibiting assignment and delegation. See Chapter 14.

¶ 21 provides for a statute of limitations that varies the statutory period under § 2-725.

¶ 22 is a choice of law provision. See Chapter 16.

¶ 23 is a dispute resolution provision providing for arbitration by the American Arbitration Association. See Chapter 13.

The rights and duties of each party are expressly stated in ¶ 2 through ¶ 6, with others impliedly found in ¶ 7 through ¶ 15. In ¶ 9 and ¶ 10 the Seller has shifted risks to the Buyer by giving no warranties.

3.   Third Pass: Implication

As mentioned, where the parties have not made their terms express, we will read in the default rules of the UCC. The parties make this explicit in ¶ 15, where they read in the UCC remedies.

There are a number of implied conditions. The most essential one is in ¶ 12, which provides that payment is conditional upon delivery. Presumably ¶ 13 also contains the implied condition that if the goods do not pass inspection Buyer may reject them.

As mentioned, this contract is unusual in that under ¶ 16 we expressly do not read in trade usage, course of dealing, and course of performance

4.   Fourth Pass: Remediation

This agreement does not have a force majeure clause that specifies excusing events, so we would read in the default rule of § 2-615.

Other than ¶ 15, there are no provisions that address remedies, so we would read in the applicable default rules.

5.   Fifth Pass: Evaluation

If I were the buyer, I would be concerned with some of the risks that have been shifted to me. In ¶ 7, for example, Buyer assumes the risk of loss upon identification. Buyer should make sure it has insurance to cover the goods while in the hands of Seller. Most importantly, Seller has promised nothing about the quality of the goods in ¶ 9 and ¶ 10. Buyer does have the right of inspection in ¶ 13, but if there are no warranties then Buyer is essentially inspection only for quantity. The Buyer might consult with experts or examine other forms to see how terms might be stated in a more favorable way.

Because the contract either adopts the default rules or changes them to advantage Seller, Buyer would actually be better off ordering the goods without entering this contract.

The agreement does seem to be written in a straightforward way with no weaknesses with language.

If you are interested in having students work with this contract, it is the subject of the CALI lesson Exploring a Contract: The Sale of Goods.

Exercise 2. Company Master Terms

First Pass: Orientation

Ascertain the general theme of this contract from the description of the instrument, the caption, and the recitals:

Description of the Instrument: Company Master Terms

Caption:

> These Company Master Terms ("Master Terms"), made this ____ day of _____, 2002 ("Effective Date"), by and between Company Inc., a Delaware corporation having an address at 555 Madison Avenue, New York, NY ("Company") and The University of Erehwon having an address at #32 Campus Drive, Erehwon ("Customer").

Recitals:

> Company offers software and services to scale from course websites, to an entire online campus and that allows institutions to establish and manage accounts for a stored value card system and security access system. Customer wishes to adopt the Company technology to enhance its own educational programs, and Company is willing to provide the Company technology to Customer for this purpose.

In addition, this agreement has a "Scope of Agreement:"

1. SCOPE OF AGREEMENT.

1.1 Exhibits and Schedules. These Master Terms describe the general terms by which Customer may license Software (as defined below) and purchase Services (as defined below) and Equipment from Company as set forth in a Schedule. The specific terms related to the license of Software and purchase of Services and/or Equipment are described in the appropriate Software or Service Schedules, and Exhibits thereto (collectively referred to as "Schedules"). Each Schedule and these Master Terms together constitute a separate agreement (the "Agreement") between Company and Customer. Schedules may be added or deleted from time to time by the agreement of the parties, but Customer is only authorized to license Software or purchase Services hereunder to the extent that one or more applicable Schedules is executed and in force.

1.2 Order of Precedence. The provisions of any Schedule will take precedence over these Master Terms, to the extent that they are inconsistent. In the event of any inconsistencies between the terms of these Master Terms and any referenced, attached, or preprinted terms and conditions on the purchase order, these Master Terms shall take precedence.

Section 1.2 is a great example of "time travel" by a drafter. The drafter has asked "what if" there is an inconsistency between parts of the agreement and has worked out a hierarchy to answer that question.

The primary exchange of promises is found in Parts 3 and 6. What is the relationship between the parties? In case of any confusion, Company clarifies the relationship in § 9.12:

> **9.12 Relationship.** Company and Customer are independent contracting parties. This Agreement shall not constitute the parties as principal and agent, partners, joint venturers, or employer and employee.

The parts of the contract.

We have already looked at the *description of the instrument* and the *caption*.

The *closing* is properly signed by agents of both parties. It is good practice to state that the corporate entity is signing "by" the individual.

There is *language of transition* preceding the first term and preceding the closing:

> Therefore, in consideration of the following mutual covenants and agreements, the parties agree as follows:

> IN WITNESS WHEREOF, the parties hereto have executed these Master Terms as of the date first written above.

Definitions. Part 2 consists of definitions. We will generally look at the defined terms as we go along. Let's spend a moment looking at a couple of uses of definition.

"Customer Content" -- where is the term used? A good practice is to use the "find" function of your word processor to locate each use of a definition. Here, you would find that it isn't used at all!

"Agreement." This term is not defined in the Definitions section, but is used throughout the document in a bewildering variety of ways:

1.1 Exhibits and Schedules. These Master Terms describe the general terms by which Customer may license Software (as defined below) and purchase Services (as defined below) and Equipment from Company as set forth in a Schedule. The specific terms related to the license of Software and purchase of Services and/or Equipment are described in the appropriate Software or Service Schedules, and Exhibits thereto (collectively referred to as "Schedules"). **Each Schedule and these Master Terms together constitute a separate agreement (the "Agreement") between Company and Customer.**

5.1 Term. These Master Terms and the agreement between the parties shall commence as of the Effective Date and shall continue until the expiration or termination of all Schedules.

5.2 Default. Either party may, at its option, terminate **these Master Terms and any or all Schedules**

5.4 Effect of Termination. Termination of the Agreement shall not relieve either party of any obligation

9.5 Modification and Waiver. Any modification, amendment, supplement, or other change to **this Agreement or any Schedule attached hereto** must be in writing and signed by a duly authorized representative of Company and Customer. All waivers must be in writing. The failure of either party to insist upon strict performance of any provision of **this Agreement**, or to exercise any right provided for herein, shall not be deemed to be a waiver of the future of such provision or right, and no waiver of any provision or right shall affect the right of the waiving party to enforce any other provision or right herein.

9.13 Entire Agreement. An Agreement, which includes these Master Terms, and the applicable Schedule(s) and Exhibit(s), constitute the entire, full and complete **Agreement** between the parties concerning the subject matter hereof, and they collectively supersede all prior or contemporaneous oral or written communications, proposals, conditions, representations and warranties, and prevails over any conflicting or additional terms of any quote, order, acknowledgment, or other communication between the parties relating to its subject matter.

If I were the Company, I would suggest looking at definitions during the Evaluation pass.

Boilerplate terms are found in Part 9, Miscellaneous. The rest of the provisions seem to be *operative terms*.

We now look at the transaction against a larger background. What does the Company want from the Customer? What does the Customer want from the Company?

Because this transaction involves software licenses, services, and goods, the applicable law is complex. Services are generally governed by the common law while Sale of Goods is governed by the Uniform Commercial Code. Some jurisdictions treat software licenses under the common law, some as sale of goods, and some have applicable statutes. This is unlikely to be an area of government regulation.

Second Pass: Explication

Separate out the boilerplate terms:

Severability:

> **9.1 Severability.** Should any term or provision of this Agreement be finally determined by a court of competent jurisdiction to be void, invalid, unenforceable or contrary to law or equity, the offending term or provision shall be modified and limited (or if strictly necessary, deleted) only to the extent required to conform to the requirements of law and the remainder of this Agreement (or, as the case may be, the application of such provisions to other circumstances) shall not be affected thereby but rather shall be enforced to the greatest extent permitted by law, and the parties shall use their best efforts to substitute for the offending provision new terms having similar economic effect.

This provision probably sets out the default rule. See § 4.6.

Choice of Law and Choice of Forum

> **9.4 Governing Law.** This Agreement shall for all purposes be governed by and interpreted in accordance with the laws of the Commonwealth of Virginia without reference to its conflicts of law provisions. Any legal suit, action or proceeding arising out of or relating to this Agreement shall be commenced in a federal court in the Commonwealth of Virginia, and each party hereto irrevocably submits to the non-exclusive jurisdiction and venue of any such court in any such suit, action or proceeding. The U.N. Convention on Contracts for the International Sale of Goods shall not apply to this Agreement.

This is a well-drafted provision. See § 16.5. But why Virginia? What connection does Virginia have to this transaction? The answer is: None. The reason the Company chose Virginia law is that Virginia is one of two states that have enacted UCITA, the Uniform Computer Information Transactions Act!

Can the drafter choose a body of law that has nothing to do with the transaction? The general rule at common law and under the UCC is no, there has to be some "reasonable relationship" between the transaction and the chosen law. UCITA § 109, however, requires no connection. Official Comment 2.a. states in part, "Parties may appropriately wish to select a neutral forum because neither is familiar with the law of the other's jurisdiction. In such a case, the chosen State's law may have no relationship at all to the transaction."

Of course, this is a bit circular. In order for the rule to apply that no connection is necessary, Virginia law would have to apply. A party could argue that Virginia law does not apply because under the rules of the forum state, there has to be some reasonable relationship between the transaction and the chosen law. Montana could well make the determination that such a rule is contrary to its "policy," a traditional exception to choice of law provisions.

The second sentence: you have to bring the claim in Virginia. This seems more problematic, as one wonders why Virginia would entertain a suit where neither party has any connection. On the other hand, this provision purports to be "non-exclusive." If so, what is it doing in the contract?

The final sentence could be significant in an international transaction. There is a UN Treaty, the UN Convention on the International Sale of Goods. It applies when both parties are citizens of signatory countries. Note, however, it applies only to goods and not to services or computer information.

Assume that we have a situation involving the sale of goods where the buyer is an American company and the seller is a Canadian company. The first sentence says that the law of Virginia applies. But the law of Virginia includes the law of the land, federal law that pre-empts state law. Therefore the UNCISG is the law of Virginia and would apply. The drafter, however, specifically opts out of that result in the final sentence.

Modification and Waiver

> **9.5 Modification and Waiver.** Any modification, amendment, supplement, or other change to this Agreement or any Schedule attached hereto must be in writing and signed by a duly authorized representative of Company and Customer. All waivers must be in writing. The failure of either party to insist upon strict performance of any provision of this Agreement, or to exercise any right provided for herein, shall not be deemed to be a waiver of the future of such provision or right, and no waiver of any provision or right shall affect the right of the waiving party to enforce any other provision or right herein.

The agreement "Must be in writing and signed." This is curious in light of the invocation of UCITA and the computer orientation of the Company. Modern law requires an "authenticated record" rather than a "signed writing."

"All waivers must be in writing." The failure to insist on strict performance is not a waiver of the future right. Don't believe a word of it. A waiver is a surrender of a right that lulls the other party into thinking that the right will not be enforced. Waivers frequently arise by conduct and by their nature are not written.

For example, assume the contract requires payment on the first of the month and gives the seller the right to terminate if timely payment is not made. In Month 1, the Customer pays on the 5th and the Company does nothing. In Month 2, the the Customer pays on the 6th and the Company does nothing. In Month 3, the the Customer pays on the 4th and the Company does nothing. In Month 4, the Customer pays on the 5th and the Company terminates the agreement. Did the Company waive its right to terminate for late payment? Yes. What about the requirement of a written waiver? It waived that. See Chapter 11.

Assignment and Delegation

> **9.6 Assignment.** No right or obligation of Customer under this Agreement may be assigned, delegated or otherwise transferred, whether by agreement, operation of law or otherwise, without the express prior written consent of Company, and any attempt to assign, delegate or otherwise transfer any of Customer's rights or obligations hereunder, without such consent, shall be void. Subject to the preceding sentence, this Agreement shall bind each party and its permitted successors and assigns.

This provision seems to change the default rule. See Chapter 9. The general rule is that parties are free to assign rights and delegate duties. Does it make sense here that the parties want to deal only with the entity with which they contracted?

Notice

> **9.8 Notices.** Any notice or communication permitted or required hereunder shall be in writing and shall be delivered in person or by courier, sent by facsimile, or mailed by certified or registered mail, postage prepaid, return receipt requested, and addressed as set forth above or to such other address as shall be given in accordance with this Section 9.8, and shall be effective upon receipt.

See § 16.5.5. Notice effective on receipt can be dangerous, but perhaps less so with large corporations which cannot dodge delivery.

Force Majeure

> **9.9 Force Majeure.** Except with regard to payment obligations, neither party will be responsible for any failure to fulfill its obligations due to causes beyond its reasonable control, including without limitation, acts or omissions of government or military authority, acts of God, materials shortages, transportation delays, fires, floods, labor disturbances, riots, wars, terrorist acts or inability to obtain any export or import license or other approval of authorization of any government authority.

This provision seems to state the default rule. See Chapter 9. Make sure you "time travel" to think through whether events that might happen to a party in your situation are enumerated. For example, if you are a public agency, will your performance be excused if your budget is slashed?

Merger Clause

> **9.13 Entire Agreement.** An Agreement, which includes these Master Terms, and the applicable Schedule(s) and Exhibit(s), constitute the entire, full and complete Agreement between the parties concerning the subject matter hereof, and they collectively supersede all prior or contemporaneous oral or written communications, proposals, conditions, representations and warranties, and prevails over any conflicting or additional terms of any quote, order, acknowledgment, or other communication between the parties relating to its subject matter.

See Chapter 6.

All we have left now is Parts 3 through 8, the operative terms. What are the promises of each party?

As we have seen, Parts 3 and 6 contain the essential promises of each party. Review what they are.

Part 4 is concerned with Confidentiality. Determine what Customer can and can not do. What happens if you don't do it?

Parts 7 is concerned with the special kind of promise called a warranty. We will look at those terms during the Remediation pass, because the terms largely determine what the remedies are for breach of that promise.

Part 8 is also concerned with remedies, but you have to read between the lines to figure out what is the promise the breach of which entitled a party to a remedy. Because it turns out to be a warranty, let's also look at that during the Remediation pass.

The duration of the contract is found in Part 5. Paragraphs 5.2 and 5.3 are also remedies provisions. Can either party terminate the agreement before that date? What happens if you do?

Third Pass: Implication

Paragraph 5.2 tells us a party can terminate if there is a material default. What is a "material default"? Note that there are more conditions. If there is a material default, the party claiming default must notify the other party and give them 30 days to correct it. Only then can the first party terminate the agreement.

What happens if Customer does not pay Company? See §§ 6.1 and 6.2. When does nonpayment become material?

Notice that the Warranty provision in § 7.1 states that the "Equipment and Software will substantially conform to the applicable Documentation, *provided that Company has received all amounts owed under this Agreement and Customer is not in default of any part of this Agreement*." Additional conditions are that "Customer must notify Company in writing of the deficiency within the warranty period and must install any generally-released Corrections, Upgrades and Updates."

Fourth Pass: Remediation

Conflict Resolution

> **9.2. Conflict Resolution.** In the event of a dispute between the Parties relating to the terms and conditions of this Master Terms or any Schedule, or the performance of the Parties hereunder, the Parties shall first attempt to resolve the dispute by internal discussions involving their appointed representatives within thirty (30) days of the dispute arising.

Arbitration

> **9.3 Arbitration. If any dispute, controversy or claim cannot be resolved to the satisfaction of both Parties pursuant to Section 9.2 above within Section 9.2's thirty (30) day period, either Party may, submit the matter to binding arbitration to be finally settled in accordance with the Commercial Arbitration Rules of the American Arbitration Association (the "AAA") then obtaining, by a panel of three arbitrators; provided, however, that this clause shall not be construed to limit or to preclude either Party from bringing an action in a court of competent jurisdiction for injunctive or other provisional relief as necessary or appropriate. Each Party shall have the right to appoint one arbitrator from the list of arbitrators supplied to the parties by the AAA, and the two arbitrators so appointed shall appoint the third. Any award or**

determination of the arbitration shall be final, non-appealable, and conclusive and binding upon the parties, and any court of competent jurisdiction thereon may enter judgment. Any award shall include interest from the date of damages incurred for breach or other violation of this Agreement, and from the date of the award until paid in full, at a rate to be fixed by the arbitrators. The prevailing party may recover its costs of arbitration, including reasonable expert witness fee and reasonable attorneys' fees.

Specific Performance and Attorney's Fees

9.7 Remedies. The parties agree that any breach of this Agreement would cause irreparable injury for which no adequate remedy at law exists; therefore, the parties agree that equitable remedies, including without limitation, injunctive relief and specific performance, are appropriate remedies to redress any breach or threatened breach of this Agreement, in addition to other remedies available to the parties. All rights and remedies hereunder shall be cumulative, may be exercised singularly or concurrently and shall not be deemed exclusive except as provided in Sections 5, 7 and 8. If any legal action is brought to enforce any obligations hereunder, the prevailing party shall be entitled to receive its attorneys' fees, court costs and other collection expenses, in addition to any other relief it may receive.

Note that the attorneys' fee provision changes the default rule.

Warranty Terms

8. INDEMNIFICATION

8.1 Company. If Customer receives a claim that the use of the Software or Equipment infringes a patent, copyright or other intellectual property right, Customer must promptly notify Company in writing. Company shall, at its own expense and option: (i) defend and settle such claim, (ii) procure Customer the right to use the Software or Equipment, (iii) modify or replace the Software or Equipment to avoid infringement; or (iv) refund the applicable fee paid for the current term. In the event Company exercises option (i) above, it shall have the sole and exclusive authority to defend and/or settle any such claim or action, provided that Company will keep Customer informed of, and will consult with any independent attorneys appointed by Customer at Customer's own expense regarding the progress of such litigation.

8.2 Exceptions. Company shall have no liability to Customer under Section 8.1 or otherwise for any claim or action alleging infringement based upon (i) any use of the Software or Equipment in a manner other than as specified by Company; (ii) any combination of the Software or Equipment by Customer with other products, equipment, devices, software, systems or data not supplied by Company (including, without limitation, any software produced by Customer for use with the Software) to the extent such claim is directed against such combination; or (iii) any modifications or customization of the Software or Equipment by any person other than Company ("Customer Matter").

8.3 Customer. Customer shall, at its own expense, defend or, at its option, settle any claim, suit or proceeding brought against Company arising out of a Customer Matter and shall pay any damages finally awarded or settlement amounts agreed upon to the extent based upon a Customer Matter ("Company Claim"); provided that Company provides Customer with (i) prompt written notice of such Company Claim; (ii) control over the defense and settlement of such Company Claim; and (iii) proper and full information and assistance to settle or defend any such Company Claim.

8.4 Exclusive Remedy. THE FOREGOING PROVISIONS OF THIS SECTION 8 STATE THE ENTIRE LIABILITY AND OBLIGATIONS OF EACH PARTY, AND THE EXCLUSIVE REMEDY OF EACH PARTY WITH RESPECT TO ACTUAL OR ALLEGED INFRINGEMENT OF ANY INTELLECTUAL PROPERTY RIGHT.

These terms refer to UCC § 2-212(3), which provides for a warranty that there is no infringement of intellectual property. In 8.1, the Company agrees to make good on such a claim, unless, as provided in 8.2 and 8.3 it is the Customer's fault. And in any event, under 8.4 the Customer may not recover consequential damages.

7. DISCLAIMERS AND REMEDIES

7.1 Limited Warranty. Unless otherwise indicated on an attached Schedule, Company warrants to Customer, subject to the remedy limitations set forth herein, that during (i) a period of twelve (12) months from the Available Date of the Equipment manufactured by Company or third-party Equipment sold by Company, unless otherwise specified in the applicable Schedule(s) and (ii) a period of ninety (90) days from License Available Date for the Software manufactured by Company, that such Equipment and Software will substantially conform to the applicable Documentation, provided that Company has received all amounts owed under this Agreement and Customer is not in default of any part of this Agreement. Customer must notify Company in writing of the deficiency within the warranty period and must install any generally-released Corrections, Upgrades and Updates. Company's sole obligation is limited to repair or replacement of the defective Software or Equipment in a timely manner.

7.2 Disclaimer of Warranty. EXCEPT FOR THE LIMITED WARRANTY IN SECTION 7.1 ABOVE AND ANY SPECIFIC WARRANTIES PROVIDED IN AN ATTACHED SCHEDULE(S), THE SOFTWARE, EQUIPMENT AND ALL PORTIONS

THEREOF, AND ANY SERVICES ARE PROVIDED "AS IS." TO THE MAXIMUM EXTENT PERMITTED BY LAW, COMPANY AND ITS LICENSORS AND SUPPLIERS DISCLAIM ALL OTHER WARRANTIES OF ANY KIND, EITHER EXPRESS OR IMPLIED, INCLUDING, WITHOUT LIMITATION, IMPLIED WARRANTIES OF MERCHANTABILITY AND FITNESS FOR A PARTICULAR PURPOSE. EXCEPT AS SPECIFICALLY PROVIDED IN AN ATTACHED SCHEDULE(S), NEITHER COMPANY NOR ITS LICENSORS WARRANT THAT THE FUNCTIONS OR INFORMATION CONTAINED IN THE SOFTWARE WILL MEET ANY REQUIREMENTS OR NEEDS CUSTOMER MAY HAVE, OR THAT THE SOFTWARE WILL OPERATE ERROR FREE, OR IN AN UNINTERRUPTED FASHION, OR THAT ANY DEFECTS OR ERRORS IN THE SOFTWARE WILL BE CORRECTED, OR THAT THE SOFTWARE IS COMPATIBLE WITH ANY PARTICULAR OPERATING SYSTEM. COMPANY AND ITS LICENSORS MAKE NO GUARANTEE OF ACCESS OF ACCURACY OF THE CONTENT CONTAINED ON OR ACCESSED THROUGH THE SOFTWARE.

7.3 Limitations of Liability. TO THE MAXIMUM EXTENT PERMITTED BY LAW, IN NO EVENT WILL COMPANY OR ITS LICENSORS BE LIABLE TO CUSTOMER OR ANY THIRD PARTY FOR ANY INCIDENTAL OR CONSEQUENTIAL DAMAGES (INCLUDING, WITHOUT LIMITATION, INDIRECT, SPECIAL, PUNITIVE, OR EXEMPLARY DAMAGES) ARISING OUT OF THE USE OF OR INABILITY TO USE THE SOFTWARE, EQUIPMENT OR ANY PORTION THEREOF, DEFECTS IN WARRANTY, ANY SERVICES, OR FOR ANY CLAIM BY ANY OTHER PARTY, EVEN IF COMPANY AND/OR ITS LICENSORS HAVE BEEN ADVISED OF THE POSSIBILITY OF SUCH DAMAGES. IN NO EVENT SHALL COMPANY'S LIABILITY EXCEED THE AMOUNT OF FEES PAID FOR THE PARTICULAR SOFTWARE, EQUIPMENT AND/OR SERVICE LICENSED UNDER EACH SCHEDULE HEREUNDER FOR THE CURRENT TWELVE (12) MONTH PERIOD.

These provisions are very typical warranty provisions. Section 7.2 effectively disclaims the implied warranties, using the techniques of both UCC § 2-316(2) and (3). See Chapter 12. This provision also disclaims warranties under UCITA. The § 2-313 gives an express warranty that is substantially limited in time and qualified by various performances by the Customer. Finally, § 7.3 excludes consequential damages under UCC § 2-719(3) and limits the remedy under UCC § 2-719(1).

Fifth Pass: Evaluation

The Company might want to look more closely at some of its definitions.

I would alert the Company that its choice of law provision might not be upheld. If it is not, is the Company adequately prepared?

Are there provisions the Customer believes are too one-sided? How might those provisions be negotiated?

Appendices

A. Bibliography

B. Sources for Drafting Exercises

C. Chart: Coordinating the book with casebooks

Appendix A

BIBLIOGRAPHY

Annotated Bibliography

Please see the text of DRAFTING AND ANALYZING CONTRACTS for an annotated bibliography of my favorite works on drafting.

Bibliographies

Collins & Hattenhauer, *Law and Language: A Selected Annotated Bibliography on Legal Writing,* 33 J. LEGAL EDUC. 141 (1983).

Dick, LEGAL DRAFTING 227-30 (2d ed. 1985).

Dickerson, MATERIALS ON LEGAL DRAFTING 164-68 (1981).

Dickerson, THE FUNDAMENTALS OF LEGAL DRAFTING Appendix A (2d ed. 1986).

Hill, *A Selected List of Materials on the Drafting of Legal Instruments and Statutes,* 2 REC. ASSN. B. CITY N.Y. 172 (1947).

Hill, *I Take My Pen in Hand … Selected Materials on the Art of Legal Writing,* 17 REC. ASSN. B. CITY N.Y. 105 (1962).

Jackson & Bollinger, CONTRACT LAW IN MODERN SOCIETY 1033-34 (2d ed. 1980).

Mellinkoff, LEGAL WRITING: SENSE & NONSENSE 219-21 (1982).

Searcy, *Legal Drafting — A Select and Annotated Bibliography,* in Dickerson, MATERIALS ON LEGAL DRAFTING 164-68 (1981).

Grammar and Usage

Dickerson, *The Difficult Choice Between "And" and "Or",* 46 A.B.A. J. 310 (1960).

Freeman, THE GRAMMATICAL LAWYER (1979). This book collects the English usage columns that were originally published in THE PRACTICAL LAWYER. The column continues with a new author.

Garner, A DICTIONARY OF MODERN LEGAL USAGE (1987).

Kirk, Legal Drafting: *The Ambiguity of "And" and "Or"*, 2 TEX. TECH. L. REV. 235 (1971).

Kirk, *Legal Drafting: Curing Unexpressive Language*, 3 TEX. TECH. L. REV. 23 (1971).

Maugans, THE GRAMMATICAL LAWYER II (1996).

McCarty, *That Hybrid "and/or"*, 39 MICH. ST. B.J. 9 (1960).

Mellinkoff, DICTIONARY OF AMERICAN LEGAL USAGE (1992).

Legal Drafting -- General

Bloss, *How to Review a Contract*, 91 CASE & COM. 38 (1986).

Brown, *Specifying Remedies in Contract Documents*, 38 CAL. ST. B.J. 293 (1963).

Burnham, *Drafting in the Contract Class*, ST. LOUIS U. L.J. 44, 1535 (2000).

Burnham, *The Hazards of Plain English*, 8 THE COMPLEAT LAWYER 46 (Summer 1991).

Butt & Castle, MODERN LEGAL DRAFTING (2001).

Child, *Some Pointers on Legal Drafting*, 35 PRAC. LAW. 13 (March 1989) (adapted from Child, DRAFTING LEGAL DOCUMENTS chs. 6 & 7 (1st ed. 1988)).

Chomsky & Landsman, *Introducing Negotiation and Drafting into the Contracts Classroom*; 44 ST. LOUIS U. L.J. 1545 (2000).

Cook, LEGAL DRAFTING (rev. ed. 1951).

Darmstandter: HEREOF, THEREOF, AND EVERYWHEREOF: A CONTRARIAN GUIDE TO LEGAL DRAFTING (ABA 2002).

Dempsey, *The Dangers of Junk Documents*, 7 CAL. LAW. 45 (Oct. 1987).

Dick, *Legal Language*, 2 CAN. B.J. 204 (1959).

Dick, *Comparisons in Legal Drafting*, 4 EST. & TR. Q. 195 (1978).

Dickerson, LEGISLATIVE DRAFTING (1954). The second edition of FUNDAMENTALS OF LEGAL DRAFTING (1986) incorporates this work.

Eggleston, Posner & Zeckhauser, *The Design and Interpretation of Contracts: Why Complexity Matters*, 95 Nw. U. L. Rev. 91 (2000).

Farnsworth, *Some Considerations in the Drafting of Agreements: Problems in Interpretation and Gap-Filling,* 23 Rec. Assn. B. City N.Y. 105 (1968).

Feldman & Nimmer, Drafting Effective Contracts (2002).

Goldberg, *Hints on Draftsmanship,* 5 Prac. Law. 39 (March 1959).

Hager, *Let's Simplify Legal Language,* 32 Rocky Mtn. L. Rev. 74 (1959).

Haggard, Contract Law from a Drafting Perspective -- An Introduction to Contract Drafting for Law Students (West 2003). The last third of this book consists of short exercises, with a Teacher's Manual to help you work through them.

Haggard, Legal Drafting in A Nutshell (1996).

Haynsworth, *How to Draft Clear and Concise Legal Documents,* 31 Prac. Law. 41 (March 1985).

Hill, *A Comment on Language and Norms in Complex Business Contracting*, 77 Chi.-Kent L. Rev. 29 (2001).

Hillman & Rachlinski, *Standard-form Contracting in the Electronic Age*, 77 N.Y.U. L. Rev. 429 (2002).

Hyland, *In Defense of Legal Writing,* 134 U. Pa. L. Rev. 599 (1986).

Keeton, Guidelines for Drafting, Editing, and Interpreting (2002).

Kirk, *Legal Drafting: How Should a Document Begin?,* 3 Tex. Tech. L. Rev. 233 (1972).

Kirk, *Legal Drafting: Some Elements of Technique,* 4 Tex. Tech. L. Rev. 297 (1973).

Kuney, The Elements of Contract Drafting (West 2003).

Lindey, *Let's Write Better Contracts,* 3 Prac. Law. 33 (Jan. 1957).

Littler, *Legal Writing in Law Practice,* 31 Cal. St. B.J. 28 (1956).

Macneil, *A Primer of Contract Planning,* 48 S. Cal. L. Rev. 627 (1975).

Martin, *50 Tips for Writing the 21ˢᵗ Century Contract That Stays Out of Court*, FLA. ST. B.J. 22 (November 2000).

Maxey, *Fundamentals of Draftsmanship — A Guide for the Apprentice in Preparing Agreements,* 51 PA. B. ASSN. Q. 47 (Jan. 1980).

Maxey, *Fundamentals of Draftsmanship — A Guide in Preparing Agreements,* 19 LAW NOTES 87 (1983).

Mellinkoff, *How to Make Contracts Illegible,* 5 STAN. L. REV. 418 (1953).

Mellinkoff, THE LANGUAGE OF THE LAW (1963).

Nehf, *Writing Contracts in The Client's Interest,* 51 S.C. L. REV. 153 (1999).

Parham, *The Fundamentals of Legal Draftsmanship,* 52 A.B.A. J. 831 (1966).

Privette, SIGN HERE: EVERYTHING YOU NEED TO KNOW ABOUT CONTRACTS (Doubleday 1985).

Ramachandra, MODERN COMMERCIAL DRAFTSMAN (1989).

Ramsfield, THE LAW AS ARCHITECTURE: BUILDING LEGAL DOCUMENTS (West 2000).

Rutherford & Vietzen, LEGAL DRAFTING (1994).

Seller & Harper, THE MYTH OF THE PAPERLESS OFFICE (MIT Press 2002).

Siviglia, WRITING CONTRACTS: A DISTINCT DISCIPLINE (1996).

Slawson, *The New Meaning of Contract; Standard Forms May No Longer Haunt the Consumer,* 21 TRIAL 26 (1985).

Thomas, *Problems in Drafting Legal Instruments,* 39 ILL. B.J. 51 (1950).

Tilton, *Basic Considerations in Designing Forms,* 26 PRAC. LAW. 55 (July 1980).

Legal Drafting -- Particular Contracts

ABA Family Law Section, PREMARITAL AND MARITAL CONTRACTS: A LAWYER'S GUIDE (1993).

Bicks, CONTRACTS FOR THE SALE OF REALTY (1973).

Chaney, ART OF COMMERCIAL CONTRACT DRAFTING (2001).

Decker & Felix, DRAFTING AND REVISING EMPLOYMENT CONTRACTS (1991).

Farber, ENTERTAINMENT INDUSTRY CONTRACTS (1992).

Felsenfeld & Siegel, SIMPLIFIED CONSUMER CREDIT FORMS (1978).

Freund, ANATOMY OF A MERGER (1975).

Friedman, CONTRACTS AND CONVEYANCES OF REAL PROPERTY (1998).

Friedman, PREPARATION OF LEASE (1969).

Harding & Farber, INTERNET COMMERCE CONTRACTS (1997).

Hart, DRAFTING TECHNIQUES UNDER THE UCC (1962).

Jones, *Internet Content Licensing: New Challenges and Best Practices*, 722 PLI/PAT 543 (2003).

Leader, DRAFTING EMPLOYMENT AND TERMINATION AGREEMENTS (1993).

Leeds, RESIDENTIAL REAL ESTATE CONTRACTS AND CLOSINGS (2002).

Lindey & Parley, SEPARATION AGREEMENTS & ANTE-NUPTIAL CONTRACTS (1964).

Mandel, THE PREPARATION OF COMMERCIAL AGREEMENTS (1978).

Marceau, DRAFTING A UNION CONTRACT (1965).

Mayers, DRAFTING PATENT LICENSE AGREEMENTS (4th ed. 1998).

Moskin, COMMERCIAL CONTRACTS - STRATEGIES FOR DRAFTING AND NEGOTIATING (2002).

Richard, *Frequently Litigated Computer Software Contract Clauses: Contract Drafting Advice for the Computer Lawyer*, 657 PLI/PAT 53 (2001).

Risdon, DRAFTING CORPORATE AGREEMENTS (2002).

Roditti, COMPUTER CONTRACTS (1987).

Rosen, S<small>ETTLEMENT</small> A<small>GREEMENTS</small> <small>IN</small> C<small>OMMERCIAL</small> D<small>ISPUTES</small>: N<small>EGOTIATING</small>, D<small>RAFTING</small>, <small>AND</small> E<small>NFORCEMENT</small> (2002).

Shippey, A S<small>HORT</small> C<small>OURSE</small> <small>IN</small> I<small>NTERNATIONAL</small> C<small>ONTRACTS</small> (2002).

Stark, C<small>OMMERCIAL</small> L<small>EGAL</small> D<small>RAFTING</small> W<small>ORKSHOP</small> (2002).

Sweet, W<small>ORKING</small> <small>WITH THE NEW</small> AIA C<small>ONTRACT</small> F<small>ORMS</small> (1987).

Volz, & Trower, T<small>HE</small> D<small>RAFTING</small> <small>OF</small> P<small>ARTNERSHIP</small> A<small>GREEMENTS</small> (7th ed. 1986).

Plain Language

Asprey, P<small>LAIN</small> L<small>ANGUAGE</small> <small>FOR</small> L<small>AWYERS</small> (2d ed. 1996).

Beckerleg, *Legal Writing in Plain English: A Text with Exercise*, 48 F<small>ED</small>. L<small>AW</small>. 63 (2001).

Benson, *The End of Legalese: The Game is Over*, 13 N.Y.U. R<small>EV</small>. L. & S<small>OC</small>. C<small>HANGE</small> 519 (1984-85).

Crump, *Against Plain English: The Case for a Functional Approach to Legal Document Preparation*, 33 R<small>UTGERS</small> L.J. 713 (2002).

Dick, *Plain English in Legal Drafting*, 18 A<small>LBERTA</small> L. R<small>EV</small>. 509 (1980).

Dickerson, M<small>ATERIALS</small> <small>ON</small> L<small>EGAL</small> D<small>RAFTING</small>, ch. 11 (1981).

Dickerson, *Plain English Statutes and Readability — Part 1 — History, the Problem, and the Case for a Statute*, 64 M<small>ICH</small>. B.J. 567 (1985).

Dickerson, *Readability Formulas and Specifications for a Plain English Statute — Part 2*, 64 M<small>ICH</small>. B.J. 714 (1985).

Federal Trade Commission, W<small>RITING</small> R<small>EADABLE</small> W<small>ARRANTIES</small> (1983).

Flesch, T<small>HE</small> A<small>RT</small> <small>OF</small> P<small>LAIN</small> T<small>ALK</small> (1962).

Flesch, H<small>OW</small> <small>TO</small> W<small>RITE</small> P<small>LAIN</small> E<small>NGLISH</small>: A B<small>OOK</small> <small>FOR</small> L<small>AWYERS</small> <small>AND</small> C<small>ONSUMERS</small> (1979).

Hill, *Why Contracts are Written in Legalese*, 77 C<small>HI</small>-K<small>ENT</small> L. R<small>EV</small>. 59 (2001).

Kellogg, *How to: A Plan for Drafting in Plain English*, 56 C<small>AL</small>. S<small>T</small>. B.J. 154 (1981).

Kimble, *A Plain English Primer,* 33 PRAC. LAW. 83 (1987).

Kimble, *Plain English: A Charter for Clear Writing,* 9 COOLEY L. REV. 1 (1992).

Kleinberger, *Plain Language for Lawyers,* 42 BENCH & B. MINN. 22 (1985).

Mellinkoff, LEGAL WRITING: SENSE & NONSENSE Appendix I (1984).

Mowat, PLAIN LANGUAGE HANDBOOK FOR LEGAL WRITERS (1998).

Redish, HOW TO DRAFT MORE UNDERSTANDABLE LEGAL DOCUMENTS (1979).

Rothenberg, PLAIN-LANGUAGE LAW DICTIONARY (1981).

[Symposium] *Plain English in the Law,* 62 MICH. B.J. 941 (1983):

> Felsenfeld, *The Future of Plain English*
>
> Hathaway, *An Overview of the Plain English Movement for Lawyers*
>
> Alterman, *Plain and Accurate Style in Lawsuit Papers*
>
> Block, *Promise v. Performance*
>
> Ciaramitaro, *Plain English in Consumer Contracts*
>
> Ciaramitaro, *Plain English in Insurance Contracts*
>
> Cohn, *Effective Brief Writing: One Judge's Observation*
>
> Hathaway, *Bibliography of Plain English for Lawyers*
>
> Hathaway, *Plain English in Judicial Opinions*
>
> Kuzara, *Plain English in Legislative Drafting*
>
> Mester, *Plain English for Judges*
>
> Pratt, *Plain English in Legal Education*

PLI, DRAFTING DOCUMENTS IN PLAIN LANGUAGE (1979).

PLI, DRAFTING DOCUMENTS IN PLAIN LANGUAGE 1981 (1981).

Sutin, *Drafting Conventions for Unconventional Drafting*, 5 PRAC. REAL EST. LAW. 61 (March 1989).

Taylor, *Plain English for Army Lawyers*, 118 MIL. L. REV. 217 (1987).

Till & Gargulo, CONTRACTS – THE MOVE TO PLAIN LANGUAGE (1979).

Thomas, *Plain English and the Law*, STATUTE L. REV. 139 (1985).

Weise, *Plain English Will Set the UCC Free*, 28 Loyola L.A. L. Rev. 371(1994).

Wydick, *Lawyer's Writing*, 78 MICH. L. REV. 711 (1980) (a review of Flesch, HOW TO WRITE PLAIN ENGLISH: A BOOK FOR LAWYERS AND CONSUMERS).

Computers and Logic

Allen, *Symbolic Logic: A Razor-Edged Tool for Drafting and Interpreting Legal Documents*, 66 YALE L.J. 833 (1957).

Allen & Engholm, *Normalized Legal Drafting and the Query Method*, 29 J. LEGAL EDUC. 380 (1978).

Braeman & Shellenberger, FROM YELLOW PADS TO COMPUTERS (2d ed. 1991).

Casen & Steiner, *Mathematical Functions and Legal Drafting*, 102 LAW Q. REV. 585 (1986).

Chaim, *A Model for the Analysis of the Language of Lawyers*, 33 J. LEGAL EDUC. 120 (1983).

Dunahoo, *Avoiding Inadvertent Syntactic Ambiguity in Legal Draftsmanship*, 20 DRAKE L. REV. 137 (1970).

Meyer, *Jurimetrics: The Scientific Method in Legal Research*, 44 CAN. B. REV. 1 (1966).

Perritt, HOW TO PRACTICE LAW WITH COMPUTERS (1988 & Supp.).

Saxon, *Computer-Aided Drafting of Legal Documents*, 3 AM. B. FOUND. RES. J. 685 (1982).

Sprowl, *Automating the Legal Reasoning Process: A Computer that Uses Regulations and Statutes to Draft Legal Documents*, 1 AM. B. FOUND. RES. J. 3 (1979).

Ethics in Drafting

Burnham, *Teaching Ethics in the Contracts Class*, 41 J. LEGAL EDUC. 105 (1991).

Kuklin & Bailey, *On the Knowing Inclusion of Unenforceable Contract and Lease Terms,* 56 U. CIN. L. REV. 845-915 (1988).

Llewellyn, *What Price Contract — An Essay in Perspective,* 40 YALE L.J. 704 (1931).

Luban (ed.), THE GOOD LAWYER (1984).

Note, *Preventing the Use of Unenforceable Provisions in Residential Leases,* 64 CORNELL L. REV. 522 (1979).

Purdy, *Professional Responsibility for Legislative Drafters,* 11 SETON HALL LEGIS. J. 67 (1987).

Schwartz, *The Professionalism and Accountability of Lawyers,* 66 CAL. L. REV. 669 (1978).

Stolle & Slain, *Standard Form Contracts and Contract Schemas: A Preliminary Investigation of the Effects of Exculpatory Clauses on Consumers' Propensity to Sue,* 15 BEHAV. SCI. & LAW 83 (1997).

Online Sources for Forms

Internet Legal Research Guide (http://www.ilrg.com)

findforms (http://www.findforms.com)

us legal forms (http://www.uslegalforms.com)

findlaw (http://www.findlaw.com)

Appendix B

Sources for Drafting Exercises

Materials useful for teaching drafting are found in many sources other than books on drafting. This guide to sources notes materials that may be found in texts. Note that some are older editions or out of print.

I. Casebooks.

Brown & Dauer, PLANNING BY LAWYERS:

> Cases and materials on drafting, 405-63
> Applications to particular transactions:
>> Real Property (co-ownership agreement), ch. 10
>> Business Planning (shareholders' agreement), ch. 11
>> Family Law (pre-nuptial agreement), ch. 12
>> Insolvency, ch. 13
>> Franchising (adhesion contracts), ch. 14

Child, DRAFTING LEGAL DOCUMENTS: Principles and Practices, *passim*

Crandall & Whaley, CONTRACTS: drafting questions, *passim*, and a problem on promise and
> condition, 856

Dickerson, MATERIALS ON LEGAL DRAFTING:

> Revision of a service agreement for clarity, 106-110
> Simplified documents, 295-310
> Problem materials on specific topics, *passim*

Farnsworth, Young & Sanger, CONTRACTS:

> Notes on drafting follow many of the cases
> The Supplement contains these forms:
>> Real Estate Broker's Agreement
>> Professional Football Player's Contract
>> Importer's Standard Form
>> Exporter's Standard Form
>> Automobile Purchase Order
>> Automobile Retail Instalment Sale Contract
>> Standard Construction Agreement (American Institute of Architects)

Fuller & Eisenberg, BASIC CONTRACT LAW: contains occasional notes on drafting. Older editions should also be consulted.

Jackson & Bollinger, CONTRACT LAW IN MODERN SOCIETY:

Essay on drafting, 1029-34
Form contract with questions raised, 1034-35, 1317-20

Knapp, Crystal & Prince, RULES OF CONTRACT LAW contains these sample contracts:

Contract for Sale of Residential Property
Requirements Contract for Purchase of Coal
Contingent Fee Agreement between Lawyer and Client
Employment Contract between Professional Corporation and Doctor
Construction Contract between Owner and General Contractor
Commercial Lease
Contract of Sale between Automobile Dealer and Consumer
Installment Contract for Sale of Automobile
Manufacturer New Car Warranty

Macneil & Gudel, CONTRACTS: Chapter 1 § 3 contains an essay on drafting as a lawyer function and problems

Mueller, Rosett & Bussel, CONTRACT LAW AND ITS APPLICATION: Lawyer's retainer letter, 295-329

Reitz, CONTRACTS AS BASIC COMMERCIAL LAW:

Contract in *Campbell Soup Co. v. Wentz*, 68-72
Record of *Universal Film Exchanges Inc. v. Viking Theatre Corp.*, 667-740

Summers & Hillman, CONTRACT AND RELATED OBLIGATION:

Contract and litigation in *White v. Benkowski*, 37 Wis. 2d 285, 155 N.W.2d 74 (1967), 5-28
Materials on planning and drafting, 358-74
Comparison of the agreement in *Lucy v. Zehmer*, 196 Va. 493, 84 S.E.2d 516 (1954) and a formbook agreement for the sale of real property, 388-93
Various notes on drafting follow many of the cases

Sweet, LEGAL ASPECTS OF ARCHITECTURE & ENGINEERING: contains various notes on drafting construction contracts

Vernon, CONTRACTS: THEORY AND PRACTICE:

> Revision for clarity of AIA form, 2-28 to -36
> Pre-drafting planning and fact-gathering, 3-40 to -41
> Problem: contractor and subcontractor, 4-36
> Liquidated damages clause, 6-91 to -92
> Sweet, *The Lawyer's Role in Contract Drafting*, 43 Calif. St. B.J. 362 (1968), Appendix

II. Sources Other Than Casebooks.

ALI-ABA COURSE MATERIALS JOURNAL often contains representative contracts with discussion

Biskind, SIMPLIFY LEGAL WRITING: sample provisions redrafted, 11-37

Brody, Rutherford, Vietzen & Dernbach, LEGAL DRAFTING

Child, DRAFTING LEGAL DOCUMENTS

Danzig, THE CAPABILITY PROBLEM IN CONTRACT LAW: excerpts from the contract in *Jacob and Youngs v. Kent*), 109-112

Dickerson, THE FUNDAMENTALS OF LEGAL DRAFTING (2d ed.):

> Revision of a residential lease, 307-16
> Agreement between legatees, 317-21
> Insurance form provisions, 322-23

Felsenfeld & Siegel, DRAFTING CONTRACTS IN PLAIN ENGLISH:

> Revision of a promissory note, 3-5, 241, and *passim*
> Revision of a contract for the sale of a cooperative apartment, 6-9, 242-44, and *passim*
> Revision of an insurance contract, 10-20, 245-53, and *passim*

Haggard, CONTRACT LAW FROM A DRAFTING PERSPECTIVE

Kuney, THE ELEMENTS OF CONTRACT DRAFTING

Rutter, *A Jurisprudence of Lawyer's Operations*, 13 J. Legal Ed. 301, 339-48, 382-92 (1961) (fact patterns and analytical outline)

Wincor, CONTRACTS IN PLAIN ENGLISH:

    Problem: negotiation of an international licensing agreement, 46-58
    Problem: negotiation of rights in intangibles, 60-73
    Approaches to negotiation, 75-90

III.   **Word lists.** Words that should be used with care when drafting are listed in the following sources:

PLI, DRAFTING AGREEMENTS IN PLAIN LANGUAGE:

    Long words with readable substitutes, 105-06
    Gender-neutral substitutes, 422-23
    Objectionable words (from Dickerson, *Fundamentals*) and preferred expressions, 426-29

PLI, DRAFTING AGREEMENTS IN PLAIN LANGUAGE 1981:

    Words to replace, 250-54

Biskind, SIMPLIFY LEGAL WRITING: choosing the right word, 64-110

Dick, LEGAL DRAFTING (2d ed.):

    Synonyms, 125-28
    Archaic words, 153
    Preferred expressions, 153-58

Dickerson, THE FUNDAMENTALS OF LEGAL DRAFTING (2d ed.):

    Live words, 187-88
    Objectionable words, 207
    Synonyms, 207-09
    Preferred expressions, 209-13
    [These lists are reprinted in Dickerson, MATERIALS ON LEGAL DRAFTING at 289-90, 290,
         ___ and 291-94 respectively]

Felsenfeld & Siegel, WRITING CONTRACTS IN PLAIN ENGLISH:

    Substitutes in a loan note, 125-26, 146-47
    Gender-neutral substitutes, 141
    Heavy words, 154

Mellinkoff, LEGAL WRITING: SENSE AND NONSENSE:

Archaic, 187-88
Synonyms, 189-91
Old formalisms, 191
Law Latin, 193-94
Law French, 195-96
Flexible, 197-98
Legal argot, 199-200
Terms of art, 201-03
[The Word and Phrase Index at 223-33 cites the location of words and phrases in the text]

Piesse & Smith, THE ELEMENTS OF DRAFTING:

Useful words, 100-03
Sources of mistakes, 103-07
Words relating to time, 108-15

Weihofen, LEGAL WRITING STYLE:

Words to watch, 20-35
Unnecessary words, 38-44
Repetition, 45-52
Simplicity, 59-60
Latin, 62
Formal and simple, 99

Wincor, CONTRACTS IN PLAIN ENGLISH:

Alarm words, 21-22
Contract phrases, 28-38

CHART: COORDINATING THE BOOK WITH CASEBOOKS

As indicated in the Introduction, this book can be used to supplement a first-year Contracts casebook. The chart that follows indicates where the subject matter covered in each chapter of Part I of this book may be found in a number of leading casebooks.

CHAPTER	Calamari, Perillo & Bender, 3rd ed.	Crandall & Whaley, 3rd ed.	Barnett, 3rd ed.	Dawson, Harvey & Henderson, 8th ed.	Epstein, Markell & Ponoroff	Farnsworth, Young & Sanger, 6th ed.
1. Offer & Acceptance	1-163	1-133	275-376	323-455	44-175	119-193
2. Consideration	164-254	149-256	601-698	188-322	344-401	22-85
3. Indefiniteness	39-90	133-147		290-322	177-192	251-262
4A. Enforceability (Public Policy)	879-914	584-664	571-600	511-542	304-328	423-450
4B. Unconscionability	399-407	674-702	1009-1026	688-713	329-343	400-422
5. Capacity	340-352	665-674	935-963	543-561	275-282	300-311
6. Parol Evidence	299-320	485-515	467-487	456-511	508-546	555-570
7. Interpretation	321-339	516-548	377-402	390-415	547-594	571-663
8. Mistake	382-399	549-584	1027-1060	601-645	241-258	786-799
9. Force Majeure	608-622	714-722	1064-1068	646-687	729-736	817-820
10. Promise & Condition	408-470, 540-574	747-856	839-856	714-868	679-715	664-699
11. Modification & Discharge	864-878	205-211, 450-451, 826-856	634-650	561-600	153-176, 395-401, 716, 676-678	280, 327-341, 570
12. Warranties		343-352	813-838	511-527, 625-640	622-674	367-384
13. Damages	626-701	257-373	59-178, 913-932	1-187	911-968	469-554
14. Third Parties	742-776	879-916	517-567	869-940	1001-1039	857-892

CHART: COORDINATING THE BOOK WITH CASEBOOKS

CHAPTER	Fuller & Eisenberg, 7th ed.	Knapp, Crystal & Prince, 5th ed.	Macaulay, Kidwell & Whitford, 2d ed.	Murphy, Speidel & Ayres, 6th ed.	Murray, 5th ed.	Rosett & Bussel, 6th ed.
1. Offer & Acceptance	403-505	161-216	I 229-294, II 157-241	245-348	78-234	577-634
2. Consideration	46-151	40-73	I 295-317	36-109	240-321	430-456
3. Indefiniteness	541-585		II 89-156	400-407	54-77	51-77
4A. Enforceability (Public Policy)	164-193	598-632	I 509-531, II 76-88	572-613	586-618	257-271
4B. Unconscionability	62-84	564-597	I 684-760	534-571	546-576	361-381
5. Capacity	364-368	507-525	I 535-548	450-469	300-308	332-345
6. Parol Evidence	587-610	381-430	II 271-368	614-637	428-468	542-573
7. Interpretation	611-642	349-380	II 243-270	638-658	476-495	51-77
8. Mistake	694-739	633-651	II 28-75	470-497	496-524	392-413
9. Force Majeure	751-756	652-704	II 579-729	802-861	742-746	
10. Promise & Condition	920-962	743-806	II 399-578	738-802	619-658	675-737
11. Modification & Discharge	109-151	679-704	II 369-398	703-722, 1034-1038	312-317, 469-475, 704-714	414-429
12. Warranties		483-506	I 656-683	723-738	184-186	
13. Damages	225-322	807-1008	I 33-228	191-229, 862-1029	767-845	102-168
14. Third Parties	794-833	705-742		1077-1124	859-906	828-848